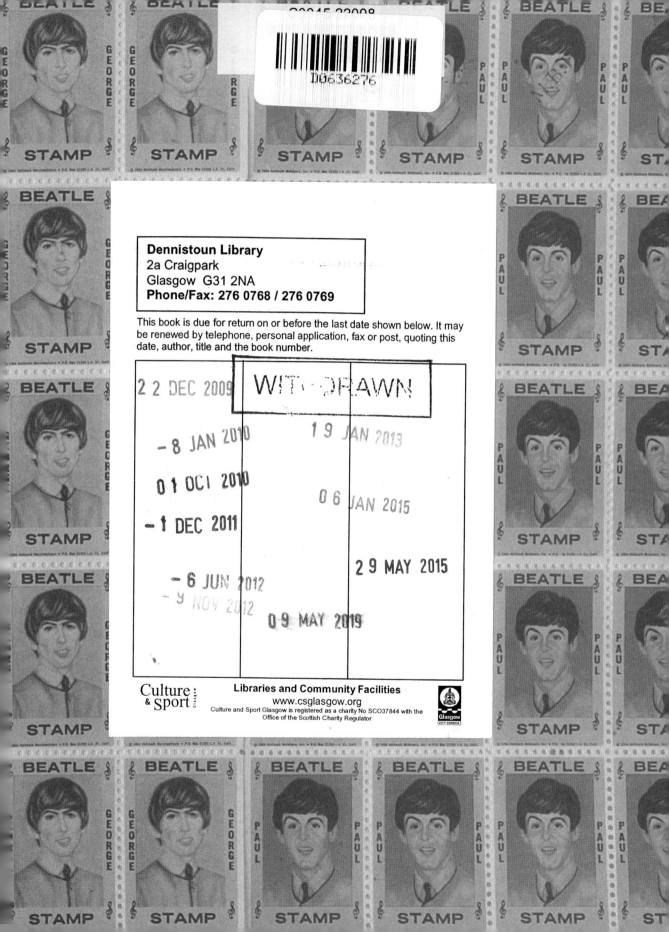

Confessions
of a
Collector

PRIME MINISTERS

OGDEN'S CIGARETTES.

OGDEN'S CIGARETTES.

EMPIRE STADIUM
WEMBLEY

WORLD CHAMPIONSHIP
1966
Jules Rimet Cup
FINAL TIE

ENTER AT
K
TURNSTILES

SATU

ENTRANCE

FOOTBALL

CUT ON LINE BELOW   JOHN

OFFICIAL
BEATLES FAN

THE BEATLES

POST CARDS

Confessions of a Collector

HUNTER DAVIES

Quercus

Contents

CARLISLE EDUCATION COMMIT

STANWIX COUNCIL SCHO

Report for Term ending 25 JUN 1943

Name .... Hunter Davies

Form .... Class II   Age....

Subject.				Possible Marks.	Actual Marks.	
Scripture	...	...	...			
Arithmetic	...	...	...	10	8	Shoul
Do.						had 1(
Do.						comple
English	...		...	10	7	
Do.	...					
Composition	...			10	5	
Reading	...	...		10	8	
Recitation	...	...		10	9	
Spelling	...	...		10	10	
Handwriting	...			10	10	
Geography	...	...				
History	...	...				
Nature Study	...					
Art	...					
Craft	...			10	8	
Needlework	...					

Hunter the Gatherer

I'm a born-again collector. I collected avidly as a boy, and then I stopped, for reasons I can't remember and probably wasn't even aware of at the time. Other things took its place, such as living, and I forgot all about collecting.

But then, equally mysteriously, it all came flooding back – the joys and delights and agonies of collecting. Like most born-agains, I found I was even more obsessive and passionate than those who'd never lapsed. But I envy those who kept the faith and never gave up, if just for one thing. Oh, if only I still had all those little, stupid, piddling scruffy things I collected as a boy, none of them valuable, even now, but so full of memories and emotions.

Childish Things

I collected stamps, like everyone I knew at the time seemed to, and indeed as every child should, as it's awfully educational. I didn't pay for them, not that I recall, apart from maybe the odd packet of assorted stamps from Woolworths bought with birthday money. My stamps were mostly steamed off envelopes that came through our

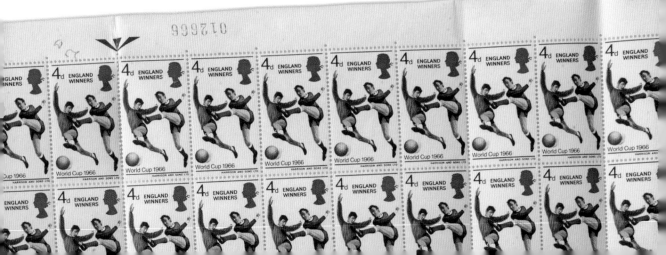

door, or were saved for me by relatives and other grown-ups. I especially prized foreign stamps. It was wartime, so we didn't see a lot of foreign letters, apart from ones from Canada. (We had relations there who sent us food parcels and vests. That used to make me really furious, the vests. Why couldn't they send me something really useful, like Yankee comics?)

I swapped stamps I had doubles of with friends; collecting can be a very sociable activity at any age, but particularly so when you're young. I stuck my stamps in a cheap little album, paperback not hardback, probably also bought from Woolies as a Christmas present. But at least it was a proper album, arranged by country. For each nation, it gave you the population, capital, currency and various other details. Told you it was an educational hobby. I used hinges, as proper collectors did, but I was very clumsy and ended up with lots either gummed together or sticking to my fingers and clothes.

ABIDING PASSION I started with stamps, and went back to them when I rediscovered collecting, but my real passion is for football memorabilia of all kinds. Below, a sheet of stamps celebrating England's 1966 cup win; above, a press pass for the England v. Germany World Cup qualifier in October 2000; right, a cigarette card showing Willie Evans of Spurs (1931–6) and Wales.

I loved to lie in bed and read my album, slowly turning over each page, scrutinizing every stamp in close detail, sideways and upside-down, hoping to find marks and messages I might have missed. I spent a lot of my childhood ill in bed. I had awful asthma for which doctors prescribed different medications, such as powder you burned and inhaled and little red fat rubber balls you squeezed to create a spray. None of them seemed to work. I had endless tests to see if I was allergic to anything. One of them consisted of pricks along my arm that came up like the perforations on the edge of a stamp.

In fact, the only thing that ever seemed to ease my breathing and make life bearable, allowing me to get up and walk around, perhaps even go outside and play football, was my little stamp album. By immersing myself in all those countries – wondering where on earth Azerbaijan was, and would I ever get a stamp from there? – I found that very slowly, almost unawares, my asthma would lift. I discovered this little miracle for myself. Even when I did it consciously, opening my album in order to distract myself, I would still get relief. So, stamps weren't only educational but also therapeutic.

I also collected football photographs, torn from the newspapers. I never had proper scrap albums for doing this, or proper glue, and stamp hinges

didn't work on large pieces of cheap newsprint. So my mother helped me make paste from flour and water. When I stuck my heroes into my home-made album, they'd all be soggy and wrinkled, but overnight, after the paste had dried, they'd come to life, appearing next day almost three-dimensional, standing stiffly to attention on the pages.

Because I was born in Scotland, my football heroes were Scottish, and whenever Scotland played England I'd listen to the radio, my ear glued to the set and my little heart beating. One of my heroes, whose photie I was always looking out for, was Billy Houliston, a bullet-headed footballer who played for Queen of the South, our local team when we lived in Dumfries. Not even many Scottish people have heard of him now. When I was aged 11, we moved across the border to Carlisle, where I started following Carlisle United, but I couldn't afford to go to games or buy programmes.

I was too late for cigarette cards as they had all but ceased just before the war. How I envied boys of the pre-war years who'd got loads of those colourful sets of little cards on every conceivable topic – and all for free. During the war, we had nothing like that, as paper was rationed and comics, when you could get them, were pathetic affairs, the pages grey and smudgy. But every adult, women and men alike, smoked cigarettes. In fact, our brave lads at the front were even given their own cigarette rations, so there were always lots of empty fag packets lying around.

There were dozens of different brands, many in very colourful, attractive packets, which my friends

ALLSORTS My areas of collecting are nothing if not eclectic, and tend to overlap. The cat post-card, right, might belong in my post-card collection, but its subject matter puts it firmly under Suffragettes. The Sean Connery card is related to my Paintings collection, as I acquired some nude pen-and-ink studies of the actor (see page 63).

8

and I collected. We'd follow people smoking in the street, hoping they'd throw away their packet, then we'd scramble in the gutter, fighting each other if it was a brand we hadn't got. We didn't keep the whole packet but tore off the fronts, holding them like packs of cards. Sweet Afton was my particular favourite. We had a good joke about Player's cigarettes. We'd ask boys who weren't in the know why, when you opened a pack of Player's, you could hear a voice going 'ONE, TWO, THREE, FOUR . . .'? The answer was right there on the packet: 'It's the tobacco that counts.' Hee hee.

I also collected marbles, trying to win them off other boys by playing games in the gutters. There were no cars, not where we lived – well very few – so you were safe playing in the streets and around the empty kerbs.

Other boys collected comics, but I could never afford them, so I had to rely on being able to borrow them. Girls, I supposed, collected dolls, but I never really had a clue what girls got up to. Almost all the stuff I collected was free – picked up, swapped or donated. Some kids had enough money to buy packets of really good stamps, not mixed rubbish, and had properly bound albums to put them in, but I don't remember feeling envious. Most of my friends had the same resources as me, namely very little. Anyway, there was a war on. We were supposed to be saving waste paper to defeat Hitler. I never quite understood how that worked: Were we supposed to throw piles of old paper at him?

My parents didn't earn enough to give me pocket money, so the only time I had anything to spend on myself was at Christmas and birthdays, when I got some money from relations. When I was 13, though, I started work as a paper boy. I used my earnings to put down a deposit on a bike, a Raleigh Lenton Sports – which I paid off on the never-never, 13/11 a week – rather than spending it on my collections.

But I still kept my stamp album and football photos safe under my bed, at least my side of the bed, which I shared with my brother. And I kept adding to my collections whenever I could. In Dumfries, and in Carlisle, I thought it was just me and my immediate friends who collected stamps and ciggie packets, or who ogled a Raleigh Lenton in the bike shop window. It was only much later I realized that what I was doing was common to all boys from all classes in the 1940s and 1950s, in the South as well as the North. I suppose the war had made us feel very insular and self-sufficient. Collecting seemed as natural as breathing. It was what you did.

And then, aged 18, I went off to university, and never really lived at home again for any length of time. I forgot all about my various little collections. Eventually my mother threw them all out. Even if she'd asked me, I probably wouldn't have stopped her, as I'd lost interest by that stage.

They were childish things, which I had put away. They'd served their purpose, amused and distracted me, put me in the playground swim, and had been a help and solace when I was ill and alone. Now I was interested in bigger, better, more important, more exciting, grown-up activities. Or so I told myself.

WOWSKI.—*Inkle and Yarico.*
" Your London Girls with roguish trip,
Wheedle wheedle wheedle,
May boast their pouting under lip,
Diddle daddle deedle ;
But Wows can beat a hundred such,
Fiddle fuddle feedle ;
Whose upper lip pouts twice as much,
O pretty double wheedle !

Come, come, Wowski, don't look shy,
Diddle daddle deedle !
But haste with me, your fortune try,
Wheedle wheedle wheedle !
And when you a Prize have gain'd,
Thousands, Ten or Twenty,
I'll be bound, there'll soon be found
Suitors for you plenty.

The Lottery will be drawn 14th This Month,

Born Again

I'm not quite sure how and when I got the bug again. It was a gradual thing, over many years, and it took me a while to realize it. But one day I woke up, took a long, hard look at myself and exclaimed, 'I'm a born-again collector!'

There are two types of collector. First, there's the Serious Collector, who goes out of his or her way to collect, and actively searches out items. You don't have to spend serious money, or acquire masses, to fall into this category but you do have to be serious enough about your hobby to consciously go forth and collect.

Then there's the Accumulator, a much more passive beast. He or she accumulates by never knowingly throwing things away. I suppose I've always been like that, even during the dormant decades. As a student, or in your first rented digs, you don't have much space to store things, but I started hoarding stuff even then, keeping billets doux from my loved one and replies from national newspapers and mags saying 'go away, don't bother us with your silly articles'. With marriage, and the acquisition of our own home, I at last had a room I liked to call my own. That's when the Accumulator in me really started to come out. Very little was ever thrown out, not from my part of the house. I kept all the bits and pieces, scraps and oddments to do with my work, book projects, interests and hobbies, and family affairs.

It was only after 20 years or so that I moved on from being an Accumulator to being a Serious Collector. I'm not quite sure why. Age was one factor, getting into my forties and looking back on my life, plus having a bit

LOTTERY MANIA
I got interested in the Lottery while researching a book on past winners. This flyer comes from the early 1800s (see page 155).

10

more time to myself after the kids had grown up. It also had a lot to do with giving up football, which I had played for about 20 years every Sunday morning on Hampstead Heath. I carried on too long, despite cartilage operations on both knees, and have paid the penalty ever since.

I'd turn out every Sunday at 11, knacker myself, be in agony all week, moaning and groaning, using patent heat treatments and ointments, then somehow manage to unplug the heat pads when Sunday came round again and stagger onto the pitch. Eventually I came to my senses and acknowledged that while I was still fit enough to play football, I was not fit enough to recover from it.

I was distraught for months. Life, especially at the weekends, seemed so empty. I hated watching my son and all my local friends, some even older than me, still playing. I must take up something else, I told myself, something that won't do in my knees or be too strenuous, that will get me out of the house, out of myself, be a harmless distraction, keep me out of mischief. I already had various piles of things I'd kept over the years, personal mementoes I'd accumulated, but for some reason, rather than concentrate on any of them – though I did do that later – I decided to become a Serious Stamp Collector. Probably I was thinking of all those happy hours I'd spent as a little boy.

Over the next ten years or so, stamps became my main collecting obsession. Until, for various reasons, I rather changed course. I found that I loved the act of collecting so much that I wanted to expand, go into other areas, where I felt more connected, more passionate, more knowledgeable. Today, I probably have about a hundred collections in all, though many of them are small, specialist branches of bigger subjects. It's made it very difficult to arrange them into 16 broad divisions for this book. I've had to fiddle things a bit, and there are many overlaps, but even doing that has given me pleasure. Collecting my collections, that's become my latest collecting hobby.

UNCLE TOM'S AUTHOR I found I could acquire letters and scraps of paper bearing the autographs of famous people at reasonable prices, so this became another collecting area of mine. Below: a letter written by Harriet Beecher Stowe, who wrote *Uncle Tom's Cabin* (1852), and an engraving of the author.

Stamps

Stamps seemed the obvious thing to go into, when I decided I was a born-again collector. There are so many of them around, on letters every day. There were stamp shops on the high streets of every town, at least in the 1970s when my interest was rekindled, not so many today, alas. In London, around the Strand, there were about 40 stamp shops and outlets, with come-hither windows, enticing reception areas, excitements promised in hidden-away store rooms. There was a wide choice of stamp magazines to pore over and a variety of societies to join.

WORLD IN MINIATURE
A selection of stamps, some from Britain's former colonies and dominions and others from elsewhere in the world. The stamp-collecting world embraces all ages and classes.

ROYAL PHILATELIST
(right) A British Guiana 2-cent stamp from the reign of George V. The king was an avid philatelist and whenever he was in London, he would spend three afternoons a week organizing his collection, which eventually ran to 328 albums.

Stamp-collecting is a huge hobby, no question, probably the biggest collecting hobby in the world. In the UK, there are reckoned to be 2 million regular collectors, according to some of my friends in the stamp trade. Others went so far as to estimate 4 million, counting those with albums stashed away, not looked at for a long time. You get some very rich dealers, handling stamps worth millions, and some very rich, distinguished collectors, while down at the grass roots, there are still large numbers of children in school stamp clubs, swapping their spares or hoping their granny will take out a Post Office subscription for them for new issues. It's a royal hobby, after all, unlike most, with a king – George V – who was obsessed by stamps and a organization that calls itself the Royal Philatelic Society. You don't get that with Beatles memorabilia.

I was astounded by this new world I'd arrived into. So different

from my childhood dabblings, steaming stamps off envelopes, buying packets of assorted Commonwealth. For a start, I couldn't understand the languages. Stamp catalogues were incomprehensible, with technical words and abbreviations that were new to me. I think it was three months before I knew that 'cover' meant envelope. Even the simple process of sticking stamps in albums had been revolutionized. Sticky stamp hinges had gone. Real stamp collectors now shuddered at the very thought of them. I quickly gathered that the merest hint of extra glue on the back of a precious stamp would ruin it, if you were a serious collector.

All the experts seemed so clever and knowledgeable. I'd never thought of stamps as a learned activity, but dear God, there are some great brains out there in the world of philately, who made me feel very ignorant, not to say small and silly. However, I was in such a hurry to get started, as if spurred on by unknown demons, that I rushed at everything.

I started buying anything of interest I saw, with little planning or logic, teaching myself as I went along. Collecting stamps can be a very academic, intellectual exercise, if you do it properly. Which I didn't. I went to stamp fairs advertised in the local papers, haunted the stalls under the arches at Charing Cross and elsewhere, went round the proper dealers in Covent Garden, worshipping at Stanley Gibbons in the Strand. I decided to acquire a copy of every British stamp up to modern times – that is, up to the last war.

Saga of the Penny Blacks

Having completed that self-created task, I started looking seriously at Penny Blacks. I discovered that a Penny Black, in poor condition, with no margins and lots of thins (i.e., with worn-away, thin bits) could be had for only £10. But once you start, you discover scores of variations. The Penny Black comes in 11 different plates, unseen to the naked eye (at least, to my naked eye), containing different combinations of letters. I eventually puzzled out what the letters in the two bottom corners of the stamps meant. It was a means, so I gathered, of deterring forgeries. On a sheet of 240 stamps – which you bought for £1, as of course there were 240 pennies in an old pound – there were 240 different variations. The combinations started on the top line with the letters AA, AB, AC etc. They didn't go to the end of the alphabet, only up to L one way and the other way down to T. But I realized I could look for Penny Blacks with my initials on, HD, and also for the rest of my family as by chance their first names are all between A and T.

After about a year, having by then got hold of lots of stamps with HD on them, I embarked on a self-imposed and rather grandiose task – to recreate a whole sheet of Penny Blacks, starting with the letters AA through to TL, all 240 of them.

I bought cheapo examples, usually between £10 and £20, as I wasn't worried about condition, just the letters. I often bought job lots, blind, in auctions, ten cheapo Blacks for £80, hoping there would be letters I hadn't got, then I tried to swap or sell the doubles to dealers. Which rarely worked. They'd offer me a fiver, at best. So I mainly kept the doubles, thinking 'well, they are Penny Blacks, everyone has heard of them'.

I then started framing my spare Penny Blacks, neatly, and gave them to people as presents, with a brief explanation underneath, certifying that this was a genuine 1840 Penny Black, dead kosher. I recall giving one to Lew Grade on his birthday, when I was doing a book about his family; he was well impressed. People who have everything, and can afford everything, are rarely not delighted at receiving a real Penny Black with their initials, as they never knew such a thing existed. I never revealed the true price, £10 or so, but merely hinted how difficult it had been, and how much more so it would have been for them, if they'd tried to track down that exact stamp themselves.

It took me seven years to actually finish that sheet. I did so enjoy the hunt, finding the missing letters. As all collectors know, it's wonderful to hit on something that is finite, which if you keep at it long enough, spend enough time and money on it, you will in the end complete. When I finally finished, I felt there was a big gap in my life.

MISSION ACCOMPLISHED
I was clearly chuffed to have finally assembled a full sheet of Penny Blacks, with all the permutations of corner letters. On the far left, you can see how the Penny Black sheet was organized, with the rows in alphabetical order, running KA, KB... and LA, LB etc.

Stamp Portfolio

After about a year, still messing around, I realized stamp prices were going up all the time, so I decided to put myself, and my money, in the hands of the real experts. I allowed Stanley Gibbons to create a small portfolio for me from their treasures, for which I paid them £4,000. I didn't tell my wife Margaret the price. In fact, I hardly told myself. I wrote it down in code, as I did for all my purchases, and then I forgot the codes, which was just as well. I let Gibbons pick the stamps, good examples of whatever they thought were bound to go up in value. This was in 1980, which happened to be a period when stamps were shooting up in price.

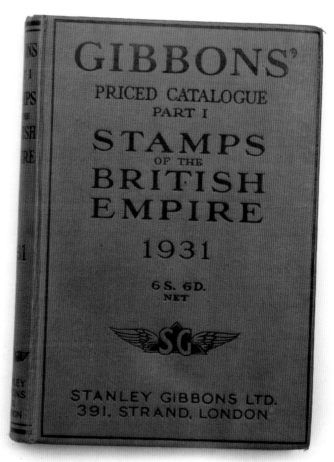

Meanwhile, I bashed on with my own little collections, such as stamps produced for the Wembley Empire Exhibition of 1924–5. Being a football fan, I had always been interested in the history of Wembley Stadium. Then I collected Columbus stamps, sparked off by writing a biography of Columbus. In 1892 the USA produced a whole set of Columbus stamps to commemorate the 400th anniversary of the European discovery of the New World, which are greatly valued by collectors. I also moved into postal history, which means the postal marks on the covers, which is what stamp collectors call envelopes.

Having started on stamps, I then began moving backwards and side-ways, into postcards, letters, ephemera of all sorts. If I went to a jumble, a car boot, a collectors' fair, or found myself in a strange town with lots of charity shops, I could wander round and pick up something of interest for one of my many collections.

I was so pleased to be back in stamps, back as a collector. Stamps had reintroduced me to the world of collecting generally, and I was moving from there into other areas. When you go to a fair, supposedly on

KING OF STAMPS
Stanley Gibbons of the Strand is an illustrious name in stamp-collecting circles. The 1931 catalogue gave detailed information on the stamps of the entire Empire.

NATIONAL ICON
One of my collection of Columbus stamps. These were the United States' first commemorative issue (1892); the series consisted of 15 stamps, ranging in value from one cent to 5 dollars, and they were instantly popular with collectors.

one theme, you do find dealers with other stuff on their stalls, not always directly related, so my mind wandered and my purse was tempted. Weekends were fun-filled again. So much for a healthy boy to enjoy, such innocent pleasures to throw myself into.

Stamp History

Rowland Hill introduced the Penny Black in 1840, the world's first pre-paid postage stamp. It was a revolutionary system, which changed the whole of communication, yet like so many Big Ideas it was very simple and you wonder now why on earth it had taken so long for anyone to think of it.

One price, a penny, covered a basic letter, whether it was going to Archway or Aberdeen. You paid the penny in advance, when you bought the stamp, not when you collected your letter from the postie or the post office, the cost depending on its weight and how far it had come. That had been the system, pre-1840, and what a faff it must have been. People would refuse to pay if the letter addressed to them looked boring or too expensive. Correspondents would try to cram in as many words as possible to save money,

POSTAL JUBILEE
An 1890 first-day cover commemorating the jubilee of the Penny Post, showing an old mail coach and a state-of-the-art mail train.

turning the pages over when they were full, and then writing sideways, in between the lines, making it hellish to read. When I did a biography of Wordsworth I dreaded having to read any letters written pre-1840.

The Penny Black was an immediate success, and was soon copied round the world. People were fascinated by it, its simple colour and shape, its appearance on sheets of 240 which had to be cut up, if you just wanted one stamp. There were no perforations on the early sheets, which is why today a Penny Black is most valued if it has four clear margins – i.e., cut out of the sheet carefully and cleanly, leaving a bit of white all the way round. Most Penny Blacks have at least one dodgy margin, where the scissors have cut into part of the design. Schoolboys started collecting them for the letters, once they'd noticed those 240 different pairs, and clubs sprang up in schools and colleges. When other countries issued stamps, teachers encouraged stamp-collecting as it was a fun way of studying geography. In 1862, Sotheby's held its first proper stamp auction.

In 1863, young Stanley Gibbons was working in his father's chemist's shop in Plymouth. His dad had allowed him one end of the counter where he had set himself up as a stamp dealer. One day, two sailors came into the ship with a bag of stamps that they had won in a raffle during shore leave in Cape Town. Well, that was their story. Young Stanley looked inside and found they were full of Cape of Good Hope triangulars, which first appeared in 1853, the earliest stamps in the world not to be stamp-shaped. Stanley offered them £5 for the bag, probably trying to look uninterested, like all smart dealers, and the sailors were delighted to accept. Stanley went on to sell the contents for £500. Thus an empire was born.

THE AVID VICTORIAN LADY COLLECTOR

In 1841, just one year after their first appearance, the following advert for spare Penny Blacks was placed in in *The Times* by a woman who was only identified by the initials 'ID':

A young lady, desirous of covering her dressing room with cancelled postage stamps, has been so far encouraged by her friends as to have succeeded in collecting sixteen thousand. These, however, being insufficient, she will be obliged if any good- natured person who may have these (otherwise useless) little articles at their disposal would assist her in this whimsical project.

Sixteen thousand, blimey, what an enormous number she had collected, when you think they'd only been out for a year. There were also twopenny blues, which had come out with the Penny Black, then penny reds in 1841. All the same, she'd gathered a vast amount, unless she was fibbing slightly. Perhaps she was trying to impress her friends, who were encouraging her whimsical idea.

CATERING FOR THE COLLECTOR

Stamp-collecting took off in the mid-19th century. By the 1860s, stamp guides were appearing, followed by special magnifying glasses, tweezers and early forms of stamp hinges.

His first stamp price lists appeared in 1864. He moved to London in 1874 and the business eventually took on offices in 1891. In 1890, *Gibbons' Monthly Journal* was published, and is still going strong. Thanks to Gibbons, all stamps have what is called an SG number, so you can look each stamp up, when searching or ordering. I can't think of any other collecting hobby in which all possible items have been so well catalogued and organized.

SG catalogues also give prices – and here troubles can start. When I first got into stamps in 1979, I bought a Penny Black for £25 from a stall, thinking 'what a bargain, considering it's almost 150 years old'. I didn't know at the time that 68 million Penny Blacks had been produced. I looked it up in my copy of Stanley Gibbons *Collect British Stamps* and its value was given as £2250 Unused and £140 Used. Mine was certainly used, but all the same, quite attractive. I took it to Gibbons' very impressive premises in the Strand, really just to boast how clever I'd been. An expert looked at it and said it was worth £5. I protested that their catalogue said it was worth £140. Ah, he replied, but those prices only refer to the best examples, in top-class condition. This one was frankly rather tatty.

Absolute beginners never realize this and to this day will think they've got a bargain, especially when other dealers advertise items 'half Gibbons' price'. Which may be true, but is meaningless. Gibbons' 2008 catalogue puts an Unused Penny Black at £8500 and a Used one at £350. As a rule of thumb, I concluded that SG prices should be divided by ten.

Postal History

My postal history collection was a spin-off from stamps. It covers envelopes, postal marks, and different frankings. One of my favourite items is a 1890 envelope, issued by the Post Office that year for the Jubilee of the Penny Post. It's so pretty, the artwork so, well, artistic, the vignettes so attractive, the subject matter so historically fascinating (see page 17).

At the top, it shows a carriage and four horses with the caption 'The North Mail making for Highgate at 8 miles an hour'. At the bottom, there's an

express train: 'The North Mail, 1890, approaching Carlisle at 48 miles an hour'. My home town is Carlisle and my London home has been in Highgate for 45 years, so naturally that caught my eye. Actually, it's not totally correct to say that we live in Highgate. Our street, when we bought this house in 1963, was in Parliament Hill Fields; that's what the estate agents called it, though the socially mobile described it as South Highgate, trying to be posh. Today, the local estate agents – none of whom had offices round here in the 1960s – call it Dartmouth Park. I usually say we live in Kentish Town. That's awfully smart.

For centuries, the North Mail coach and horses would speed this way as it belted out of London carrying passengers and post to the wilderness north of Watford. Then it all changed. By 1890, the railway had taken over. My envelope combines two of the greatest innovations of the Victorian era, and celebrates two of my all-time heroes: Rowland Hill and George Stephenson.

George Stephenson didn't invent the railways, but he was the first to make them work – with the Stockton to Darlington railway in 1825, then the Liverpool to Manchester in 1830. Within 20 years, the railways had transformed Britain, creating suburbs and commuters, taking fresh vegetables to towns the length and breadth of the land, revolutionizing the post and all forms of communications. Since the beginning of time, man had only been able to move at the speed of the fastest horse – as the 1890 Jubilee cover illustrates. After George Stephenson, and the coming of trains, the world was never the same again. I can't think of another person in history about whom this can be truly said. Can you?

Thematics

An easy way to collect stamps, which appeals particularly to children and newcomers, is to start a thematic collection – a collection on one theme. In the USA, they talk about a 'topical collection'. That doesn't mean that it's topical, as in 'of the moment', but concerned with one topic.

The most popular topics and themes include birds, flowers, cars, ships and

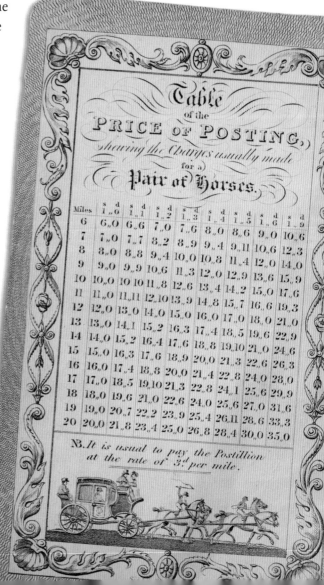

830   LIVERPOOL AND MANCHESTER RAILWAY 1830   LIVERPOOL AND MANCHESTER RAILWAY 1830   LIVERPOOL AND MANCHESTER RAILWAY 1830   LIVERPOOL AND MAN

DEFINING MOMENT

As a great admirer of George Stephenson, I was bound to be interested in the 1980 commemorative stamps marking the 150th anniversary of the opening of the Liverpool to Manchester railway, the world's first passenger line. This uncut set of stamps shows Stephenson's *Rocket* pulling a variety of wagons.

SLIDING SCALE

Left: an ornate example of a Victorian table of prices, showing the cost of posting a letter to be carried by mail coach.

railways. Places like Woolies used to sell packets of themed stamps, just to get you started. It's noticeable that the Post Office, in their endless production of commemorative stamps, tend to go for popular themes and images, knowing gullible stamp collectors will rush to buy them.

There were no commemoratives issued for many years by our Post Office. British stamps normally only ever had the face of the monarch, perhaps a bit of fancy scroll, plus the value, but no other words or lettering. Not even the name of the country. That's one of the things schoolchildren learn quite early – that Great Britain is the only country in the world that doesn't have the name of its country on its stamps. We were first to think of stamps, so we didn't need to add our name.

Our first commemorative stamps came out for the 1924 Wembley Exhibition – and had on them 'British Empire Exhibition 1924', with just two values, 1d and 1½d. They were issued again the following year, as the Exhibition was still going strong, with 1924 changed to 1925. So, in theory, there were only four Wembley stamps, but when I started collecting them I came across lots of variations, with different markings and frankings. Later came the commemoratives for the 1929 Postal Union Congress, for George V's Silver Jubilee of 1935 and then for other royal events, plus the Olympic Games in London in 1948. The flood of commemoratives, with up to a dozen new issues on different themes each year, didn't start till the 1960s.

Apart from Wembley Exhibition stamps, I decided that my main thematic collection would be stamps with a football theme or connection. Great Britain didn't issue any for many years, but I found lots of foreign commemorative football stamps, usually issued when the country in question was hosting the World Cup. The earliest football stamps I could find appeared in 1924, issued by Uruguay in honour of their football victory at the Olympic Games. They don't actually show a footballer. The first stamp with a footballer on it came out in Holland in 1928, again to mark the Olympics.

I still look out for football stamps, or football-related first covers, but only up to 1966 and England's World Cup triumph. I don't collect later issues. As with our Post Office's first-day covers and special issues, there are far too many of them, brought out purely to be collected, so I refuse them.

As an investment, whatever the Post Office suggests, they are a complete waste of time. At every stamp fair you will see boxes of first-day covers for only 50p each, often as low as a tenth of what they cost some poor granny, just a year or so earlier.

End of an Era

After ten years collecting stamps, loving every minute, having spread out all over the place, going sideways and backwards, I realized one day I had a pile of stamps in a registered envelope, bought at a postal auction, that I hadn't yet opened. There were albums of treasures whose pages I had not turned over for, well, I couldn't remember, which was a worrying sign in itself. Perhaps for over a year.

'What am I doing?' I asked myself. This is becoming a nonsense. I don't look at these stamps. No one else looks at these stamps. What's the point? I felt sickened by my own compulsions, guilty at my expenditure. I now had so many other collections, most of which I felt more passionate about, more knowledgeable about. Why was I continuing to buy stamps?

I woke up one day and said 'That's it.' I'm getting out of stamps. They're all going. I'll sell my so-called investment collection. I'm going to concentrate on stuff I really know and care about.

You can guess what happened. The valuable portfolio that Stanley Gibbons had bought for me ten years earlier, chosen by their experts, turned out not to be so valuable. Every year or so I asked if this was a good time to sell, as after all I'd only bought this little portfolio as an investment. They'd say hold on, times are not so good, you have to give it a few years. The portfolio consisted mainly of early Commonwealth stamps, about which I knew little and cared less. I put it in the vaults at the Midland Bank at King's Cross, where it lay for ten years.

Eventually, when I decided this was daftness, why keep something I wasn't interested in, and which seemed to be going down in value every year, I sold

COMMEMORATING SPORTING PROWESS Stamps issued by Uruguay (above) in honour of their victory in the football competition at the Olympic Games of 1924 in Paris. On the left are two Italian stamps marking that country's hosting of the World Cup in 1934, in which it won the trophy.

them at Sotheby's. All I got for them was £1500 – less than half what I'd paid. I'd come in on a rising market and left at the bottom of the next depression.

I also sold my reconstructed sheet of Penny Blacks and in this case got roughly my money back. So for 10 years of collecting, I hadn't made a penny, but at least with the Penny Blacks I'd assembled them myself and had fun. I'd made the mistake of going for quantity rather than quality. Instead of, for example, buying five poor Penny Blacks at £20 each, I should have bought one good one at £100. That holds true for most collections.

Thus I learned one of the basic rules of collecting – poor stuff always remains poor. A good stamp will always be a good stamp, and you are likely to get your money back, if you hang on long enough, but rubbish stamps remain rubbish, even in good times. A £20 Penny Black, for example, will still be a poor stamp ten years later, and worth little more. But a £100 Penny Black is likely to have doubled in value. Unless we're in a depression, that is.

The most important lesson I learned from all this was to buy for fun, amusement, personal interest, and not for investment. If, of course, something you have picked up or collected turns out to be valuable, then so much the better, but that should not be the first object. So, I sold almost all my so-called good stamps, including my Wembley collection, but kept some of the minor ones, just for amusement, for the memory of times past. I decided I'd made a mistake. Stamps were not really for me. Even after ten years, I still felt ignorant about them. I'd collected a huge amount, but they were giving me little real pleasure. So what was the point?

I hate to say this now, as as an ex-stamp collector I don't want to appear to be giving stamps a kicking, but I think that the great days of stamp collecting are over. Schoolchildren don't seem as keen any more, now they have TV, computer games and the internet. Stamp collecting also has an uncool, anorakish image. That's always been there, but I think now there are many other collecting areas that people consider attractive, unusual, individual and creative. You can make up your own, not follow the herd.

Anyway, I decided to concentrate on two areas that I did know and care about, where my love was pure and genuine . . .

Hunter Davies

(ADPS)

EMSWORTH PHILATELIC
8 CHRISTOPHER WAY
EMSWORTH
HANTS PO10 7QZ
TEL 0243 374349

Dear Mr.D.,   30th May 1997
            It is five years since I last contacted
you, but your name was the first to spring to mind
when I came across the enclosed—must be the
cheapest 1d Black there is:
1d Black CK Red m/cr......tear at left   £1(?)
      usual approval terms—I hope this finds you
okay. For my part, I have not yet been head-hunted
by Gibbons, so continue to plug away.
      I look forward to your reply. Best regards
to you,

            Yours sincerely,

            Tim Stephens

(Any cheques payable please to:-) Tim Stephens.

✓ 5 + 2¹
clogstamps

The Beatles

My biggest and best collection is The Beatles,
but it's a bit of a cheat in a way, in that I was fortunate enough to have
privileged access to them and so found myself with certain items that
ordinary fans, ordinary collectors, in the ordinary way of things, would
never have managed to acquire. But all the same, I was and still am a
collector of all things Beatly. Such a shame that the best items are now
astronomically expensive, most of them far out of my reach.

I got to write their only ever authorized biography by the simple means of
asking. I'd gone to see Paul McCartney when the single 'Eleanor Rigby' came
out in 1966. A year later, I went to see him at his London home in St John's
Wood with a different hat on, this time as a screen writer. I was writing the

Portraits of Ringo, John, George and Paul, from the first set of bubblegum cards to feature The Beatles, which was issued in 1964. Other shots from this same 60-card series showed the mop-topped lads donkey-riding, go-karting, and visiting the hairdresser's.

film script for a novel of mine, which was being made into a film, *Here We Go Round the Mulberry Bush*. We hoped Paul might do the theme tune for the film, but he never did. While I was with him, however, I put to him the suggestion that there should be a proper hardback book about The Beatles so that for the rest of his life, when people asked the same old dopey questions about The Beatles, he would be able to say: 'Look in the book, it's all there!'

Firstly I had to talk to the band's manager, Brian Epstein, to get his agreement. Paul, being ever so kind, and also good at PR, said he'd help me write the letter, which I sent to Brian on 31 December 1966. I still have a carbon copy of it (the original went to Brian, of course). This became my first personal item of Beatles memorabilia. I got Brian's agreement, and a publisher signed the contract, which I also still have. I spent most of 1967–8 interviewing The Beatles at their homes and in the studio, talking to their mums, and visiting places they had been, such as Hamburg.

While I was doing their biog, I naturally acquired and kept all the fan mags, booklets, sheet music, photographs, souvenirs and newspaper articles that were currently available. All of it was very cheap. While fans eagerly bought and collected Beatles photos or bubblegum cards, there was as yet no secondhand market, no dealers sold such material, nor were there any auction houses specializing in pop memorabilia.

I should imagine that many Beatles fans, when they grew up and moved on, got married and had children, forgot or threw away their teenage Beatles collections. But a huge number did not forget, or even move on. I think they realized, as most people round the world soon did, that they had witnessed, and been part of, a phenomenon of popular culture the like of which we had not seen before. Nor probably ever will again. That's what I still believe.

A surprising number of these 1960s Beatles scrapbooks have survived. They're full of items such as photos and postcards, which girls – they were nearly always girls – carefully preserved, usually going kissy kissy over their favourite one of the Fab Four. Some of these albums were bought specially, part of Beatles merchandising, with an illustration of the group on the cover, but some were just ordinary, cheapo scrapbooks. In theory, they are of little value, being by definition scraps, containing stuff torn from newspapers, but today you can find Beatles dealers asking £20–£30 for them.

As for original, 1960s Beatles material, as opposed to scraps, some things, such as early programmes and posters from their Liverpool or Hamburg days, now fetch small fortunes. When they were top of the bill at the Palladium or wherever, or going on national and international tours, thousands of posters and programmes were printed, all of them of value today. But the really expensive stuff comes from earlier on, when they were down the bill, or appearing at a Women's Institute or a local jazz club. Posters from this period – 1957–62 – were flimsy, cheaply done, and probably only a handful were produced, most of which were torn down, pasted over, left to blow away.

I looked around for material in Liverpool and Hamburg, When I

XMAS SPECIAL
Cover of the souvenir programme for The Beatles' first Christmas show, at the Finsbury Park Astoria from Christmas Eve 1963 to 11 January 1964 (see also page 33). Inside this 24-page booklet was a preview of their appearance on the Ed Sullivan Show. Other acts on the bill included Billy J. Kramer & the Dakotas, Rolf Harris, Cilla Black and the Barron Knights.

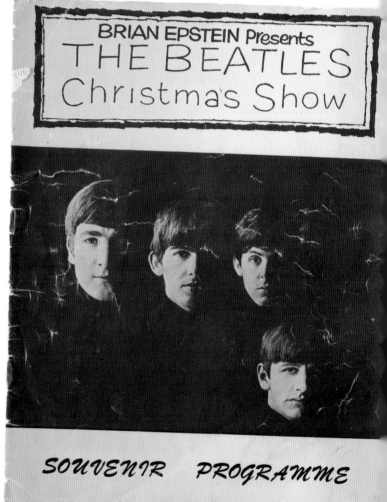

BRIAN EPSTEIN Presents THE BEATLES Christmas Show

SOUVENIR PROGRAMME

The HESWALL JAZZ CLUB

present their

★ ★ ★

★ALL★STAR★BILL

★ *Starring*

THE BEATLES

- ★ Mersey Beat Poll Winners !
- ★ Polydor Recording Artists !
- ★ Prior to European Tour !

★ *plus*

The Pasadena Jazzmen

Firm Favourites !

plus ★

'Top Twenty' Records

at Barnston Women's Institute

on Saturday March 24th, 1962

7-30 p.m. —— 11-15 p.m.

7/6   ADMISSION   **7/6**
    Strictly by TICKETS ONLY

F. W. COOPER SEAVIEW PRESS, 368, BOROUGH ROAD, BIRKENHEAD.

RARE FIND

Before they began appearing at huge venues like the Shea Stadium and the Hollywood Bowl, The Beatles played in many less exalted settings, such as the Heswall Jazz Club. This gig was notable for being the first public outing for their trademark stage attire of matching suits (they'd worn jeans and leather jackets in Hamburg).

went to the offices of NEMS, the Beatles' management company, I asked them to dig out copies of old hand-outs and other publicity material. John gave me a few bits and pieces, and so did Brian. The Beatles came to our house for tea or supper, and I went to their parties. Whenever they wrote to me, I kept every letter, every postcard. Beginning with The Beatles biography, and with each of the books I have written since, I have held on to every item relating to the project – letters, articles, leaflets, whatever. (I still have the entrance tickets for all the Roman forts I visited when I walked Hadrian's Wall for a book I wrote in 1973 – valueless today, but not to me.)

I didn't use a tape recorder when I interviewed The Beatles. I wrote everything down in little red notebooks, as I still do. I have this theory that using a tape recorder doubles your work, as you have to listen to it all over again. Anyway, I only ever write down what I think I'm going to use, editing it as I go along.

I wish now I *had* recorded the Beatles interview. I could have had dozens of hours of tape, spread over two of the most productive years in their lives. What an addition to my Beatles collection that would have been.

During the making of the album *Sergeant Pepper's Lonely Hearts Club Band* at Abbey Road in 1967, there were always some torn-up scraps of paper left at the end of each session. Words of songs were written down on the backs of envelopes, restaurant menus, airline notepaper, whatever odd bit of paper was to hand, and then corrected and changed as the sessions wore on. A fresh copy might be written out for Ringo, when he arrived, so he knew what song they were doing. Each evening the scraps were left lying on the floor for the cleaners to chuck out. Probably 95 percent were thus destroyed.

But now and again, if I wanted a copy of a song's words, because I was going to write about it, I would pick up the relevant scrap from the floor and ask if I could have it. They always said yes, fine. They had no further use for the scrap once they had recorded the song. After the book was finished, I shoved them in a drawer, along with scraps from other books.

We had a burglary at our house in the early 1970s. Amongst the things stolen were my copies of Beatles LPs that I had got The Beatles to autograph.

When I claimed on the insurance, I claimed only the replacement value of each record, which I think must have been about 30 shillings. There was no extra value in their signatures – only to me. Last year, a friend of mine sold his *Sergeant Pepper* album, signed by all four Beatles, for £15,000. I bet my burglar didn't get that for his.

I had forgotten about my Beatles lyrics, still lying in that drawer, till the 1980s, when my children became teenagers and showed a passing interest in pop music. I opened up The Beatles drawer, saw I had some handwritten lyrics, put them in clip frames and hung them on the stairs. My children weren't at all impressed. Some of their teenage friends were, and I began to worry that at some drunken party, someone would be sick all over them.

One day in 1981, Sotheby's held their first auction of pop memorabilia. I found that overnight my scraps on the wall had become worth more than the house. I worried about their safety – should I hide or sell them? But I wanted to keep them together, perhaps displayed for others to see.

I rang the British Museum and asked if they'd like to have them. I half expected a refusal, that they'd say the scraps were too trivial, but they jumped at my offer. For many years, they were on show in the BM's Manuscript Room. Then they were transferred to the new British Library in Euston Road. They are in the manuscript gallery, along with Magna Carta, Beethoven, Mozart, Wordsworth, Jane Austen. On any one day, The Beatles' display usually has the biggest crowd around it. When the Queen opened the Library, it was one of the cases she paused at. They are easy to understand.

The British Library has them on permanent loan. In my will, which I have recently drawn up, they will go to the British Library and remain on show there for ever – or so I hope . . .

TWIST AND SHOUT A dapper-looking John Lennon performing with The Quarrymen, the embryonic Beatles, in 1957. To his left is guitarist Eric Griffiths; after leaving The Quarrymen in 1958, he went on to a career in the Merchant Navy and later the Scottish Prison Service.

Collecting Beatles Souvenirs

I probably have about 1000 Beatles-related items, but I haven't got everything, not by a long way. Beatles memorabilia is so vast that most Beatles collectors tend to specialize in one area, such as the records, or the souvenirs. I can't say I'm an expert on either of those. I can't identify a rare pressing and I find it hard to get worked up about Beatles talcum. Beatles wigs, though, I find them amusing and they do have a relevance. Back in the 1960s, people did think about their hair, when they first thought about The Beatles.

With all my collections, I always prefer memorabilia I can read and study, stuff that has some sort of content or relevance, and with The Beatles, what I'm looking for – just like every Beatles collector – is contemporary material, from the 1960s. I like to think that while so much of it was cheap merchandising, cashing in, they were at least catering for real, living, screaming fans.

My general Beatles stuff, as opposed to my personal, signed material, includes the sorts of items most Beatles collectors have and is not very hard to find. Sometimes the prices are ridiculous, when a dealer is hoping some dopey tourist will think he is getting something extremely rare, but on the whole you don't have to pay more than £20–£50 for most Beatles records, souvenirs, books and mags, even from the 1960s. Beatles souvenirs fall into ten broad areas.

1 RECORDS I have original copies of every UK single and LP, which are still easy to find and not too dear, but that's about all. I gave up trying to be a proper record collector when I realized just how many rare demos, acetates, bootlegs and foreign editions there are. With many of them, I couldn't see the difference anyway, so why bother? Out there are scores of real Beatles experts, who know everything about every record, like my friend Pete Nash, so I decided not to bother. I could never compete.

However, if I see a cheapo copy of the double 'White Album' of 1968, and the number in the bottom right-hand corner is quite low, say under 1000, or a *Sergeant Pepper* album with

the moustache and all the bits intact, still uncut, then I'll make an offer, usually derisory, knowing that whatever the dealer says, there are still loads of them around.

2 PHOTOGRAPHS My most valuable are snaps taken in Hamburg, of The Beatles mucking around on what looks like the roof of a club. I also have the originals of the four portraits of The Beatles with their families, which Ringo took specially for the first edition of my biography in 1968. Three of the photos were excellent quality, bang in focus, nicely arranged, but the one of Ringo himself, plus his wife Maureen and their two children, is very fuzzy. That's because Ringo took it himself, jumping back and forward, having set the timer on his camera to catch himself in the right position. Ringo was a whizz on camera technology, but in 1968 such devices were in their infancy. I'd had all four of these photos on my wall for 40 years – then a few months ago we had a leak in a lavatory. Water seeped down the wall, sneaking in behind the four photos. Before I had realized, they got soggy and ruined.

I've also bought lots of Beatles photos from dealers and other collectors. About 20 years ago, I acquired a folder of 100 or so press photos which had come from a news agency library, with their stamp and captions on the back. This is the vital thing, to have such markings, as it lets you know these must be original prints. Some would have been used at the time, somewhere, but not all of them. The pictures desk would have had a selection in front of them, all marked up by the photographer or the agency; one or two would have made the paper, but the rest were put in their own library. Over the years, most newspapers have got rid of their old cuttings and picture libraries, storing things on computers. At one stage, there was quite a flood of such material, all very cheap, but now it has dried up.

Repro photos are easy to spot, as the photographic paper is so glossy and modern, the images a bit blurry with being copied so often, and there are, of course, no marks on the back. There must be thousands out there, as so many stalls have them, almost all of them rip-offs, reproduced without

copyright permission. I still buy them, for between £2 and £5, if it's an image I've never seen before.

Famous photos of The Beatles, taken by famous photographers and often signed by them, are often sold in special limited editions, or appear in exhibitions. They can cost hundreds of pounds. I recently bought a set from Michael Ward, who took some excellent photos of them in the Cavern.

3 POSTCARDS As with photographs, the original ones from the 1960s are the ones to collect. You can usually tell from the age and condition and also by the names of the manufacturer or distributors, such as Brel, Valex or Top Star. Early coloured ones, even if the colours are awful and overlapping, are very desirable.

Mike McCartney, Paul's brother, produced probably the best Beatles post-cards ever when he created a series of 19, based on his own photographs from the late 1950s and 60s, but they are no longer commercially available and are therefore hard to find. Bubblegum cards, which came in lots of different series, often contained less well-known photos of The Beatles, but most of them were very badly reproduced. Today, repro postcards of The Beatles are everywhere, a lot of them produced illegally, without copyright permission, using album covers or familiar images.

BUBBLEGUM BEATLES (above) Two more cards from the 1964 card set. Supposedly 'candid' shots of the band relaxing or 'zany' images of them fooling around were used to promote The Beatles' image.

4 MAGAZINES Mags wholly devoted to The Beatles, and published in the 1960s, are the ones to look out for, such as *Beatles by Royal Command*, *Beatles in Carnegie Hall*, *Beatles on Broadway*, *Beatles in Sweden*, and *Beatles in Paris*. They are not very expensive, around £15–£30 each, as so many were produced.

I also collect any mags or newspapers from the 1960s with The Beatles on the cover or featured inside. The most desirable, expensive and inter-esting are copies of *Mersey Beat*, the local Liverpool pop music newspaper which charted their early days. In the first issue, 6 July 1961, John wrote a funny account of how The Beatles were formed: 'Being a short diversion on the dubious origins of The Beatles'. The second edition is also interesting. The Beatles are on the front page with the headline 'Beatles sign recording contract', which turns out to be the Hamburg contract with Bert Kaempfert. In the accompanying photo, the caption refers to 'Paul MacArthy'.

Pop music mags and newspapers, such as *Melody Maker*, *Pop Weekly*, *Record Mirror*, *New Musical Express*, and *Big Beat*, featured The Beatles from 1962–3 and are interesting because they set The Beatles in context, showing the groups competing with them, recording their progress up the charts.

Then there are the teenage mags, such as *Fabulous*, *Marilyn*, *Valentine*, *Jackie*, mainly devoted to fashion and teenage topics, which often included special pull-out posters – the sort that girls stuck in their albums or on their bedroom walls. The Americans, at the same time, were covering The Beatles in their pop and teenage mags. As they were in Europe, particularly in Holland. Not so many in France.

I'm always looking out for any publication with a Beatles reference, as long as it's from the 1960s. I try to avoid anything from later decades, apart from 1981, the year after John Lennon was murdered in New York. I bought and have carefully kept all the John Lennon memorial issues.

5 THE BEATLES FAN CLUB You didn't have to join the Fan Club in order to get a copy of *Beatles Monthly*, which is one of my fave Beatles fanzines. It was available at newsagents and ran, in the first instance, for 77 issues, from August 1963 to December 1969. The photos were excellent and the words, even though it was all sanitized, being an official Beatles production, were informative. Its editor signed himself Johnny Dean, who didn't exist – the name was a pseudonym for Sean O'Mahoney, its publisher.

If you were in the official Fan Club, you got a membership card and regular newsletters. The club started in 1962, and the early letters came from Liverpool. When they moved to London, the address on the letters became 13 Monmouth Street. The Fan Club secretary who signed the letters in the early days was Freda Kelly, Northern Secretary, but after the move to London, letters were signed by Ann Collingham, as the National Club Secretary. There was in fact no such person. The Fan Club was run by

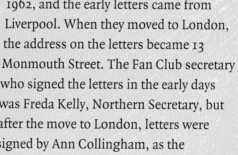

The Official
Beatles FAN CLUB
P.O. Box No. 12,
LIVERPOOL, 1.

THIS IS TO CERTIFY THAT
...SHEILA...DE...BOER...
IS AN OFFICIALLY ENROLLED MEMBER
OF THE FAN CLUB AND HAS BECOME
BEATLE PERSON NUMBER

111068

Freda Kelly
Freda Kelly
National Secretary of The Official Beatles Fan Club

PAID-UP MEMBER
Signed by the real Freda Kelly (unlike later supposed 'club secretaries'), this early Beatles' Fan Club membership card comes from the time when the club was still based in Liverpool.

ODEON SOUTHGATE

om Sunday, August 2nd, for 1 week

THE BEATLES

ARD DAYS NIGHT

OORS OPEN SUNDAY 4 p.m. WEEKDAYS 12.15

NING TIMES : SUNDAY 5.05, 7.10, 9.10
WEEKDAYS 1.05, 3.10, 5.10, 7.10, 9.15

COMPLETE PROGRAMMES COMMENCE AT—
SUNDAY 4.30, 6.30, 8.30
WEEKDAYS 12.30, 2.30, 4.35, 6.35, 8.40

Tony Barrow (The Beatles' PR man) and his staff from the same office, but they liked to pretend it was a separate entity.

One of the most fascinating products you got through the Fan Club was the annual Beatles flexi disc. It was produced every Xmas from 1963 to 1969. It was a small, flexible disc, on which The Beatles recorded a personal message for the fans, larking around, singing bits of songs, putting on silly voices. Over the years, the covers became more psychedelic. In 1970, they appeared on a compilation LP, which is now quite expensive, but the original flexis, in their jacket, in the brown envelope as posted from the Fan Club, are the most interesting ones to collect.

Almost every aspect of The Beatles' lives has had a book devoted to it, but so far I haven't seen a complete study of the history and work of The Beatles Fan Club. Long overdue.

6 BEATLES FILMS There were five Beatles films: two full-length feature films – *A Hard Day's Night* (1964) and *Help* (1965); *Let It Be* (1970), which was a documentary; *Magical Mystery Tour* (1967), which was an hour-long feature film, made initially for TV; and *Yellow Submarine* (1968), which was a cartoon. All of these produced front-of-house stills, posters, publicity material, postcards, and in different languages, as the films were shown all over the world.

7 PROGRAMMES AND TICKETS Early programmes, if you can find them, are very expensive. Once The Beatles started touring nationally, the same programme lasted the whole tour, despite being sold in different cities up and down the country. But most shows had their own posters. The Beatles did two Christmas Shows in London – at the Finsbury Park Astoria and Hammersmith Odeon – which had good souvenir programmes. Tickets, for the UK

SCREEN SUCCESS
The Beatles' first feature film, *A Hard Day's Night*, premiered in July 1964. It was so popular that, a month later, this cinema in north London produced a special poster advertising the screening times. The film was a 'mockumentary' of the band's life in Swinging London.

ASTORIA
FINSBURY PARK
BRIAN EPSTEIN presents
THE BEATLES
CHRISTMAS SHOW
EVENING 7-0
TUESDAY
DECEMBER 24
STALLS
T13   7/6
No Tickets exchanged nor money refunded
TO BE GIVEN UP

and USA, are hard to find, and are very boring anyway. Most of the interesting programmes, posters and even tickets, are available in repro versions, so serious students can study them without having to pay a fortune.

8 TOYS I haven't got many of these, mainly because of the daft prices. Dealers get carried away just because a Beatles image got stuck on a bit of 1960s tat, but I do have some jigsaws and a couple of Yellow Submarines, both in bad nick with bits missing. One of my favourites is a Beatles wig and magnet game – you pick up iron filings with the magnet and then move it around to make each Beatle's head either hairy or baldy.

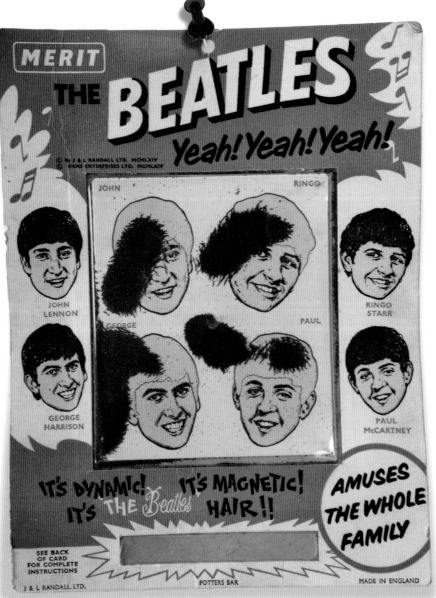

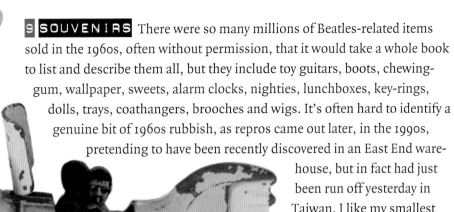

9 SOUVENIRS There were so many millions of Beatles-related items sold in the 1960s, often without permission, that it would take a whole book to list and describe them all, but they include toy guitars, boots, chewing-gum, wallpaper, sweets, alarm clocks, nighties, lunchboxes, key-rings, dolls, trays, coathangers, brooches and wigs. It's often hard to identify a genuine bit of 1960s rubbish, as repros came out later, in the 1990s, pretending to have been recently discovered in an East End warehouse, but in fact had just been run off yesterday in Taiwan. I like my smallest souvenirs the best – the badges. I have over 200, the nicest and best designed of which were those sold by the Fan Club.

10 BOOKS When I wrote my Beatles book in 1968, there were only two earlier ones I could find, both published in 1964: *The True Story of The Beatles* by Bill Shepherd, which was little more than an extended fan club magazine, and *Love Me Do* by Michael Braun, an American journalist who did a slice-of-life report, travelling with them on tour.

Today, I estimate the total number of books on The Beatles must come to around 1000 – and new ones are appearing all the time, many of them either reproducing the same old stuff (such as quotes taken word for word from my book) or on extremely esoteric topics. People who once drove The Beatles, or stood outside Abbey Road and got their autographs, have all had their books published, while true anoraks have managed to produce whole books based on just one album or one concert. My book, by the way, in its first edition, published by Heinemann, with the original dust jacket done by Alan Aldridge, sells for about £50, depending on the condition. I wish I'd kept more of them.

One thing I always noticed about Beatles mags produced in America was that they always managed to make The Beatles look American. Was it to make them more acceptable and wholesome, or was it that American photographers, artists and printers stuck to a certain style? Their faces always came out squarer, their teeth whiter, their complexions better, not at all like we pasty-faced Brits, brought up on wartime rations.

Valentine
BRINGS YOU LOVE STORIES IN PICTURES

PAUL AND JOHN
SUPER COLOUR PORTRAITS OF BEATLES

John Lennon George Harrison

C

Official Beatle Nylons
Special made for
VROOM & DREESMANN
Paul McCartney Nems Ent. Licence Stramsact.
Ringo Starr

Beatles
NYLON STOCKINGS
FIRST QUALITY 20 DEN. PLAIN

LINE ABOVE PAUL
Presented with VALENTINE
BELOW JOHN

...over story is ...The BEATLES' song ...

GOT TO D...

THEN I WAS OFF...BEING 'SOFT'
AS MY BOYFRIEND JEFF WOU...

LOOK, I'VE GOT
AN HOUR TO SPARE.
LET ME HELP YOU DELI-VER
THE 'WASHO' SAMPLES
ALONG OUR STREET.

...and Paul McCartney, Published by
...on Parlophone PMC1206.

DELL 1000 HINTS
07 141-411

...xtra-Big Portra...

BEATLE HAIRDO
& SETTING PATTERNS

BEATLE
...NGS,
...FFANTS,
...BLES,
...BS,
...OLLS,
...
...RES
...AUL,
...GE,

HELP! U also starring LEO McKERN
by WALTER SHEN...

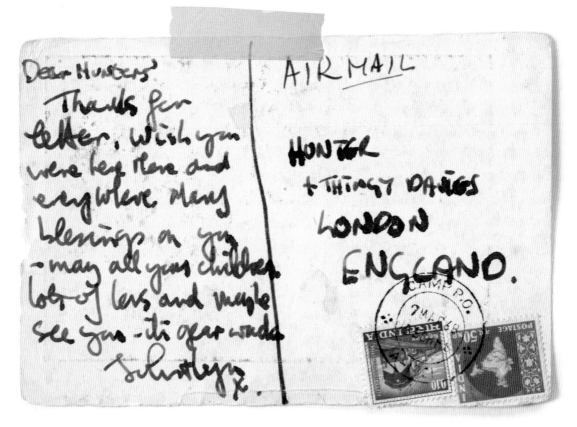

Dear Hunters?
Thanks for
letter, wish you
were here there and
everywhere many
blessings on you
- may all your children
lots of love and maybe
see you - its gear wonda
Schmtheys?

AIR MAIL

HUNTER
+ THINGY DAVIES
LONDON
ENGLAND.

Personal Beatles Material

While writing my Beatles book, I received letters and postcards from John's Aunt Mimi, who brought him up, and also his dad Alf, who did a runner in his childhood and only reappeared later in John's life. I tracked him down to a hotel on the outskirts of London where he was doing the washing-up. He gave me a photo of

himself when he'd been at sea, as a steward. He was on a charge at the time, for allegedly stealing some whisky, and in the photo you can see him holding up a number. The photo shows how John might have looked, if he'd lived to be a bit older.

I also got letters from George's mother Louise and also from Ringo's dad, his real dad, not the one who brought him up. He corrected my spelling of his surname – pointing out it should be Starkey, not Starkie.

The most interesting letters are of course the ones from The Beatles themselves. In March 1968, John sent me a postcard from

India, where The Beatles were staying with the Maharishi Mahesh Yogi. It's addressed to 'Hunter and Thingy Davies' and says, as far as I can decipher: 'Dear Hunters', Thanks for letter, wish you were here there and everywhere. Many blessings on you, may all your children. Lots of Love and maybe see you – its gear wack. John & Cyn' (Cynthia was his wife at the time). I'm not sure about 'gear wack', which was a Liverpool expression. It could be 'gear world'.

I also have some postcards from Paul, done in deliberately schoolboy writing and signed Barney, but I know it's Paul. In 1967, he and Linda stayed with us in a house we had rented in the Algarve, in Praia da Luz, and afterwards he sent us several jokey thank-you cards.

The four Beatles sent these sort of cards to each other all the time – in fact a couple of years ago, Ringo produced a rather charming little book of them called *Postcards from the Boys*, full of their jokes, smart remarks, drawings and illustrations.

Alas, biographers and collectors in years to come won't have such treasures to save and savour and study. The Beatles were a product of their time, when we all sent cards to each other. Who on Earth will ever want to treasure e-mails and texts? Ugh.

Prime Ministers

About 25 years ago, when I gave up being a proper journalist – that is, being on the staff, going to an office, hanging around – I was clearing my desk on my last day and found that I had carefully kept three letters written to me by prime ministers.

House of Commons,
London. S.W.1

21st March, 1963.

Dear Mr. Davies,

Many thanks for your letter of the 19th March. I greatly enjoyed reading the enclosure you sent me. Frankly I do not remember the incident referred to as I was only six at the time and I started following Huddersfield Town a little later on. I often however heard legends of the Preston Northend cup final and it was perhaps ironic justice that Preston beat Huddersfield also with a penalty in the last minute of extra time in the last cup final before the war.* Again, many thanks for writing.

Yours sincerely,

Harold Wilson

*After hitting the cross-bar.

Mr. Hunter Davies,

One of the letters was from Anthony Eden saying: go away, I'm not giving interviews. He was by then an old gadgy – that's a Carlisle expression, meaning 'old bloke'. Another was from Clement Attlee, who did give me an interview in his old age but warned that he was 'feeling a bit seedy today'.

The third was from Harold Wilson (see left). In his letter, he mentions the 1938 Cup Final, when Preston beat his team, Huddersfield, in the last minute of extra time. The letter is typed by a secretary, but at the end he'd added in his own handwriting, 'After hitting the cross-bar'.

As collectors know, content is all. The nice thing about this letter is that it illustrates Wilson showing off – his knowledge of football, his excellent memory, and what a big head he had.

So, I found I'd started a new collection (come on, three related items is definitely a collection) without knowing it, just by not throwing these letters away. I then set myself the task of collecting autographs of every British prime minister. It took me ten years to complete, going back to Robert Walpole in the 18th century.

PMS ANCIENT AND MODERN
(clockwise) Pitt the Elder, Balfour, Thatcher and Chamberlain. Above, Wilson's letter to me.

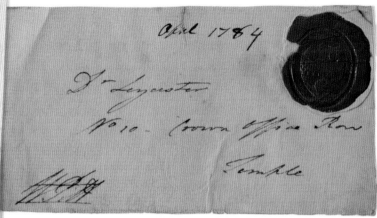

My Walpole signature is on an old document, or part of an old document. It appears to be a quarter or half of a page, on thick parchment-like paper, all handwritten in ink, authorizing a payment to someone on the Civil List. It's also signed by W.A. Yonge and George Dodington, both well-known political figures of the day. I had to look them up, as I'd never heard of them. As a historical document, it's rather lacking in content, as all Walpole appears to have written on it is his signature, but it is dated 1725, so it's pretty old. I see in the corner I have written in pencil how much I paid for it, £6. What a bargain.

With most of the very early prime ministers, such as Spencer Perceval, all I have is a scrap of paper with the PM's autograph on it, not even a bit of document. Spencer Perceval was PM from 1809 to 1812, when he was shot dead in the lobby of the House of Commons on 11 May, thereby becoming the only British PM – so far – to have been assassinated. He was shot through the heart by John Bellingham, who had a personal grudge against the government, but was also said to be deranged. I would never have known these fascinating historical details if I hadn't decided to collect prime ministers.

With later PMs, from the mid-19th century onwards, I have quite a few whole letters, with reasonably interesting contents. The longest is a two-page letter from the Duke of Wellington in 1829 about some Treasury matter. He was PM from 1828 to 1830, so he was in office at the time he wrote it. Naturally, I have tried to get autographs and letters *during* the time they were PM, but haven't always managed it. Well, it's my collection, I can fiddle my own rules. I didn't actually buy the Wellington letter – I swapped it with a dealer and gave him in exchange a T.S. Eliot letter, which the poet sent to me, saying no, he wouldn't give me an interview. I wish now I hadn't done so. I wasn't collecting famous poets at that time, nor did I realize that a small note from T.S. Eliot is harder to find than a Wellington two-pager.

Other whole letters from PMs I've managed to acquire include Lord Derby, Lord Aberdeen, Palmerston, Gladstone, Salisbury, Rosebery, Balfour, Campbell-Bannerman and Asquith. Mostly they are short letters, either declining an invitation to dinner or to speak, accepting one, or thanking someone afterwards for their hospitality. So not exactly of shattering political importance. Important prime ministerial letters today would cost hundreds if not thousands and be kept in proper museums and archives, but minor ones can be had for £30–£80, depending on the PM and the content. In the days of handwritten letters, and posts on the hour, a PM would write dozens of personal bread-and-butter letters every day to his friends and supporters, many of which were kept.

The Palmerston one, dated 1836, is from the Foreign Office, signed by him when he was Foreign Secretary. It is in effect an early form of passport. It's asking for an MP, Charles Barclay, to be given protection and help while visiting Brussels. I also have a later one, signed by Lord Salisbury, which is a more official form of passport, on a large sheet of paper, printed in italic lettering, made out in the name of a Mrs Rosabelle Lloyd. It asks for her to be allowed to 'pass freely without let or hindrance to afford her every assistance and protection of which she may stand in need'. It has been stamped by the authorities in Italy and Germany, showing where she had travelled.

I wasn't aware, until I started collecting PMs, of the existence of 'Free

Fronts'. They are the easiest and cheapest way of acquiring PMs' signatures, or those of any famous political or aristocratic figure of the 19th century. Before pre-paid postage stamps arrived in 1840, politicians could get free postage by signing their names on the front of envelopes. Postal historians collect such envelopes for their postal markings, but they often don't recognize, or can't make out, the signature, so you can sometimes find Free Fronts signed by famous politicians relatively cheaply. For instance, I have one signed by William Pitt the Younger, with a nice big red seal, which cost me only £8.

People used to try to fiddle these Free Fronts, pretending to be an MP or Lord in order to get free post (postage was very expensive until the arrival of Penny Black). This was the downfall of a conman and bigamist called Hatfield, who did the dirty on the pure and lovely Maid Of Buttermere, a saga written about by Wordsworth and more recently in a novel by Melvyn Bragg. Hatfield was hanged in Carlisle in 1803, not for his dastardly seductions but for defrauding the Post Office. The blackguard.

Gladstone's autograph is quite cheap, because he signed so many Free Fronts and wrote so many letters, cards and notes. Lloyd George is relatively expensive, presumably because he didn't sign as many, but I have three signed pieces by him, plus some original photos taken at a funeral in Wales.

I also have a 10 Downing Street letter signed by his secretary, F.L. Stevenson, thanking someone for writing. The signature is interesting because F.L. Stevenson was Fanny Stevenson, with whom Lloyd George had a romp, allegedly on the table at Number 11, before he became premier. He did marry her, though, later in life.

Churchill is the most expensive PM – for obvious reasons. He is adored by Americans, who will buy anything signed by him. Even a straightforward thank-you letter will cost hundreds of pounds. But you have to be careful – Churchill's office used an early writing machine to reply to fans. I have a few such bits of correspondence myself, as they are interesting in themselves.

Before the 20th century, you don't see much headed notepaper – Palmerston's 'passport' letter, for example, is just headed 'Foreign Office', in handwriting, though seals were used in earlier times. The first printed 10 Downing Street-headed notepaper I have is a letter from Gladstone in 1874. It's interesting after that to see how the typography changes over the decades.

Together with the autographed material, letters, postcards, envelopes and scraps, I also keep any interesting postcards and illustrations of the

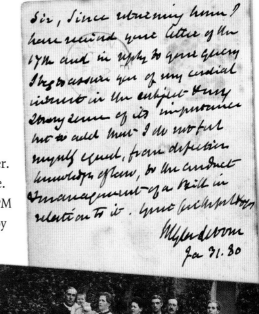

Mr. Gladstone and Family at Hawarden

PMs. Technically speaking, I have finished this collection, as I've got examples all the way back to Walpole. Not many collections have a finite point.

Oddly, one of the most difficult autographs to obtain was that of the present PM, Gordon Brown. I just wrote to him as a collector, probably one of many sending similar requests. He may have simply been too busy with

London Thirteenth Jany 26

Rt Honble
Sir Gore Ouseley Bart

Woolmers
Hertford

Liverpool

EARL ATTLEE, K.G., P.C., O.M., C.H. WESTCOTT, MARTIN'S END LANE, GREAT MISSEN
GREAT MISSENDEN 2476

29th Sept 63

Dear Mr Davies

Thank you s~ much for the excelle~
I have been a bit seedy the last few days
the delay in acknowledging.

yours sincerely

Attlee

Privy Council Office,
Whitehall, S.W.

14th May, 1940.

Dear Sir James,

I am grateful to you for your letter
and for the message of sympathy and understanding
which you have sent me. It is a help in these
difficult days to know that the action I have
taken has been understood and appreciated.

Yours sincerely

Neville Chamberlain

Sir James Marchant

GREAT BRITAIN
Commonwealth
PARLIAMENTARY ASSOCIATION
Conference
LONDON 1973

8p   10p

OF ISSUE

Harold Wilson
Alec Douglas-Home
Avon
Edward Heath
Margaret Thatcher.

LORD ROSEBERY

---

it, I wi~

as a lan~

as they ~

me, Dear ~r, Your obedien~

Servant. Wellington

I thank you sincerely
for y^r 5 kind message
to me wh I have
received & read with
great pleasure.

Winston Churchill

1945

THE PRIME MINISTER

13 May 1997

Dear Hunter,

I am very grateful to you for having taken the trouble to send me such a kind message. Your congratulations and good wishes are very much appreciated.

It was so good of you to write & I hope this kite is what you need for the collection!

Best wishes

Your ever

Tony Blair

H. Davies, Esq.

10, Downing Street,
Whitehall,

4th April, 1935.

Dear Sir James Marchant,

Thank you very much for the copy of the volume in the Whitehall Series on the War Office which you so kindly sent to me.

The education of the public in the work of the great Departments of State, which you have undertaken in the Whitehall Series, is certainly a very worthy object. I congratulate you on the volumes you have already produced and I certainly wish you well in your further efforts.

Yours very sincerely,

Ramsay MacDonald

"TOWARD UNITED NATIONS APRIL 25, 1945" 5¢ UNITED STATES POSTAGE

23267

With Best Wishes
For Christmas
And The New Year

Tony, Cherie

23

DISRAELI

pressing affairs of state to bother with such trivial things. Or maybe he was one step ahead; by limiting the supply of his autographs and letters, he may have been trying to put his own prices up hugely in the years ahead. Very canny.

But credit where credit's due: although it took me ages to get a positive response, I'm now delighted to report that he has personally sent me an example of his signature. So now I have a complete set of PMs. Collecting heaven!

By contrast, Mr Brown's predecessor at Number 10, Tony Blair, was really quick off the mark, seeing it as good public relations. Also he was keen to be liked, by anyone, so most letters to him, even from pestering autograph-hunters like me, would get a reply within two weeks.

Some PM Facts & Figures

Sir Robert Walpole, 1st Earl of Walpole (1676–1745), is generally considered by historians to have been the first British prime minister, in that he was the first politician to have that term applied to him. Before him, there had been chief ministers, but none with quite the power and position of Walpole. His starting date is usually put at 1721, when he first formed an administration. He presided over the cabinet and reported on the affairs of his government to the sovereign, staying in power till 1742.

Between 1721 and 2009, we have had 73 premierships – but that includes people like Pitt the Younger, Peel, Gladstone, Disraeli and Churchill, who came back as PMs for a second or even third term. Counting the actual different people who were PM, the total is 52.

Eighteen PMs went to Eton. The number of known or probable adulterers is 12. I got these names (except Major's) from the eminent historian A.J.P. Taylor, who added that there will be many more that we don't yet know about.

The youngest PM, on first taking office, was Pitt the Younger, aged 24. The oldest was Lord Palmerston, aged 71. The longest-serving PM was Walpole, 20 years, if you count him as the first. Eight other PMs have managed to serve for a decade or more – Pitt (18), Liverpool (14), Salisbury (13), Gladstone and North (12), Thatcher (11) and Pelham and Blair (10).

'DIZZY' Below: together with his great rival William Gladstone, the flamboyant Benjamin Disraeli epitomized the High Victorian age. As well as being a politician, Disraeli was also a novelist.

WHIPPERSNAPPER Left: when he came to office, in 1783, aged 24, William Pitt the Younger was the youngest British PM, and is almost certain to retain this record. Despite his youth, Pitt steered Britain deftly through a period of great strife and danger, including the Napoleonic Wars.

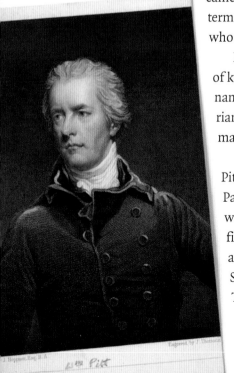

BRITISH PRIME MINISTERS 1721–2009

Sir Robert Walpole 1st Earl of Orford	1721–42
Spencer Compton 1st Earl of Wilmington	1742–3
Henry Pelham	1743–54
Sir Thomas Pelham-Holles 1st Duke of Newcastle	1754–6
William Cavendish 4th Duke of Devonshire	1756–57
Duke of Newcastle	1757–60
John Stuart 3rd Earl of Bute	1762–3
George Grenville	1763–5
Charles Watson-Wentworth 2nd Marquis of Rockingham	1765–6
William Pitt the Elder, 1st Earl of Chatham	1766–8
Augustus Henry Fitzroy 3rd Duke of Grafton	1768–70
Frederick North 2nd Earl of Guilford	1770–82
Marquis of Rockingham	1782
William Petty 2nd Earl of Shelburne, 1st Marquis of Lansdowne	1782–83
William Cavendish Bentinck 3rd Duke of Portland	1783
William Pitt the Younger	1783–1801
Henry Addington 1st Viscount Sidmouth	1801–04
William Pitt the Younger	1804–06
William Wyndham Baron Grenville	1806–07
Duke of Portland	1807–09
Spencer Perceval	1809–12
Robert Banks Jenkinson 2nd Earl of Liverpool	1812–27
George Canning	1827
Frederick John Robinson Viscount Goderich, 1st Earl of Ripon	1827–8
Arthur Wellesley 1st Duke of Wellington	1828–30
Charles Grey 2nd Earl and Viscount Howick	1830–4
William Lamb 2nd Viscount Melbourne	1834
Duke of Wellington	1834
Sir Robert Peel	1834–5
Viscount Melbourne	1835–41
Sir Robert Peel	1841–6
Lord John Russell 1st Earl Russell	1846–52
Edward Stanley 14th Earl of Derby	1852
George Hamilton-Gordon 4th Earl of Aberdeen	1852–5
Henry John Temple 3rd Viscount Palmerston	1855–8
Earl of Derby	1858–9
Viscount Palmerston	1859–65
Earl Russell	1865–6
Earl of Derby	1866–8
Benjamin Disraeli 1st Earl of Beaconsfield	1868
William Ewart Gladstone	1868–74
Benjamin Disraeli	1874–80
William Ewart Gladstone	1880–5
Robert Cecil 3rd Marquess of Salisbury	1885–6
William Ewart Gladstone	1886
Marquess of Salisbury	1886–92
William Ewart Gladstone	1892–4
Archibald Philip Primrose 5th Earl of Rosebery	1894–5
Marquess of Salisbury	1895–1902
Arthur James Balfour 1st Earl of Balfour	1902–05
Sir Henry Campbell-Bannerman	1905–08
Herbert Henry Asquith 1st Earl of Oxford and Asquith	1908–16
David Lloyd George 1st Earl of Dwyfor	1916–22
Andrew Bonar Law	1922–3
Stanley Baldwin 1st Earl Baldwin of Bewdley	1923–4
James Ramsay MacDonald	1924
Stanley Baldwin	1924–9
James Ramsay MacDonald	1929–35
Stanley Baldwin	1935–7
(Arthur) Neville Chamberlain	1937–40
Sir Winston Spencer Churchill	1940–5
Clement Richard Attlee 1st Earl Attlee	1945–51
Sir Winston Spencer Churchill	1951–5
Sir Anthony Eden 1st Earl of Avon	1955–7
Harold Macmillan 1st Earl of Stockton	1957–63
Sir Alexander Frederick Douglas-Home 4th Earl of Home	1963–4
(James) Harold Wilson Baron Wilson of Rievaulx	1964–70
Sir Edward Heath	1970–4
(James) Harold Wilson	1974–6
(Leonard) James Callaghan Baron Callaghan of Cardiff	1976–9
Margaret Thatcher Baroness Thatcher	1979–90
Sir John Major	1990–7
Anthony Charles Lynton Blair	1997–2007
Gordon Brown	2007–

HISTORY OF COLLECTING

I received a letter the other day from a student at Cambridge doing a thesis on 'The History of Collecting'. Dear God, I thought, what are our universities coming to – first media studies, now collecting studies. Why don't they stick to vital stuff like Latin and Greek and let ordinary people get on with their trivial pursuits?

This is how collectors usually react – apologetic, mocking themselves, confessing their stupid obsessions, how daft it all is, yes this is what I collect, for my sins. We only half mean it, of course. Other times we big it up. I collect therefore I am.

But I was surprised, so I wrote back to this student, at Fitzwilliam College, and asked if it was his own whim, a self-chosen subject, perhaps a cushy number, or were there academics actually studying and teaching collecting? It turned out that he'd been given a monster reading list. So I bought two of the titles myself.

Apparently, there are at least 400 learned works on collecting, judging by the bibliographies in the two books I bought. It's amazing how academics can take the joy out of life. The books were full of graphs and figures and headings I just couldn't understand. They included chapters with such titles as 'Collecting the Proper Within'. This comes from a book, published by 1995, by Professor Susan Pearce of the University of Leicester. Once I settled down, fixed my cold compresses and turned off all the phones, I found it rather informative.

She dates the various periods of collecting, starting with ancient times, when objects such as weapons, pots, metal and silver jewellery and other stuff were found in burial mounds, graves and shrines. Obviously they had been collected, but I personally don't look upon these prehistoric troves as 'collecting'. Rich men, as they've always done, acquire riches – that's what they do – while religious folk like to appease their gods or carry their possessions into the next world.

In the Classical period, the Greeks and Romans had sculptures, pottery, temples. There were also private collectors, like Cicero and Verres, the Governor of Sicily, who filled every room in his house with his collections – the first reported example of a temptation to which all collectors succumb at some time. Verres kept his

best and favourite statue in a purely private room, where no one else could see it, another mark of an obsessive collector.

During Renaissance times, it was paintings and sculpture that claimed the attention of collectors, while the pious, in abbeys and cathedrals, were gathering, and sometimes competing for, relics of saints and holy people.

In the Early Modern Period, collectors filled cabinets with 'curiosities' and oddities. Here, at last, Professor Pearce is getting near my definition of collecting. The use of the word 'curiosities' is interesting. At one time 'oddities' were what book dealers kept in the back room, locked away in a drawer for discerning male customers.

The 18th and 19th centuries saw the arrival of the Industrial Revolution, and of scientific collections of machinery, engines and instruments. The Royal Society had been founded in 1660 and gentleman scholars began to collect natural rarities. The celebrated Swedish taxonomist Carl Linnaeus made his first great collection of botanical specimens in 1737. Natural history collections became very popular with ordinary folks, too. They pasted dried flowers in books, and collected shells, fossils and geological specimens. Natural history clubs and societies sprang up all over Britain.

The Great Exhibition of 1851 inspired collectors great and small, and led to the creation of provincial museums in all our major cities. In London, the Victoria and Albert Museum opened in 1857, as the South Kensington Museum.

Now, apparently, we're in the Postmodern period. Contemporary collectors can hoard any old thing. So, at last, Professor Pearce has come to me. She identifies certain collectors as 'subversive', deliberately collecting objects that would not normally be accepted as an art form. She doesn't actually give examples, but I would think Beatles' knickers or bubblegum might come into that category.

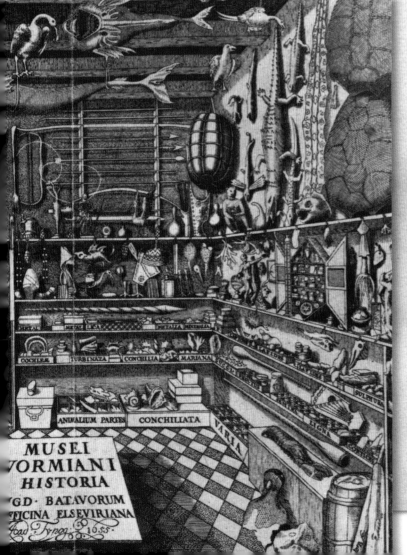

MUSEI WORMIANI HISTORIA
LGD· BATAVORUM
FICINA ELSEVIRIANA

WEIRD AND WONDERFUL The museum of natural history items belonging to the collector Ole Worm, from Leiden, Holland, in 1655. In the Early Modern Period, which Professor Susan Pearce defines as the 16th and 17th centuries, many people had cabinets filled with 'curiosities' and oddities.

Paintings

Art must have been amongst the first collectables. Someone did a drawing or painting on the wall of the cave and other people said: 'Heh, that's nice, will you do one on my wall?'

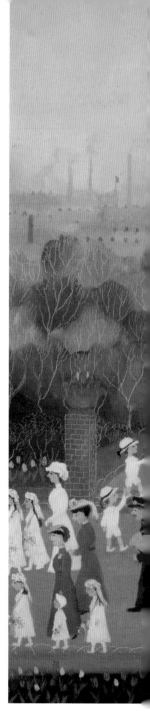

Or did statues come first? Deities, spirits or animals carved out of wood or stone would have served a purpose – they were not made purely for decoration. Religious relics have been collected ever since we had religions, shrines and holy places displaying their treasures to be admired or worshipped.

For centuries, there have been art collectors. Kings and queens, emperors and rich men, competed to acquire the choicest examples, sometimes keeping them to themselves, for their own pleasure, at other times opening them up for the unwashed hordes to enjoy.

I'm rather in awe of people who collect paintings. It seems sort of grown-up, serious, intellectual. When you see someone referred to as a 'distinguished collector' with a 'notable collection', you know it's not bottle tops. It's art.

Art can cover many objects, ranging from paintings and sculptures to antiquities, like Roman and Greek artefacts, or even older ones, from ancient Egypt and China, or from prehistoric times. Collectors, in the past, seem to have been particularly fascinated by the past. And they didn't tend to collect trivial or ephemeral objects. That seems to be a more modern interest, originating in Victorian times. Stamp collectors had to wait till 1840, when the Penny Black arrived, before they could start collecting postage stamps. Football programme collectors were just hanging around, twiddling their thumbs, until the laws of football were approved in 1863. Even then, they had to wait a few decades till someone thought of printing programmes.

Collecting a lot of the rubbish that I do, stuff which has no purpose or use, and doesn't even look all that pretty or artistic, is probably more of a 20th-century fashion. But I'm sure the impulses are much the same, the yearning to gather in, arrange and order, and then, with a bit of luck, show off. Collectors do feel they are kings, if only of their own creations.

My Paintings

However, I have acquired quite a few paintings on the journey so far, about 30 of them, mostly without any theme or pattern. Like books, they can make a room. It's hard to hang Beatles records or postage stamps on a wall, though that has been done. Paintings hang well, look well, brighten a room, give it interest, provide talking points, impress visitors and are also very useful for covering up damp patches and nasty stains.

We have one specialist collection in our house, one painter we have deliberately set out to collect. I use the word 'we' because paintings are the only thing my wife and I have ever bought together, making joint choices, either of us being able to overrule the other if we don't like something. All the other collections in our London house, or our Lakeland house, are totally my own, my affair. In fact she is blissfully ignorant of many of them, which is just as well.

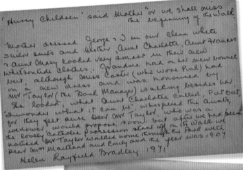

Mostly, we have acquired our paintings by chance, from people who have come our way, artists who have presented themselves.

1 MRS BRADLEY The first real painting we bought was in 1966. Until then, the walls of our North London house, where we still live today, were covered mainly with wall hangings and framed Picasso prints, the sort of stuff we had given each other as students.

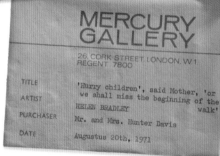

While I was writing the 'Atticus' column in *The Sunday Times*, I went to interview a grandmother in her sixties called Mrs Bradley, who late in life had started painting scenes from her Edwardian childhood in Lancashire.

Her paintings depicted rather idealized industrial scenes, with smoke and chimneys in the background, but pretty, well-dressed, colourful, happy people in the foreground. I liked the way she signed herself with a small black fly, for reasons I can't quite remember, but I think it had been her nickname when she was young. I also liked the way she wrote, in handwriting, little descriptions of each painting, as if talking to her granddaughter, which were then stuck on the back of the painting.

I bought one which she'd entitled *Fanny, Our Strong-Minded Horse*. The note on the back reads: 'The horses getting ready to walk through the village on May Saturday. Father is waiting with Fanny, our strong-minded horse. The year was 1904 – Helen Layfield Bradley, 1966.' In the foreground is a woman in pink, who was not named. I paid £20 for the painting.

She went on to have three shows at the Mercury Gallery in London, and one in Los Angeles. Her prices rocketed and people loved her on both sides of the Atlantic. 'The enchantment of the season!' enthused the *International Herald Tribune*. Jonathan Cape produced a book of her paintings in 1971, called *And Miss Carter Wore Pink*.

We bought a second painting, from the Mercury Gallery, in 1971, for £200, as the paintings had increased tenfold in price. This is called *Hurry children, said mother, or we shall miss the beginning of the walk*.

Cape published another book about Mrs Bradley, and you often see copies at jumbles and Oxfam today for only a couple of pounds, but the prices for her actual paintings have continued to soar, often reaching the £20,000 mark. She died in 1979.

2 **MARY FEDDEN** There was a short period in the early 1970s when a woman dealer was selling paintings in our area, door to door. A friend of a friend had given her our name. She rang up, said she was in our area, could she pop in. We said fine, no problem.

We wouldn't be so welcoming today with cold callers, though they try it all the time – Geordies selling fresh fish at the door or so-called charity workers selling dishcloths, while on the 'phone we get pestered by people who use Christian names, as if we are best friends, then try to interest us in special offers on gas and electricity prices or amazing investments in Nigeria. Get lost, is what I say to them all, even when they pretend to have been in contact already or been recommended to call. Back in the 1970s, I was much kinder.

This woman, middle-aged, middle-class, arrived at our front door in a small van, out of which she took some paintings. She came in, propped them up, and we gave her a glass of wine. I liked her enterprise, working all

on her own, handling the work of just a few artists without having the fuss and expense of exhibiting their work in a West End gallery. Those galleries were and are very snotty places, cold and superior rather than welcoming.

This woman didn't do a hard sell, just quietly explained about the artists she was handling and tried to work out our likes and dislikes. She had a good eye, and we liked most of what she showed us. That first evening, we bought a painting by Mary Fedden, whom we'd not heard of at the time. It features a pleasant landscape, of hills and fields, with a woman in the foreground with some donkeys. I thought it might be Lakeland, in olden times, but we gathered it was somewhere like Israel. We've grown to like it more and more, as the years have gone by, but I can't remember the price we paid.

3 BERYL COOK In 1975, when I became editor of the *Sunday Times Magazine*, a freelance sent us some transparencies of paintings by a local landlady in Plymouth called Beryl Cook. I loved them, but the art department said boring, boring, totally amateur, crude and derivative.

I was always having rows with the art department, and usually gave in, as of course they knew so much, and were awfully clever, but this time I insisted. I rang the woman myself, interviewed her on the 'phone, ran a little story. She really did run a guest house and this was her first exhibition. To help her along, I said I'd buy one. I chose one of three women sunbathing as it made me smile. I think I paid £10, or perhaps £15. I always intended to buy some more, but never did. She immediately became so popular that her prices rocketed. Now she can fetch up to £40,000.

Our Beryl Cook hung in the kitchen for years, which was silly, as it got too much sun and the colours faded. The woman's bikini at the top used to be bright red. But it still makes me smile. And it would, even if I lived in a cave ...

4 L.S. LOWRY The first Lowry painting I ever saw, in the flesh, was in 1967 at Brian Epstein's house in Chapel Street, Belgravia, London, best part. In fact he had two of them, both

B. Cook

stunning. Did I ogle them! I knew who Lowry was, his Northern origins, and had seen his matchstick drawings, but was not quite aware of his paintings, and how attractive and colourful they were.

I was impressed that Brian had two of them, but then I was impressed by everything about Epstein. He was so sophisticated, so polished, well dressed, well spoken, and of course so successful, having discovered The Beatles. I always felt scruffy and provincial in his presence. It's only now, when I look back, checking his birth date, that I realize he was only two years older than me. He seemed decades more mature.

I had interviewed Lowry himself a couple of years earlier, at an exhibition of his drawings in a London gallery. He sat in a corner, smiling to himself, amused by all the arty types, gently mocking their pretensions. I persuaded him to sign a book of his drawings, which I still have. Somewhere. Driven myself mad trying to find it. Must be in the Lake District.

I then collected all the books about him I could find. I had a fancy to do a biog, and got a publisher very keen. On the surface a boring life – unmarried, rent collector, didn't go anywhere – yet his hidden life story is so strange. He befriended a sequence of very young girls, gave them money, took them on holiday, helped with their education. Today, the tabloids would have hounded him, yet he demanded nothing from them, behaved impeccably. I couldn't get agreement from his estate, possibly because I made the mistake of saying I was interested in his girlfriends. I didn't want to do an unauthorized book, so I dropped the idea.

But I did buy my own Lowry. It's what young Northern lads from the 1960s aspired to. Make a bit of brass, get your mam a bungalow, then buy a Lowry. I wasn't quite in the Epstein class, however. Now I look at my notes on the back of my little drawing, which is just six inches square, I see it was incredibly cheap. I bought it at auction on 10 April 1980 at Thomson, Roddick and Laurie in Carlisle. It's signed and dated, 1954 – price £180.

My notes also reveal it has a title – *The Argument* – which I'd forgotten. I presume the taller figure on the right – could it be Lowry? – is having words with a woman, possibly about her rent. Or is Lowry the rent collector figure with a bowler? The matchstick dogs are very Lowryesque.

My children, with their London ways, unaware of what a loved figure

BLOOMSBURY IDYLL *The Chair, Charleston* by Vanessa Bell, a leading light of the Bloomsbury Group. Charleston is a farmhouse near Lewes in East Sussex where this avant-garde set of writers and artists retreated to work and enjoy rural solitude. You can visit it and go on a guided tour.

Lowry was for all Northerners of a certain age, used to go, ugh, I could do that. Oh, if only they had. I could have had a whole gallery by now . . .

5 VANESSA BELL In the end I summoned up the nerve to go to an actual West End gallery, and wandered round the paintings on show as if I knew what I was doing, or even what I liked. I asked to see the dealer, who of course was hidden in a back office, and enquired what his best price was on a certain painting. I wasn't sure if one did that in Mayfair, but come on, I thought, there can't be any basic difference between a dealer selling a Hockney painting or a Beatles programme. It's all a game. If they look shocked by the notion of 'best price', and pretend that what is on the item is the one and only price, what on earth do you mean, then you either shrug and walk away, or simply take it, because in fact you wanted it anyway and think it is a good price. The gallery in question was the Anthony d'Offay Gallery in Dering Street, off New Bond Street, one of the best-known London dealers and galleries of recent times. D'Offay has now retired, having passed over something like £25 million worth of his collection to the National Gallery.

My wife and I were interested in the Bloombury Group and in 1981 we heard that D'Offay had a painting for sale by Vanessa Bell, sister of Virginia Woolf. It's called *The Chair, Charleston*, which is the farmhouse in Sussex where the Bloomsbury group used to gather. A note on the back of the painting revealed that at one time it had been owned by the painter, critic and fellow Bloomsbury member Roger Fry. It shows a straw chair, a bit of the house and garden, but not much else. I was appalled by the official price – £3000. We'd never spent anything near that in our lives, even on a car, apart of course from our house – and that had cost just £5000. My wife seemed keener than me, so I didn't want to appear a meanie, but all the same, I managed to whittle the price down to £2900. Pretty cheeky and brave, as he was a fairly cold, intimidating figure. It's still our most expensive painting.

6 PRIMITIVE HAITIAN PAINTINGS At the other end of the scale, the cheapest paintings I ever acquired, and which I still love, are some I bought in Haiti, direct from street painters in the capital Port-au-Prince.

Haiti was and still is the poorest country in the Western hemisphere, with people living in the gutter, yet the colour and vitality of their art was incredible. You could see it in their 'tap-taps' – old and battered and over-loaded little buses – each one of which is hand-painted with tropical scenes, faces and figures. In alleyways and at corner shops you would see groups of people, who looked like carpenters and labourers rather than artists, painting away, selling their works for a few pounds to passers-by. I bought three paintings, just the canvases, not framed, which was all I could carry. I gave one to each of my children, who were then quite young, and hung them in their bedrooms. I'm pleased to see that they each kept their little primitive Haitian painting and still have them on the walls of their houses today.

7 JOHN BRATBY A letter arrived one day from John Bratby, RA, whom I had never met, though I had heard of his work as he was very well known at the time. In his letter he said he was assembling portraits of 'People of Today' to go in an exhibition, and would I sit for him? He lived down in Hastings and said it would only take a few hours and he'd provide lunch. I was intrigued, amused, flattered, so I went down to see him. The lunch consisted of fried bacon sandwiches, prepared by a woman I took to be his wife. He worked very quickly, slap-slapping away, while I ate my sarnie.

I asked for more details about the exhibition, but it all seemed a bit vague. I was, however, pleased by the painting and asked if I could buy it. He agreed, surprisingly quickly, and I paid him, I think, £300. I don't think the exhibition 'People of Today' ever took place, but I gather he wrote to lots of people whose names he saw in the paper, especially when he was hard up. Most of them, like me, offered to buy their own portrait.

We still have it, but at the top of the landing, hidden away. My wife always disliked it. But it still amuses me. He was an RA, after all.

8 SHEILA FELL The only real and proper collection of paintings we have are by a woman called Sheila Fell (1931–79), who was also an RA, one of the first women ever to be elected.

The connection began because she was from Cumbria, like us. We became friendly with her in the 1960s, after we had moved to London. We went to see her several times in her garret flat-cum-studio in Redcliffe Square, Chelsea. It was miles up, and the stairs were bare stone, as far as I remember. I wondered how someone so small and frail could lug up all her easels, canvases and stuff.

She had long, thick, jet-black hair set against a porcelain-pale white face. Very 1960s, very art-schoolish. She was taciturn, hesitant, worried. I once went on a radio programme with her, about young people from the North making it in London. She'd said she would only go on it if I came with her. All the way through, she was shaking, unable to do herself justice, yet she had interesting ideas, original thoughts.

I didn't know at that time that she had been befriended, as a young girl aged 24, after her first exhibition, by L.S. Lowry. He used to pay her £3 a week to help out in his studio. Sheila was just one of several girls whom Lowry took under his wing, often paying for their studies or their living expenses. Lowry remained a father-figure to Sheila for over 20 years, even going on holiday with her, watching her painting. We were all thrilled, we exiled Cumbrians, when Sheila became an RA in 1974, an honour for the county – and most unusual for a woman. Even today, the vast majority of Academicians are men.

Over the years, we acquired seven Sheila Fells, from dealers and public auctions, which we love dearly, not just for their associations, knowing the landscape so well, but for the truth, the lack of any sentimentality or choco-late-box gloss, which, alas, is the main feature of many Lake District paintings. For many years we had a huge one, six feet by four, called *Village in Cumber-land*. It was one of those that I bought direct from Sheila in the 1960s, paying her, I think, £400. It had pride of place in our London living room, looking perfect until 1986, when our son put a snooker cue through the bottom corner. Wasn't his fault, he said. It was the stupid snooker table's fault, one of those small, table-top ones.

We planned to take it with us when we moved to our Loweswater house in 1987, and had a suitably large, empty wall ready for it. But when we moved in, the builders had put a radiator on that wall. There was nowhere else it could go. So in 1988, we sold it at Sotheby's (for £3000).

In December 1990, there was a Sheila Fell retrospective at the RA. We went to see it, pleased that, ten years after her death, she had not been forgotten. In fact, she was being honoured and admired, even more than she had been during her lifetime.

As we wandered in, we saw that pride of place had been given to our former painting *Village in Cumberland*. And it looked stunning. The small hole had been repaired, and the whole painting cleaned. And it was properly lit. We had hung it so badly, so dimly. No wonder the sky had looked so dark. Today, I suppose it would go for £50,000. We later bought another Sheila Fell, a smaller one, but I do wish we had not sold the big one.

Sheila's life ended tragically and abruptly when she was aged just 48. She was called Fell, she painted fells, and she died falling down the steep staircase at Redcliffe Square. By an awfully gruesome coincidence, I had done an interview with her for *The Sunday Times* on 16 December 1979, which appeared the very morning after her sudden death.

9 SEAN CONNERY NUDES   I also have some drawings in my art collection – which were a big mistake. How I regret buying them! What *was* I thinking? In acquiring them, I broke one of my basic rules of collecting, which I thought I'd learned the hard way when I collected stamps.

I was doing a book on Sean Connery that was going to take me a year. Naturally, I started collecting books about him, postcards, theatre programmes, film stills, all quite cheap, all easy to pick up. I like having a new subject – and a new excuse to spend Saturday mornings tracking down rubbish, I mean treasures. Then suddenly I saw in a Christie's catalogue that they were selling seven nude studies of him, done in pen, ink and wash, dating from the early 1950s when he earned money by modelling for life classes at Edinburgh College of Art. A woman who had been an art student at the time, later an art teacher, had recently discovered them in a folder she'd totally forgotten about. The estimate was £800–£1200. Hmm, not quite rubbish, in fact mad really, far more than I'd spend on something in my usual collections, but on the other hand, it would be brilliant to have some unpublished material I could use. And if I got old Sean to sign them, it would double their value. I couldn't lose.

So I went along, on 14 December 2004, to Christie's in South Kensington to bid for lot 193. It was a Film and Entertainment sale with a lot of James Bond-related items. I couldn't believe some of the prices being paid, such as £14,000 for a fibreglass coat-of-arms from *On Her Majesty's Secret Service*, and £20,000 for a moon buggy as seen in *Diamonds are Forever*.

I thought I'd have no chance with the nude drawings, but amazingly I got them – for only £800. (That's a secret by the way, as I never told my wife.) I felt very pleased, I'd beaten the field, stolen a march on the dealers, but looking back, I think I was the only bidder. Sean was amused when I let him see them, and he signed the four he liked best. I spoke to the woman who had drawn them, Hilary Buchanan, and got her permission to use them. But then, after eight months, the book project collapsed. I gave the more rubbishy James Bond books and mags to a charity shop, but I put the nudes back into Christie's – convinced I could get at least double what I paid.

They were in Christie's sale on 5 December 2006, lot 165, estimate £1000–1500. I even paid for an illustration in the catalogue. But they didn't get a single bid. Oh, the ignominy! And I thought I'd been so clever, convinced that whatever happened, they would be a good investment. Just as well I never told my wife what I'd paid. They are now deep in a drawer, hidden from sight, hidden from my mind.

Never buy purely for investment. If only I'd stuck to my own rules . . .

CUMBRIAN ARTIST One of our seven paintings by Sheila Fell – *Haystacks in Cumberland*.

BOND IN THE BUFF Life-class sketches of Sean Connery by Hilary Buchanan. Not my smartest bit of collecting, but nice drawings for all that.

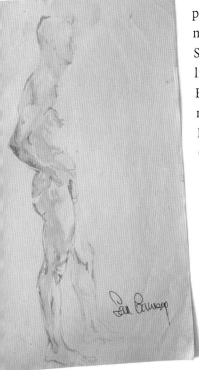

COLLECTING AND CLASS

You get snobbery and class consciousness in collecting, just as in many other walks of life. Whenever you read the obituary of someone who's described as a Great Collector, saying that he or she has left a fine collection, you can be sure it wasn't postcards, bottle tops or airline sick bags. Chances are it was Old Masters or Chippendale furniture.

Collectors are collectors, with the same instincts, obsessions, desires and daftnesses, but traditionally they have segregated themselves into devotees of High and Low Art. In modern times, the latter – hoarders of unconsidered trifles, everyday objects that might otherwise get thrown away – are by far the more numerous. They have been accorded higher status these last 30 years, once the great auction houses like Sotheby's and Christie's started selling things like pop memorabilia and football programmes. Often for vast amounts of money. Not stupid, our auction houses.

All the same, class distinctions linger on. Even in small-time, small-town auction houses, you'll see the words 'Property of a Gentleman' on items whose owners don't want their identity revealed. You never see 'Property of a Dustman/ Unskilled Labourer', yet they are just as likely to have collected some excellent examples of early tin-openers, snuff-boxes, 19th-century pencil sharpeners, *Beanos* or Dinky Toys, now worth a great deal of money.

Collectors of, and dealers in, paintings, sculpture and antique furniture – High Art – consider themselves aficionados of taste, distinction and great learning. At smart auction houses, they still tend to wear suits, even coats with astrakhan collars. Yet in the same auction house, the following week, when it's Cup Final programmes, the dealers and collectors will be in jeans and jumpers – bidding up to £20,000 for what the High Arties consider impossibly Low Tat.

Just to confuse things, you also get social distinctions within certain areas of collecting. In china, for example, there are poshos who are into fine bone china like Spode who look down on chavs who collect cheap pottery souvenirs like coronation mugs. (For some reason coronation plates are considered much classier items.) Likewise, members of the Royal Philatelic despise gullible people who collect first-day covers.

There's also an intellectual snobbery at work in the great big wonderful world of collecting. People who collect Old Masters reckon they have refined aesthetic sensibilities, whereas people who collect Beryl Cooks are, frankly, the ignorant Great Unwashed. It's a fact that people with 'taste' often feel they have to do down the preferences

of others. The art critic Brian Sewell saves his finest, most savage writing for paintings and painters he doesn't like.

Wordsworth believed you needed education and effort, intellect, sensitivity and hard mental work to truly appreciate the finer points of poetry, so naturally lesser mortals wouldn't manage it. He also thought that the *hoi-polloi* wouldn't appreciate the beauties of the Lake District, which was why he was against the railway coming to Windermere, bringing the industrial hordes from Lancashire.

Snobbery is not so overt these days, but there's still a feeling that those who collect everyday objects are somehow intellectually inferior. Yet whenever I meet people with big collections of Beatles souvenirs or football programmes, I am always struck by how very knowledgeable they are. They do appreciate the

finer points, and are well aware which the more important items are. They are constantly using their powers of judgement in discarding or ignoring what's fake and phoney and discriminating about what has intrinsic merit and, yes, beauty.

About ten years ago, while working on a walking book, I visited Chatsworth House in Derbyshire to meet the Duchess of Devonshire – Deborah Mitford, as was. There can't be a grander house in all England, with its Old Masters and fine furniture, 175 rooms, 27 bathrooms, 359 doors and thousands of lush acres. When the Duchess left her study briefly to find something, I noticed a cut-out image of Elvis, stuck in the side of a mirror on the mantelpiece. I presumed one of her children or grandchildren had put it there.

So when she returned, I asked her who the Elvis fan was. 'Me!' she exclaimed. 'It all started three years ago. I was watching some TV programme about Elvis. I suppose I knew about him at the time, because of my children's interests, but I hadn't taken a great deal of notice. It suddenly struck me how amazing he had been – and there and then I decided to study him.'

She'd been to Graceland, gone on tours with other Elvis fans, bought loads of Elvis souvenirs. That very day, her secretary was busy making a telephone bid on her behalf at an auction of Elvis material. The Duchess' favourite item was a telephone in the shape of Elvis, holding a guitar. When you picked up the receiver, he started singing and playing. 'Isn't that marvellous?!'

Collecting, you see, is democratic and classless, open to all, regardless of brow or breeding.

REGAL ROLLERS Prince Rainier III of Monaco (1923–2005) was a major collector both of stamps and of luxury vintage automobiles. I consider all collections to have equal merit, or equal demerits. It's how far you take them, the choices you make, your enthusiasm and knowledge, that's worthy of respect and admiration, rather than the actual subject matter.

Yours faithfully
Rowland Hill

Famous Autographs

It was through tracking down prime ministers that I came across a whole host of golden dealers who specialize in autographs. They have fairs, often in Mayfair or West End hotels, as opposed to Bloomsbury where the postcards and book people gather. They tend not to sell through retail outlets like shops or stalls. They work mainly from home, usually in nice parts of the country, carrying their choicer goods with them in their Volvos to big fairs once or twice a year.

At the bottom, more downmarket, end they sell autographs of minor pop and TV stars, retired footballers, astronauts you've never heard of. At the top end, they are dealing in literary or historic manuscripts, acting for museums and galleries and wealthy collectors round the world. They wear pin-striped suits, even the women, and take themselves very seriously, because of course they are serious, intellectual, professional people.

The leading manuscript dealers – which is what they prefer to call themselves, not autograph traders – produce very high-class catalogues, excellently illustrated on glossy paper. They are worth getting, as they are very informative, meticulously giving the background to each document and letter, explaining when and to whom it was written. You usually get sent one or two for free, if you appear to be a serious collector, but they soon stop if it's clear you're a cheapskate, wanting their knowledge, but unwilling to pay.

However, even these top-enders have boxes in the corner of their stalls at fairs, or separate sections in their catalogues, which contain special offers, cheapo examples of famous signatures, names on scraps without any content. The dealers can be dreadfully offhand with people whose only interest is in these scraps, as opposed to proper manuscripts, which they are more than willing to show you, but can usually be prevailed upon to take your money, while looking sniffily in the air.

It was from these dealers, at both ends of the market, that I bought a lot of my PM stuff in the early days. I'd imagined, when I first stumbled upon prime ministers' autographs, that I had chanced upon a new speciality, that I'd be a lone collector. But as ever, in the big wide world of collecting, you are never alone. There are always other people out there ahead of you, with more money, time, energy and knowledge, scooping up the good stuff. I found that almost all professional manuscript dealers – I'd better call them that from now on, so as not to offend – have a box or section marked 'Prime Ministers', making it very easy to ratch through for bargains, or missing items.

They usually also have a box marked 'US Presidents'. A lot of the main dealers are international operators, with clients all over the world, attending fairs in the US and Europe. I did think of going into presidents, when I was getting near the end of prime ministers, but held back when I saw the prices and realized the extent of the competition. British prime ministers, on the whole, are not collected by non-Britons. That does tend to keep prices fairly reasonable, unless of course it's Churchill.

By going round these dealers, looking at their stuff, I soon found myself eyeing the other boxes, marked with different categories, and flicking through them. I noticed that I already had quite a few signatures they were selling, letters from famous people, dead and alive, which I'd acquired over the years. Why not add to what I already have? So whoosh, I was off again.

The Allure of Famous People

I have this image of the Roman legions when they invaded Britain, advancing through the country, their banners flying, shields and swords at the ready, marching in step, led by handsome centurions through villages and settlements – and women swooning, especially if they caught sight of Julius Caesar. Okay, so he only made two short trips, in 55 and 54 BC, but there were plenty of famous senators and other important Romans stationed in Britain. I'm sure some of the local men also rushed to gape, perhaps even clapped, or at least looked on in awe and wonder.

The famous, the rich, the successful and even the notorious have always attracted attention. People have wanted a glimpse of them, or of some object they had touched. Religious relics, the bones and garments of saints, or of kings and queens, have for centuries been collected and displayed for true believers to touch and revere.

In 1745, when Bonnie Prince Charlie marched south from Scotland through England, and for a time it looked as if he might take over the nation, people came out to see him and cheer him on, while women rushed to cut off locks of his hair. In the centuries when not many wrote letters, and fewer people could read (which made autograph hunting a bit limited), hair from the famous was seen as a valuable memento. By the 19th century, locks of hair had become collectable items, swapped, bought and sold, with dealers willing to pay good prices.

When William Wordsworth lived in his final years at Rydal Mount, near Ambleside, Poet Laureate and Grand Old Man, he had a gardener who also cut his hair. Wordsworth groupies, unable to catch sight of or secure an audience with the great man, would lean over the wall and the gardener would slip them a lock or two, for a suitable remuneration of course.

I once visited the Harry Ransome Collection at the University of Texas in Austin, which has one of the world's greatest collections of literary manuscripts. I came across a collection of poets' hair, framed in glass cases, from Keats, Shelley, Wordsworth and others, originally acquired by some wealthy Victorians who displayed these cases in their studies or libraries, to be admired by their friends or to impress fellow collectors.

Hair, as a collectable, has now gone out of fashion, though The Beatles often received letters asking for hair. Fans in a frenzy at their early concerts, when they were allowed within touching distance, would often try to snip off a few locks. The market in hair has now, sadly, fallen. Can't remember when I last heard of a hair dealer. I say sadly because, as a collector, I want all collections to thrive, however bizarre.

FOUNDING FATHER

Not an artefact from my collection, unfortunately. This lock of George Washington's hair was 'taken from the General's head in 1779' and is now in the possession of the Historical Society of Pennsylvania.

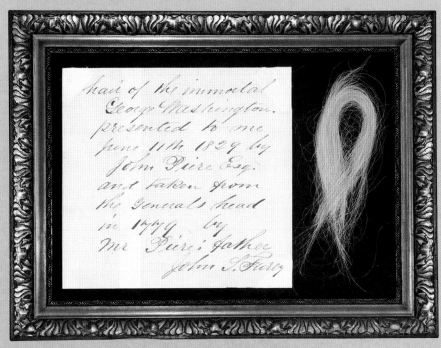

In the 1960s, there were two or three groupies who allegedly made plaster casts of the erect penises of famous pop stars they had slept with, catching the imprints in soft clay before it was too late. I've never seen any examples, but groupies have boasted about them in their kiss 'n' tell memoirs.

Will DNA samples, taken from famous people, be collected in future? Or semen specimens from pop stars or footballers? Once they are hard-up, and have sold off their gold discs or winners' medals, they could be offering themselves to the highest bidder.

Poet Laureates

Having started with PMs, it seemed natural to think about PLs – Poet Laureates. And as with PMs, I already had, by chance, some material from a couple of Poet Laureates I'd met, purely in the way of work.

The very first person I ever interviewed, and saw the result published with my name on, was John Masefield in 1963. I'd been working on *The Sunday Times* for three years by then, and had met some famous people in my job as the assistant on the 'Atticus' column, but in those days, we didn't get by-lines. Today, the titchiest, pottiest little story, rewritten from a handout, gets a huge by-line.

Arranging to see Masefield was all done by letter and went on for months, with endless changes and delays, which meant I ended up with a series of six

little blue notelets, immaculately hand-written from his home, Burcote Brook, near Abingdon. I see from his notepaper that he had a telephone, Clifton Hampden 277, but I don't remember ever ringing him. Perhaps I'd been told he never answered it, preferring to be contacted by letter. He was 84 at the time and had been made Poet Laureate in 1930 by Ramsay MacDonald. During our chat, he reminisced about Thomas Hardy. It was like meeting a creature from another age. I was suitably reverential in my interview, with no silly remarks or cheeky questions.

About fifteen years later, in the late 1970s, I had some dealings with John Betjeman. I was editing a book about London, dreamt up by the publisher Anthony Blond, and we wanted someone to write about London churches.

LETTER FROM A LAUREATE
One of the notelets sent to me by John Masefield, whom I interviewed early in my journalism career, in 1963.

I expected Betjeman would turn me down, as the money on offer was very low – only £100 – but he surpised me by agreeing to do it. I went to see him in some very dark, dingy flat in the East End. One of the things about poets through the centuries, even Poet Laureates, is that very few have ever made much money from their poetry, so they've usually been eager and willing to take on other work, as Wordsworth did, getting himself appointed Stamp Distributor for Westmorland.

While I was with Betjeman, it came out that I was born in Scotland, brought up in Carlisle. He insisted I should have his two volumes of *Border Antiquities*, published in the 1800s, leather-bound, not in great nick, but with some excellent illustrations. I said no, I couldn't possibly take them. He'd bought them years ago for a few bob from a barrow in Farringdon Road. He now had no room for them, and said he'd be pleased if I gave them a good home.

I asked him to sign them and he did – as John McBetjeman, a joke which will confuse any future collectors. John Lennon did a similar thing when I asked him to autograph a photo – signing it 'Winston Lennon'. (Beatles' collectors will know the significance: his full name was John Winston Lennon, having been born during the war when Churchill was our saviour.)

The Farringdon Road bookstalls, by the way, were amazing, a long line of them on shoogly wooden trestle tables, with books spilling on to the pavement or lying in gutters. The stallholders were incredibly scruffy, more like tramps than dealers, and you wondered if they really knew their stock, but they did. I used to haunt these stalls in the 1960s, when I was on *The Sunday Times*, round the corner in Grays Inn Road, but they all went long ago. You don't get street markets like that selling books any more – they only seem to sell rubbishy cheap clothes. Even Camden Lock, which originally had several bookstalls, has now totally changed character.

My Poet Laureate collection, now I look at it – which I haven't for a long time – includes letters or bits of paper signed by Robert Southey, William Wordsworth, Alfred Lord Tennyson, Alfred Austin, Robert Bridges, Cecil Day-Lewis, Ted Hughes, plus John Masefield. For Wordsworth I have only a scrap, a simple sig – he is highly desirable, on both sides of the Atlantic, and a letter from him is worth thousands. They practically give Alfred Austin's signature away, however. He was Poet Laureate after Tennyson and was ridiculed for his laziness and lousy poetry. Now he's almost forgotten, except for two lines on the Prince of Wales's illness:

POET LAUREATES

John Dryden 1668–89, Thomas Shadwell 1689–92, Nahum Tate 1692–1715, Nicholas Rowe 1715–18, Laurence Eusden 1718–30, Colley Cibber 1730–57, William Whitehead 1757–85, Thomas Warton 1785–90, Henry Pye 1790–1813, Robert Southey 1813–43, William Wordsworth 1843–50, Alfred Tennyson 1850–92, Alfred Austin (above) 1896–1913, Robert Bridges 1913–30, John Masefield 1930–67, Cecil Day-Lewis 1968–72, John Betjeman 1972–84, Ted Hughes 1984–98, Andrew Motion 1998–2009, Carol Ann Duffy 2009–

Across the wires, the electric message came
'He is no better, he is much the same.'

On the whole, the position of Poet Laureate has not been greatly revered. Many have turned it down, such as Walter Scott and Philip Larkin, while others were not apparently asked, such as Keats, Browning and W.H. Auden.

Ben Jonson is often said to have been the first Poet Laureate, but the first to officially have the title was John Dryden, appointed in 1668. The salary, still the same, is £100 a year. Traditionally, the Poet Laureate was meant to produce verses in celebration of some national or royal event, but not all have done so.

Andrew Motion, Poet Laureate from 1998 to 2009, did at least try to do his bit, producing poetry for big occasions, though it wasn't always highly applauded. And he put himself around, on radio, in the press, at literary festivals, pontificating on things poetic, trying to raise interest in literature generally.

With best wishes
from
Daphne du Maurier
1985

December 19th. 1971.

KILMARTH
PAR
CORNWALL

Dear Mr Roest,

Thank you for your letter, and it was kind of you to write. I am very glad indeed that my books and stories are widely read in the Netherlands.

I shall be extremely busy directly Christmas is over, because I intend to start on a new novel, therefore I would much prefer it, please, if your editor could have waited until the spring for an interview, as once I am working I keep very strict hours and do not care to be distracted by visitors, even from my own family. Also, the weather would be better for a reportage on Cornwall. I do hope you will understand.

Yours sincerely,

Literary Letters

I have written lots of books these last 40 years, so naturally I have received letters from fellow writers, some well known, others not, all of which I have carefully kept. I have two separate folders of Literary Letters. One is marked 'Literary', while the other is marked 'Women Writers'.

This second folder includes letters to me from Margaret Drabble, Antonia Fraser, Edna O'Brien, Jilly Cooper, Fay Weldon, Brigid Brophy and Deborah Moggach. I've also got letters from women writers I have interviewed, such as Muriel Spark. I went to see her in Italy when I was presenting Radio 4's *Bookshelf*. Then there are letters I have gone out and bought for my collection, including ones written by Daphne du Maurier and Richmal Crompton, the creator of *Just William*.

I have a nice letter from Dame Rebecca West, a fan letter, about my biography of George Stephenson, and also an irate letter from Doris Lessing. I had apparently given the impression in an article that she had said 'personal questions about the Booker Prize were irritating and a trick' when in fact those words had not been used by her but by Tom Maschler, her publisher. I can't now remember the truth of it, but she does go on to thank me for writing stuff about the Booker. She ends by giving me her home 'phone number, asking me to ring her 'early in the morning or late at night'.

Dear Mr Atticus.

Like Jeeves, I do my best to give satisfaction; but in this case I must ask to be excused. I have always been shy of publicity, and now much prefer to be a period piece in privacy. There is some point in it for dear E.B, who has never been given adequate applause, being so modest. Give my best regards to M. Wiggin when you see him.

Yours sincerely,

Among male writers, I have letters written to me by Siegfried Sassoon, declining an interview; Harold Acton, also saying 'no' to an interview (and then another letter from Acton saying 'yes'); C.P. Snow, thanking me for an interview; plus letters from Desmond Morris, Anthony Burgess, Ian McEwan, and Alan Bennett. Letters I have bought include ones by William Thackeray, just a couple of words, Somerset Maugham and Captain W.E. Johns, author of the *Biggles* books.

The most irate literary letter I have ever received came from John le Carré – real name David Cornwell – who accused me of the most awful things, too outrageous to even print, not in his lifetime anyway. I must have caught him on a bad day.

Perhaps the most interesting modern literary autographs I possess came through a North London Literary Lunch Club I founded in 1983. I had left proper journalism for good, deciding from now on to work full-time at home, as a writer and general hack. I'd put off doing this for some years, though I could have done so much earlier. What I used to do was work six months at home, then six months at *The Sunday Times*, doing whatever job Harry Evans, the editor, gave me, which ranged from Women's Editor to Editor of the colour magazine.

PARK HOUSE, HAMPTON COURT
EAST MOLESEY, SURREY
ENGLAND
Jan. 12th 1965

Dear David.

There are now 80 Biggles books. Glad you like them. I served right through the First World War, Pilot in the R.F.C. & flew many planes. & knew most of the aces. I was shot down in 1918 by the German ace Udet

Best of luck

W.E. Johns

Lunch with the Literati

I was very pleased not to have to go out to work any more, listen to office politics, hear people moaning about their expenses, the size of their office or their secretaries (which every minor executive had in those days, to answer their phone and type out their letters). The only thing I found I missed was the lunches. So my wife suggested I should organize my own. There must be other people like me in North London, writers working from home who would quite like to meet up for lunch once a month and rubbish their publisher, agent and other writers.

I had made a list of 40 writers I knew, or knew of, who lived within two miles of me. I wrote to them all, and most said yes, would love to join. John le Carré was one of the few who said 'no'. (The later row was nothing to do with that.) He wrote to say he would 'prefer to meet his brother and sister writers in the next world, not this'.

The people who turned up for the early lunches, held on the last Wednesday of every month in a Camden Town or Hampstead restaurant, included Kingsley Amis, Salman Rushdie, John Hillaby, Bernice Reubens, Eva Figes, Victoria Glendinning and Jessica Mitford, though she was just visiting from the US. During the first few lunches, I got them all to sign their name on a sheet, as a record.

The lunches ran for about ten years, then petered out. I had to give up when I started presenting *Bookshelf* on Radio 4 as our recording day was always a Wednesday.

We had a bit of a scene during the first lunches, thanks to Kingsley Amis. I had decided we should add up the whole bill, for food and drinks, then each pay an equal share, rather than having the waiters going round working out 30 individual bills. This seemed to work well the first time, then some of the younger women writers started complaining. One week, when the share was £5 each, one woman said that £5 was what she was allowing herself for a *whole* week for food and drink. So she couldn't pay and would have to leave.

It was then discovered that Kingsley Amis was ordering whisky all the way through the lunch, not drinking cheap Greek wine like the rest of us, and was therefore greatly inflating the total bill. I took it up with him, but

✖✖✖✖✖✖✖✖✖✖✖✖✖✖✖✖✖✖✖✖✖✖✖✖✖✖✖✖✖✖✖✖✖✖✖✖✖

March 30, 1983

Dear Writers,
Thanks for coming. We will meet every last Wednesday in the
month from now on - here, unless anyone has a better idea.

Please bring friends or any other writers or such like who
live inNorth London ish and are based from home.

I wrote to 40 people in all, mostly people I knew. I'm sure
I missed many likely people out, tho all by accident.

Of the 40,   18 wrote and said yes, yup, be here today

Kingsley
who ?

       8 said lovely idea, can't make it the first
Wed but will come on later Weds. They were -
Fay Weldon, Salman Rushdie, Gillian Tindall, Michael Palin
Shiva Naipaul, Peter Nichols, Julian Barnes, Victoria
Glendening

David CORN-
WELL PISSIS
IN IS ShOE
Kingsley's

2 said no   AJP Taylor said he never has lunch, but
wd come any dinner time as he likes the idea and
loves this place, so he said.
      David Cornwell wished us luck but
said he prefers to meet his brother and sister
writers in the next world not this...

10 never replied , the rotten lot, tho perhaps
some of them have turned up today.

For those who don't know the immediate area, well it's fun filled
tho v scruffy. Turn right out of the rest, then second left and
it's the actual TVx AM studios. Go on into the High Street.
There's a brilliant book shop on the right, Compendium, perfect
for cranks, druggies and feminists. That's their specialities.
Then carry on right, over the bridge, and you come to Camden Lock.
Lots of shops. Trific xixx walk along the canal, either way, right
to the Zoo or left passed the TV AM Egg cups...

Hunter Davies
Nigman Dobbs
Mervyn Jones.

Next time
If you can come, or plan
to anyway, could you
sign below? Thanks...

John Hillaby

James Cameron

Alan O'Brien

Joan Bakewell.

Kingsley Amis

Stanley Price

Gary Goodwin

Margaret Drabble
Roxy Holmes
Nicholas Amer (a delighted friend)
Owen Weymouth
Paul Ableman Ann and Bernard Kops.
Eva Figes Michael Digwell
Gillian Freeman
John Hurd

76

he refused to cut out the whisky, so I had to change the system. From then on, everybody had to stump up for their own drinks individually.

Other Autograph Collections

I have five other files with letters and autographs of the famous. One is marked 'Politicians' – which means politicians who did not become prime ministers. It's not very exciting, though it does contain nice letterheads from the House of Commons and House of Lords. The writers include Enoch Powell, Ernest Marples, Norman St John Stevas, James Prior, Roy Hattersley, Neil Kinnock, Marcia Falkender, Denis Healey, Jonathan Aitken, Randolph Churchill, Ken Livingstone, Willie Whitelaw, Teresa Gorman, Nicholas Fairbairn, Edwina Currie and Tony Benn – who has signed himself 'Anthony Wedgwood Benn', before he became simply Tony Benn. Now I look at them properly, some are more interesting than I'd remembered.

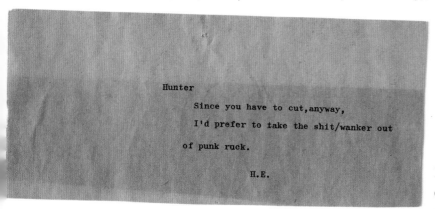

Hunter
        Since you have to cut, anyway,
          I'd prefer to take the shit/wanker out
of punk rock.

            H.E.

LUNCHING LUMINARIES
(left) My note to those who turned up at the first writers' lunch I organized in 1983, emblazoned with their signatures.

Another file is entitled 'Journalists, Publishers, Broadcasters', and that is pretty boring, unless you happen to be interested in the media. Most of them are people I have worked with, in some capacity, or fellow toilers in the various fields. It includes letters from Keith Waterhouse, Richard Ingrams, Basil Boothroyd, James Cameron, Alan Coren, Ray Gosling, Miles Kington, Melvyn Bragg, Ned Sherrin, Simon Jenkins, Simon Hoggart, Jill Tweedie, Sue Lawley, Anna Ford, John Birt, Harry Evans, Tina Brown, William Rees-Mogg, Veronica Wadley, Paul Dacre. The publishers are not as well represented, but then people don't normally know their names, but they include Tony Godwin, Gail Rebuck, Graham C. Greene, Anthony Cheetham, Tom Maschler, Carmen Callil and Victoria Barnsley.

There is a faded note from Harold Evans when he was editor of *The Sunday Times* and I was editing the colour magazine which reads: 'Hunter – since you have to cut, anyway, I'd prefer it if you take the shit/wanker out of punk rock.'

I also have a 'Theatre and Show Business' file, which is strange, as I haven't really moved in those circles. In fact I don't think I'd opened it for five years. It starts, to my surprise, with signed pieces from Sir Henry Irving, Sir Charles Wyndham and Edmund Kean – stuff I must have bought cheap in some bargain box. There's a signed Laurence Olivier photo, plus letters to me from Wayne Sleep, Nigel Havers, Trevor Nunn, Michael Palin, Lew Grade, Colin Welland, Maureen Lipman, Ken Loach, Michael Frayn, Henry Livings, Arnold Wesker, Peter Nichols, John Osborne, Ruby Wax, Jennifer Saunders and Robbie Coltrane. So I suppose I must have met more luvvies than I'd remembered.

At the end of this file, I have a subsection called 'Artists', which I had truly forgotten. It contains pieces signed by the Victorian artists William Frith and Lord Leighton, but also more modern items, some illustrated, from Mel Calman, Ralph Steadman and Peter Blake.

I have one folder marked 'Assorted', so I opened it with some excitement, wondering what I might have classed as assorted. It starts off quite impressively with a letter to me from U Thant, Secretary General of the UN, in 1967, and one from John Kenneth Galbraith, the famous American economist, written from Harvard University in 1977. It also has some scientists and engineers, such as George Stephenson, his son Robert, Joseph Paxton and Thomas Brassey. There's also a Rowland Hill letter, to my surprise and delight, as I have no memory of buying it. It's a whole letter, edged in black, written from Hampstead in 1871. Along with it is a letter from the Nobel

HUNTER'S HEROES

My box file of 'Assorted' autographs contains such gems as the signature of Robert Stephenson (above), plus an entire letter from Rowland Hill, excusing himself from a ballot at the Reform Club on grounds of ill health and asking his correspondent to vote in his stead.

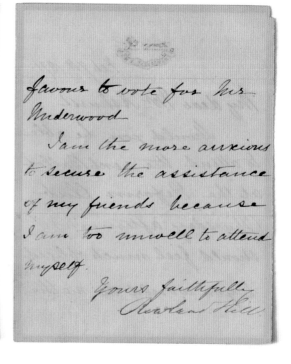

Prize-winning chemist Dorothy Hodgkin. There's also Damon Hill, the racing driver (not sure what he's doing there), Sir Clive Sinclair and the Duke of Marlborough.

As I closed this album, out fell a glossy photocopy of Karl Marx's death certificate. It records his death in Kentish Town in March 1883 while living in Maitland Park Road. The cause of death was laryngitis and he was aged 64, male. I suppose I must have picked it up from some stall because it had to do with Kentish Town, near where I live.

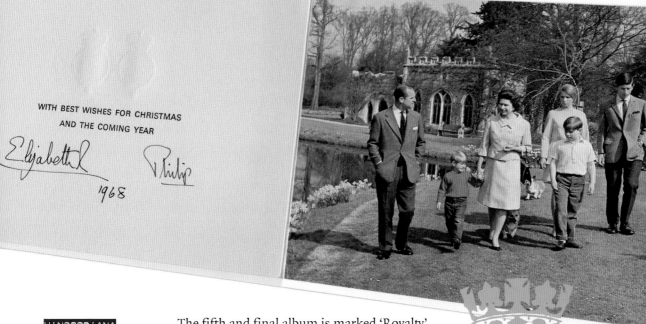

WITH BEST WISHES FOR CHRISTMAS
AND THE COMING YEAR
Elizabeth R
Philip
1968

WINDSORIANA
The Queen and Prince Philip's Christmas card of 1968, showing very youthful princes Charles, Andrew and Edward, plus the obligatory corgis in tow. Right, the entwined monogram of Edward VIII and Wallis Simpson, a fateful match that led to the Abdication Crisis of 1936.

The fifth and final album is marked 'Royalty'. It begins with a photo – well, a print of an illustration signed by Queen Victoria, plus a note in pencil by Prince Albert to the Queen at Osborne House. I see I paid £20 for the two items. There's also a letter from Queen Alexandra, 1909, which is simply a list of presents, and an invitation from Edward VIII and Wallis Simpson which has a fancy crest in the shape of 'WE' – but inside it's blank.

I also have something I did pay a bit of money for – a 1968 Xmas card from the Queen and Prince Philip, signed by both – plus some Royal items I got for nothing. In 1981, we were invited to a Royal Garden Party. Naturally, I kept all the cards, envelopes and covering letters. Well, I am a collector.

FAMOUS COLLECTORS

The world's first collector is often said to have been Noah. He certainly was a prime example of the scientific collector. The Bible would have us believe that he collected two of all the known animals on the planet, and every creeping thing, and put them in an Ark, safe from the flood – thus achieving an entire set, which to this day is the dream of most collectors.

Lucky Noah. Or you could say, poor old Noah. Once his task was finished, his collection complete, what was there left for him to do? He was, of course, trying to save the creatures, preserve them for posterity, which was why he had to find a male and female of each species. Modern collectors often try to persuade themselves that they too are rescuing objects from destruction, whether the unloved and ignored or the rare and precious. This paper carrier bag will be thrown out, unless I keep it. My Old Masters? – no really, I'm just a custodian.

Noah wasn't a typical collector, as it was in a sense his job, ordained by God. In my definition, collecting has to begin voluntarily, be a self-imposed task, for whatever worthy or unworthy reasons. When it gets a grip, and you can't help yourself, well that's a different matter.

Most Roman emperors, like Julius Caesar, collected precious objects, statues and pottery, a mark of their taste as well as their power and prestige. A bit like many modern art collectors.

Christopher Columbus was one of the greatest scientific collectors, but then he had one huge advantage. In 1492, he explored places no other European had yet set foot in. He brought back samples of cotton, tobacco and rubber, plants and vegetables, and recorded unknown things like hammocks and canoes. He also brought back several half-naked Indians, whom he exhibited in a grand procession round the streets of Barcelona.

His journals show his delight and amazement at what he has seen, emotions readily understood and appreciated by all collectors, but what he was really after was gold. He needed that to impress the Queen and King of Spain, who would then fund future trips, which he hoped would bring him honour and glory. He was a collector – but you could argue he was motivated by greed, wealth, fame, prestige. Just like many explorers who came after him.

Sir John Soane (1753–1837) seems to have been a pure collector. He was in love with beautiful things and wanted to surround himself with them, then preserve them intact, frozen in time. Which is what happened, as you can see if you visit his wonderful house in Lincoln's Inn Fields in London, which he made into a museum in his own lifetime, while he was still living there. Soane was architect to the Bank of England, and a professor of architecture, so there are many architectural drawings and models in his collections, but he also collected books, paintings, prints, plaster casts, and sculptures.

Between 1900 and 1951, another wealthy architect, Charles Paget Wade, who had inherited a manor house in the Cotswolds, collected over 20,000 items of craftsmanship – old bikes, clocks, locks, cow bells, butter churns. Like Soane, he filled his home with them – but then, finding he had left no room for himself, decamped to an old outhouse in the grounds. Wade's house, Snowshill, is now owned by the National Trust.

Sigmund Freud collected topics, making endless lists of things like dreams, case histories

abortion campaigner Marie Stopes, and picked up a copy of the first rules of ping-pong for free. His collection, when he died, was worth around £100,000.

Modern-day celebrities collect a variety of things. Rockers Rod Stewart, Eric Clapton and Phil Collins are model railway enthusiasts. Johnny Depp collects insects, while Quentin Tarantino likes board games. Whoopi Goldberg goes for bake-

and jokes, but he was also a great collector of physical objects, mainly antiquities. He specialized in small ornaments – rings, statuettes, masks and pottery – from ancient Egypt, Greece, Rome and Renaissance Italy. He managed to bring about 3000 of his treasures with him to London when he fled from Vienna in 1938. Patients lying on his couch in his consulting room found themselves surrounded by his *objets d'art*. His house in Hampstead is now open to the public, the famous couch still covered with a multi-coloured Persian rug, making it look a bit like a Turkish brothel. When I visited, I counted 40 different artefacts on his desk.

The writer Ian Fleming specialized in first editions that he thought had 'started something'. He paid £4 for Marie Curie's doctoral thesis on radium, 15 shillings for *Married Love* by the pro-

lite jewellery and Tom Hanks collects typewriters. Leonardo DiCaprio and Nicolas Cage both collect dinosaur skeletons, and once competed for one at auction. Meanwhile, artist and Turner Prize winner Rachel Whiteread has a collection of 200 dolls' houses, amassed over 20 years. She has used some in her work, so it's more than just collecting.

Andy Warhol had a good eye for the interesting as well as the bizarre, but was unusual as a collector in not being at all bothered by having dozens, if not hundreds, of the same thing – whether it was cookie jars, wristwatches, carpets or baskets. You can see this same tendency in his art. When Sotheby's sold off his collections in 1988, they needed six catalogues to list everything. The sale lasted ten days and realized $30 million. That's the way to do it.

JUBILEE YEAR.

COMMENCING   JUNE 20TH 1886.

VICTORIA

QUEEN OF GREAT BRITAIN AND IRELAND
EMPRESS OF INDIA.
BORN MAY 24TH, 1819.
ASCENDED THE THRONE JUNE 20TH, 1837.

China

Collecting china is one of the world's most popular hobbies. China in the general sense – meaning pots and plates, vases and ornaments made from earthenware or glass – was found in burial mounds and graves, from the ancient to the medieval world, along with silver plates and other precious items. It showed how well you had done in life, to have accumulated such objects, but presumably these objects, collected in life, must also have been displayed in life, kept in cabinets or on shelves to impress family and friends. Otherwise, what was the point? Surely they were not collected and kept solely for the funeral?

PATRIOTIC POTTERY

With the great rise in the popular appeal of the British monarchy in the Victorian era, china plates, mugs and vases with a royal theme began to be turned out by the thousand for people to display their patriotic pride. This mass production makes most coronation and jubilee crockery largely worthless, though they're still very pleasing to look at and historically interesting, like this Golden Jubilee souvenir plate of 1886.

But china-collecting also had a cultural aspect, the importance of which has increased with time, placing it on a higher plane than, say, collecting Beatles bubblegum cards. China was admired for its craftsmanship, considered as a work of art, and its leading makers greatly renowned. The best-known examples often had social and historical content, depicting famous figures and scenes, conveying a narrative.

China, from China the country, has always been prized and was exported to Europe for centuries. In Britain, we have also had our own china production, most famously based in the Potteries in Staffordshire, and the best items from the best manufacturers, such as Wedgwood and Spode, have always been collected.

One of the world's best-known pieces of china is the Portland Vase in the British Museum. It was probably made in around 30–20 BC, so is over 2000 years old, the finest surviving example of Roman cameo glass. It's decorated with classical friezes, and is meant to represent the divinity of the imperial family. It might have been originally intended for Julius Caesar, or possibly Cleopatra and her lover Mark Antony.

The Portland Vase was one of the great classical treasures that young gents in the 17th and 18th century went to look at when they were passing through Italy on the 'Grand Tour', till the Italian family who owned it fell on hard times. In 1786 it was sold, via a Scottish antique dealer, to the Duke of Portland, a former British prime minister whose family owned it until 1945.

Part of its attraction, and fame, rests on its interesting history, the dramas of the people to whom it once belonged. It happens to be pretty useless as a vase. Over the centuries, the Portland Vase has been broken into 200 different fragments – and then, at several stages, carefully pieced together again. I look at my little collection of rubbishy china objects, at the cracks and chips, the dirt and discolouring, and think, well, at least they're in one piece. For the most part, anyway.

The best, most famous pieces of china are like the Portland Vase, and, like many famous works of art, are known for their history and legends as much as for their content. China is a vast subject – there's so much to learn and to understand: thousands of books have been written about it, there are learned journals and societies devoted to it, choice examples are displayed prominently in the world's leading museums and galleries and historic homes. It is rather humbling to enter such a world, even on the periphery, at the very bottom of the pile. I confess that I've always felt something of an outsider when it comes to serious china-collecting (my sort of collecting areas seem awfully trivial and ephemeral compared with classic china), but I am naturally in great awe of the experts who know so much.

China is also – how can I put this – very much a woman's subject, perhaps because of its domestic history and use. Looking round the stalls and dealers, there are always a lot of women doing the china dealing and buying compared with other collectables. Plus a lot of gay men. Nothing wrong with any of that. I'm just observing. It all adds up to a world I don't feel part of.

Coronation Crockery

Is there a collecting gene? Does it run in families, through inheritance or environment? We have three children, so you'd expect one at least to have some sort of collection. One is like my wife, going through life with no clutter. One is pretty untidy, but does not collect. The other has no collections, but loves jumbles and car boots. We'll call her a half-collector.

My parents didn't collect – how could they? – having no money, no space, never owning their own home. Slight exaggeration. They did have a cocktail cabinet, which was strange, as they never drank cocktails. It was a working-class status symbol, in which they kept three brass candlesticks and a set of brass monkeys: Hear no evil, see no evil, speak no evil. They were a collection, in that the brass ornaments had no use, but were regularly polished and admired. I liked to imagine they were family heirlooms, but in fact they were won at the Glasgow Fair in 1934. It was either them or goldfish.

Strange to relate, my grandfather collected string. I can see him now, playing Ludo with me, whistling a silent whistle, unravelling balls of string. He picked them up in the street, or from neighbours, the more tangled the better. Recycling, we now call it.

I have a brother and two sisters – only one of whom has ever collected, my sister Annabell who lives in Leighton Buzzard. Does that prove it's in the blood? But she only collects one thing, coronation mugs. So do I. Snap.

I'm not sure if purists would regard coronation mugs as china. Even I can tell that most of my mugs are mass-produced junk, sold in Woolies or street markets. The decorations are often cheap transfers, which come off in the wash. The point of them is of course their age, and the event they are commemorating.

You also get regional variations, mainstream coronation events given a local setting, such as 'Silloth Celebrates the Jubilee'. As Silloth is in Cumbria and I collect Cumbrian objects, I'd buy that mug, just for its local angle. Over the centuries, some well-known potteries, such as Royal Doulton, have turned out coronation mugs and they tend to be better quality.

Although I am ignorant of the actual quality of the china, and can't translate the marks or recognize most of the makers, I look out for what I consider pretty mugs, with nice colours and decorations and lettering.

Coronation mugs are obvious, corny, so I try to look upon mine ironically, telling myself they are very postmodern. Lots of people collect them, and, unsurprisingly, there are loads of them

LONG TO REIGN OVER US

From right to left: two mugs commemorating the coronation of George VI in 1937, and an older example marking Queen Victoria's Diamond Jubilee in 1897.

around, as millions appear every time we have a coronation, mostly handed out free to schoolchildren. China manufacturers must hate the present Queen, hanging on for so damn long.

In a way I'm surprised I ever became interested in them. Partly it was the free element, being given one when I was at school, then my children receiving them in their turn. The mugs came into the house without being invited, and then were never chucked out, because of course I never knowingly chuck *anything* out. But the main reason for my interest was the realization, some years ago, that in the year of my birth, 1936, we had three kings. George V died on 20 January – when I was just two weeks old – followed by Edward VIII, who abdicated on 11 December, and then came George VI. He lasted till 1952, when his daughter, Elizabeth II, took over. Considering how young I am, five monarchs in my lifetime isn't at all bad. A good enough excuse to collect coronation and jubilee mugs.

I like my old ones best – for Victoria's diamond jubilee in 1897, for George V's coronation in 1911 and his silver jubilee in 1935. They're a bit cracked and faded, but aren't we all? I also have some coronation plates, particularly a nice one for Queen Victoria (see page 82). Plates tend to be more expensive, having been produced for collectors to cherish, while

the mugs were mainly cheap souvenirs made for tourists or schoolchildren.

The one thing against collecting coronation mugs, and for that matter any sort of china, is the dust they collect. They also need space. That's why I usually prefer flat stuff, which can be put in folders or drawers – and the dust ignored. Funnily enough, my wife, the non-collector, the chucker-out, is quite fond of my 30 or so coronation mugs. Her favourite is a pretty pink one, made by Mason's, for the present Queen's silver jubilee in 1977. She says it's rewarding, cleaning it, as it comes up a treat. I do like her to have some pleasures ...

Pottery from Portugal

I'm not sure what the difference is between china and pottery. My coronation mugs I see as china, because they are sort of white, while pottery I see as brown in colour, like peasant ware – mass-produced utility articles with no pretensions to being works of art.

By this definition, I have one china collection, my coronation mugs, and one pottery collection, our Portuguese plates. I say 'our' because my wife and I bought them together and she was responsible for bringing ʅ. She is a world-class packer. Yet all she did was wrap them wspaper in our suitcases and not once did they ever get ıazing.

years ago we lived in Portugal for six months, in Praia da Luz on the Algarve, then bought a little house in the next bay, Porto de Mos. We had it as our holiday home for 20 years – and filled it with local furniture. Hand-painted tables, chairs, beds and plates. Most of the stuff was fairly rough and primitive, but my dears, so authentic. We loved the local plates, especially the fishy ones – with paintings of fish on them – or flowers, or ʹ ʹ ll so pretty. You ı everywhere in

Redolent of happy times in the Algarve, these hand-painted Portuguese plates have a rustic charm all their own. Purely for display, mind – apparently the glazes are toxic.

the late 1960s, for a few *escudos*. This was at a time when the main form of local transport was horse and cart and grannies sat on the beach, all in black.

I went back last year for a holiday. The horses and carts have gone, even the oldest gran is in a bikini and the market stalls are the same as everywhere – selling horrible, cheap clothes and nasty, mass-produced, characterless china. But up in the mountains, in Monchique, I found a dusty shop selling the traditional hand-painted plates and dishes. I bought some to add to my collection.

Not to use, of course. You'd probably die if you did. It was about 1975 when a very posh English friend of ours called Alison, an Algarve resident for many years, burst in when we were eating and said 'STOP!' She'd just read in a Portuguese newspaper that a dodgy form of lead had been used to glaze these peasant plates. So we brought them all back to England, for display purposes, and they stand to this day on the Welsh dresser. We have three rows of them, little works of Portuguese native art. They include a pig dish, which I think might originally have been for toast. I use it for olive stones. Hmm, so can I really count that as a collectable … ?

I might have given the impression that my wife is a chucker-out, which is true, and that she doesn't collect anything herself, also true, and thinks I'm mad spending all my time and money on junk. But there is one type of collectable that, though she does not buy or collect the items for herself, she is willing to receive as a present. Isn't that kind and thoughtful of her?

Over the years, for Christmas and birthdays, when I get stuck, or when I feel I haven't got her enough or anything decent, I've bought her two or three old plates, picked up when I've been going round the stalls and car boots. Pretty plates, with nice patterns, usually in green or brown, not in boring old blue. The world and his wife, especially his wife, likes blue plates.

These plates get used – they're not stashed away like my other collections. We bring them out all the time and they're constantly being put in the dishwasher. Both of us have always preferred odd plates and bowls to anything that smacks of a dinner service. We use a variety of them, ringing the changes all the time. So when I buy her plates as a present, they are for domestic use, not as collectables or for display. If by chance I find something she particularly approves of, her face lights up.

Clarice Cliff

Three or four years ago, I overheard my wife saying she liked Clarice Cliff. She was reading a magazine at the time, which I couldn't see, so I didn't know at first whether Clarice Cliff was a place or a person. Now I know that she was a woman, a star ceramic designer of the 1930s, the epitome of Art Deco pottery.

Her background was interesting. She wasn't trained in the normal sense, at a London art college, but started at 13 as an ordinary factory girl in one of the Staffordshire potteries, wearing a pinny. She was born in 1899, but by the time she was 30, she had become a leading designer with her own name stamped on her pottery and her own lines, notably 'Bizarre'. She became a role model for many working-class girls of the time, a public figure, seen as an independent modern woman – though in real life she lived at home with her parents in their terraced house till she was quite old and had an affair with her married boss.

Her pottery is incredibly colourful and vibrant, even I can see that, and very 1930s in design and shape. Today, once again, it is highly popular. Her best pieces fetch far more than I'm prepared to pay, as an outsider, knowing little about pottery. But so far I have bought two pieces, one of which is a nice bowl that cost £80 at auction, which to me was a lot. I won't let my wife use it for day-to-day purposes, certainly not at that price. We keep it on a shelf in our bedroom, with glass eggs inside it. Very tasteful.

Daddy, what did *YOU* do in the Great War?

World Wars

I was aged three in 1939, so my early childhood was dominated by the war. It was quite good fun, actually, listening for the sirens, going into air-raid shelters in the middle of the night, watching the sky criss-crossed by searchlights and lit up by explosions.

HARD TIMES
Souvenirs from war and its aftermath. Left: a famous First World War poster. Below: Britain was broke after the Second World War, and rationing went on into the 1950s.

At school, we knitted squares out of old wool, which the teacher stitched together for blankets for our brave soldiers. I used to feel sorry for the poor sods who got my squares. They were always full of holes. One day the teacher asked kids whose dads were POWs to put their hands up. They each got a food parcel, lucky beggars. I came home and moaned: 'Why aren't you a prisoner of war, Dad?' He was in the RAF, but a humble pay clerk.

Rationing was a fact of life. It began in 1939, with petrol rationing, then came food rationing in 1940, followed by clothes rationing. Before the war, 70 percent of our food had been imported. Suddenly, we had to provide our own, doing clever things with carrots and potatoes, nettles and dandelions, eating fish we'd never heard of and meat made out of cardboard, or so it seemed. Ah, but we were healthy. No fatties then. The parts of ration books that were of interest to me were the sweetie coupons, D's and E's, which you patiently saved up for a bar of chocolate. When you finally got one, it tasted of sawdust.

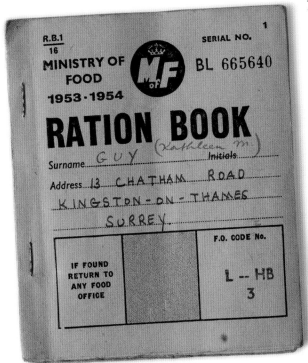

My mother used to give us mashed parsnips, swearing they were the same as bananas, which of course we'd never tasted. After the war, when bananas first arrived – oh, the excitement! But I was dead disappointed. They didn't taste at all like parsnips.

I hadn't realized, until I started collecting ration books, that it had gone on for so long – till the mid-1950s – or that soap was rationed, along with meat, tea, eggs, sugar, bacon, fats. You were allowed only so many ounces a week and had to be registered with a grocer who put his stamp inside your ration book when he took the appropriate coupons, or points.

I also hadn't known, which I should have done, that other countries directly or indirectly involved in the war were also living on rations, across Europe and in the USA. I recently got hold of some German ration books –

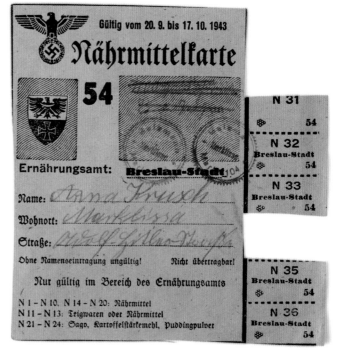

British and German civilians alike had to tighten their belts and pull together to help the war effort. Above: a German food ration card, issued to one Anna Krusch from the city of Breslau (now Wroclaw in Poland). Below: a clothing book from austerity-era Britain.

very similar to ours, with coupons allowing so many grams of sugar, meat, bread, potatoes and the like each week. In Britain, potatoes and carrots, plus bread and fish – which we grew or caught at home – were not rationed, but there were big queues whenever new supplies arrived.

I have about 30 ration books, from different periods, for different items, and they have been used by two generations of my family – my children and now grandchildren – for school projects, taken in and shown off. Granddads do have their uses. Social history, innit.

But oh I do wish I'd kept something which was at the bottom of our garden when we moved into our North London house in 1963. I thought it was garden refuse, perhaps a rhubarb patch, as it was all under snow. When spring came, it turned out to be an old corrugated-iron Anderson air-raid shelter. I stupidly replaced it with a shed. Today, I could be giving conducted tours. Plus sharing my memories …

Other Second World War Memorabilia

Having started on ration books, which are easy to find, and cost very little, I then started looking out for other bits of Second World War memorabilia, such as identity cards, notices, leaflets, posters and letters.

Wartime letters, written by unknown soldiers at the front, are very common, often with photos or other mementoes stuck inside, all so poignant and sad. Sad because it's possible the soldiers never returned and, if they did, it's sad in a different way that their letters are now being sold for £2 on a junk stall. Either their families didn't care, didn't recognize their worth, or at some later stage their effects got sold off to a rag-and-bone man, possibly even paid to clear the attic.

One interesting Second World War letter I have in my collection is a long, cheerful one from 1944, passed by the field post office, from a soldier called F. Morby from Edmonton, North London. He is writing to a girl called Ciss, saying he wished he was at home and could go dog racing with her at Haringey. He says he never got the parcel she said she'd sent, with some cake and chocolate, so he advises her if she sends any more to mark it 'Books' on the outside. As a PS, he has a small souvenir for her – a passport-sized photograph of a German soldier in full uniform, with his name on the back, handwritten in German. 'I am enclosing a photo of a GERMAN prisoner we have got,' our Edmonton soldier boasts.

I don't normally go in for artefacts. They take so much space, need

NEWS FROM THE FRONT

After the D-Day landings in Normandy and the Allied advance across Occupied Europe, a soldier named F. Morby sent back this letter to his nearest and dearest, enclosing a photo of a German POW.

cleaning or looking after, but in my Second World War stuff I do have a genuine gas mask. Not one I wore but one I bought at a Cockermouth car boot a few years ago, so presumably it did have a local Cumbrian face inside it at one time. It even still has its cardboard container. If only I'd kept the air raid shelter, I could have gone down into it, on school tours, wearing my gas mask.

First World War

I also have some First World War material, not that I was there, alive and present – I'm not that old – but just because, on the wartime memorabilia stalls, items from the different periods tend to get mixed up together.

I don't collect wartime medals, army insignia, uniforms and badges, but I do look out for interesting written or printed material to read and study, or to admire for the artwork or illustrations. One of the best-known posters from the First World War is a man playing with his two children and one child saying 'Daddy, what did YOU do in the Great War'. I have a postcard version of it, sent from France.

Militaria is a subject in its own right, with a vast body of knowledge and institutions associated with it. It is one of many specialities I've never got into, only fluttering about in the wings.

A selection of
different postcards
sent from the
Western Front in the
First World War.
Right: a terse, official
missive, and below,
a picture postcard
of a shattered Ypres
and a cheery ditty to
raise morale.

I have quite a few letters from ordinary
soldiers at the front, which had to go
through the censor. They used to issue pre-
printed cards for soldiers at the front, in
which you ticked the statements that
applied to you, such as 'I am quite well/
I am sick/ I am wounded/ I am being sent
down to the base/ I have received your
letter/parcel/telegram/ I have received no
letter from you lately/for a long time.'
Goodness knows what loved ones thought
when they read these impersonal cards,
with the options ticked in pencil. Better
than nothing, I suppose.

You could send a comic postcard from
the front, to cheer up the folks back home.
I have one which shows some smiling tommies, bayonets at the ready, with
the caption 'Just a line to let you see/ We're still
all-right and mean to be/ Still all gay and not
down-hearted/ Any more than when we parted.'

Some of the postcards, despite being passed
by the censor, look pretty frightening, such as
one that shows a bombed-out hospital in Ypres.
Another shows a group of
soldiers next to a burnt-out
farm (see page 99). The caption
on the back says: 'A wayside
group of gallant Indian caval-
rymen, some of whom enjoyed
their share in a charge through
the cornfields at High Wood on
July 14, 1916 with the Dragoon
Guards. Being Indians, of
course, they were still cheerful.'

Looting, or at least liberating, German possessions seems to have been
allowed, if not actively encouraged, during the First World War. I have a
good quality black-and-white photo of a group of 'Happy "Tommies"
wearing Hun Helmets' (see page 96). This was an official battle picture
produced by the *Daily Mail* newspaper and passed by the censor. The
soldiers in question, all laughing and joking, are sporting elaborate German

NOTHING is to be written on this except
the date and signature of the sender. Sentences
not required may be erased. If anything else
is added the post card will be destroyed.

I am quite well.

I have been admitted into hospital
(sick) and am going on well.
(wounded) and hope to be discharged soon.

I am being sent down to the base.

I have received your (letter
(telegram.
(parcel.

Letter follows at first opportunity.

I have received no letter from you
(lately.
(for a long time.

Signature
only. } Will

Date 23/9/14

[Postage must be prepaid on any letter or postcard addressed
to the sender of this card.]

YPRES

40419-45. — Ypres 1919. Hospi

THERE'S GLADNESS IN REMEMBRANCE

Just a line to let you see
We're still all-right & mean to be.
Still all gay & not down-hearted
Any more than when we parted.

Pickelhaube helmets, the ones with a spike on top, at jaunty angles, presumably taken from captured or dead Germans.

Most of my collections are impersonal and mass-produced, with no particular individual stories attached to the items in them, or details of who owned these objects before me. But with all these wartime letters and documents, the flesh-and-blood human beings jump right out, despite their being completely unknown to me and probably long forgotten, perhaps even by their own families. I like to think, in this instance at least, that I am not merely a collector, but a curator and keeper of memories and existences long gone.

" Daily Mail " WAR PICTURES

HAPPY "TOMMIES" WEARING HUN HELMETS. 73.

OFFICIAL PHOTOGRAPH.
CROWN COPYRIGHT RESERVED.

Silks

I have a pretty decent collection of First World War postcards, especially the 'silks'. They're called silks because that's what they are partly made of, beautifully embroidered pieces of gauze-like cloth that are mounted on the front of postcards. Some of them open up, and have another little decorated card inside, which you could sign, thus making it even more personal and special.

The embroidery is delicate and intricate, weaving in messages with flowers and flags and other decorations. They were sent from the front by our soldiers in the First World War, and were made specially by French

women. Judging by a message like 'We'll come out all right' (see above), I imagine they were still stitching away while the war was going on. Mostly the messages were from a loving husband to his wife, or to his mum or his sister. You don't often see silks addressed to a father or a brother.

Some of them have embroidered flags and banners that clearly represent particular regiments. That's where I fall down, not knowing enough about military history, but I still love their beauty and finesse.

When I first started buying them, for £2 or £3, 20 years ago, I would re-use them myself, rubbing out the names, as they were often in pencil, and sending them to my wife or sisters on their birthdays. I used to spoil them. Now they are too expensive to entrust to the post, so I keep them safe in albums.

I find them all heartbreaking. Especially when I read the handwritten messages in the little pockets. 'May 18, 1918, France. From your own boy, I'll be home soon – Wilf . . .'

COLLECTING TYPES

One topic that has obsessed academics is the systematization of collectors and collecting. They can describe its history, back to ancient times, its various manifestations, but naturally, as academics, they are keen to analyze why we do it, and then create pigeonholes into which they can slot all collectors and collections.

Psychoanalysts, who ascribe deep sexual motives to everything, have identified a type of collecting they refer to as 'Fetishism'. Quite amusing, I suppose, with a small sliver of truth, but pretty daft really. Sociologists analyze collecting in terms of 'Colonizing' and 'Possessing'. Then there are the collectors whom they refer to as 'Separationists'. These are the people who acquire objects that have been taken from their original context – African spears, Egyptian masks, Eskimo headgear and so on – and have ended up in some penthouse in New York.

After long and serious deliberation, lasting well over five minutes, I suggest that we keep it simple and whittle things down to four main types of collecting:

1 SCIENTIFIC This was the basis of the collections that went on to form many of the world's great museums. By collecting old skulls, bones, remains of statues, pottery, plants, shells and the like, people in the past were attempting to educate themselves and others – to give meaning, to suggest patterns. They often had a hidden agenda, perhaps to prove the existence of God, or the truth of an evolutionary theory. At the same time, they experienced wonder and amazement as they explored what nature and man had created. Items they treasured could be big or small, valuable or worthless, ugly or beautiful. What connected them was the enquiring mind behind the collection.

2 ARTISTIC In this case, the collector is inspired mostly by the notion of Beauty – not to

REVISITING THE PAST Another of my First World War postcards, a colour-tinted photo of the Battle of the Somme in 1916. Objects like this would definitely fall into the category of 'Souvenir' collecting, since they bring the past alive for me and reveal the human stories behind great historical events.

learn something, or educate others, but to enjoy and admire objects for their own sake. This is what those who collect Old Masters, rare china, sculpture and fine furniture tell themselves, and sometimes it's a bit of a fib. Investment possibilities, or social prestige, come into it as well. But I like to think there always have been a large number of collectors whose main reason for collecting *is* Beauty – how things look and feel to them, how they appeal to their tastes and sensitivities. The way in which people appreciate anything is of course very often determined by the styles, fashions and education of the period, and by experts in and arbiters of what is considered to be good taste.

3 STATUS Normally wealth is the vital determining element here, rather than science or beauty, but it can happen lower down the collecting scale with people collecting in order to give themselves importance and standing, even if they have a small cheque book. Those with fat wads use dealers, experts, galleries and auction houses to build their collections as they are usually too busy making money, or too ignorant, to research things for themselves.

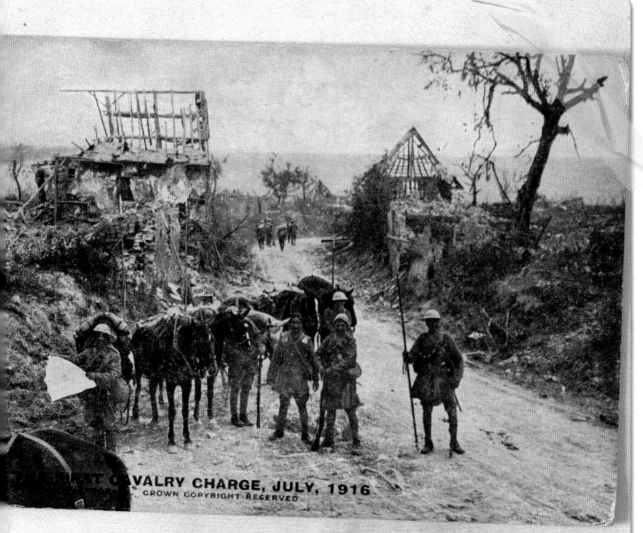

CAVALRY CHARGE, JULY, 1916
CROWN COPYRIGHT RESERVED

This is not to say that those motivated by status do not acquire expertise and taste, but that without money, and the desire to display it, they would never have got round to collecting in the first place. It has always happened: popes, kings, noblemen and dictators would compete with other popes, kings, noblemen and dictators to show off their trophies from around the globe.

Status collecting was fairly limited in the old days. Ordinary people didn't have the money or space. Now that you can hardly move for billionaires, status collections are everywhere, from California to China, Carlisle to Camden Lock.

4 SOUVENIRS This might suggest the collecting of cheap, tatty, mass-produced, shoddy goods – which of course is brilliant fun – but I'm thinking of souvenirs in the general sense, of objects that bring back memories of times past, including historical events you never experienced yourself, such as the 1914–18 war. By looking at the objects, I feel I understand more.

Postcards are obvious souvenirs, as are stamps, football programmes, toys, games, autographs and most forms of ephemera. It doesn't mean they are not educational, or pretty, or sometimes have become quite valuable status symbols, but in their original forms they were rarely seen as works of art. Now of course we like to give them added value – seeing them as part of social history.

FIRE! FIRE!! FIRE!!!

Great Salvage Sale.

Bargains in
WOMEN

Come early and have your choice.

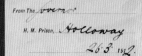

MRS. PANKHURST ARRESTED IN VICTORIA STREET. FEB. 13. 1908.

LOT 1.—Splendid assortment of **Fat Cooks**, would suit a copper. Once round their waists, twice round the Gasworks.

LOT 2.—Several good old **Gin Tasters**, slightly imperfect.

LOT 3.—Cheap line of **Old Maids**, (we don't think) who have never known the meaning of a good night's kiss. Samples on approval.

LOT 4.—A few **Suffragettes** just arrived from Pentonville.

Old Sports, but wished wooden legs, they have been

We Want Our Vote!

From The Governor's
H. M. Prison, *Holloway*
26·3·1912

To Mrs. *Warrie,*
32 Doughty Street
N.C.

15710 Harrison.

Dear Madam,

In reply to your letter of the 23rd instant referring to the above named prisoner I beg to inform you that she will not be entitled to a visit during her sentence

Yours faithfully

Acting Governor.

Advice on Marriage.
TO YOUNG LADIES.

1. Do not marry at all.

2. But if you must avoid the Beauty Men, Flirts, and the Bounders, Tailor's Dummies, and the Football Enthusiasts.

3. Look for a Strong, Tame Man, a Fire-lighter, Coal-getter, Window Cleaner, and Yard Swiller.

4. Don't except too much, most men are lazy, selfish, thoughtless, lying, drunken, clumsy, heavy-footed, rough, unmanly brutes, and need taming.

5. All Bachelors are, and many are worse still.

6. If you want him to be happy, Feed the Brute.

7. The same remark applies to Dogs.

8. You will be wiser not to chance it, it isn't worth the risk.

A SUFFRAGETTE WIFE.

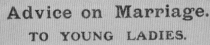

100

Suffragettes

About 20 years ago my wife was researching a book about early feminists, women who changed the world by improving the lot of their fellow women. Christmas was coming up and in a shop off Charing Cross Road I saw a set of signatures by the Pankhursts, mother and daughters, nicely framed. So I thought, heh, this will do for her present. Clever old me.

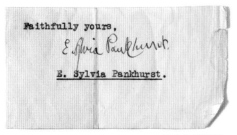

I bought it and made a pencil note in code of what I'd paid, not because it was a present but because this is what I always do when I purchase something. I don't want other people finding out how dopey I have been.

My wife looked puzzled when, pleased as Punch, I handed them over: 'I'm not doing the Pankhursts. And they're just signatures. Why would I want them?'

'I was just thinking', I said, 'as you're working on this feminist book, wouldn't it be amusing to have this, as a sort of inspiration, hmm, my petal?'

'I've got enough inspiration, thank you.'

HARD STRUGGLE

Left: a selection of Suffragette-related items from my collection. Clockwise from top: postcard of Mrs Emmeline Pankhurst being arrested; letter from the governor of Holloway, refusing visiting rights; and three examples of anti-Suffragette agitation.

Starting My Suffragette Collection

So that's how I began my Suffragette collection. It's now pretty enormous, up there in my top ten collections, but it's the only one I can remember starting in this way.

Having got the Pankhursts' autographs, I began looking out for photographs of them. They appeared on lots of postcards just before the First World War – on marches, being arrested, giving speeches. I also tracked down Suffragette magazines, leaflets, posters and original letters, some of which came from Holloway Prison.

Once the Suffragette movement got into its stride, in the early 1900s, there were lots of different organizations, some with very similar titles.

Some were pacifist, wanting to achieve their ends by peaceful means, while others were becoming violently militant. But they were all after the same thing – Votes for Women.

The National Union of Women's Suffrage Societies was the biggest of the Suffragette organizations. It was non-militant and not party political, brought together by its President, Millicent Garrett Fawcett, in 1897. Its publication was *The Common Cause*. The Women's Social and Political Union, founded by Emmeline Pankhurst in 1903, became increasingly militant, even resorting to violence and bombing. Their paper was *Votes for Women*, which later became *The Suffragette*, following the departure of its original editors, Emmeline Pethick-Lawrence and her husband.

Militancy was at its height prior to the First World War, but then when war came, women were as caught up in it as men, going into the munitions factories to replace the men who'd gone to the front, and doing other jobs that men had done. Female suffrage (for women over 30) became law as soon as the war was over in 1918.

VOTES FOR WOMEN.

Photo. by Kay, Mancheste

Miss CHRISTABEL PANKHURST, LL

Organising Secretary, National Women's Social an Political Union, 4, Clement's Inn, Strand. W.C.

Feminists and Chauvinists

The best fun and cheapest to buy, at least when I started collecting Suffragette stuff, are the comic postcards. When you begin a new collection, not knowing where you are going, what's rare or what's common, you tend to be all over the place. But I soon realized the comic cards fell into two types.

Firstly, there are pro-Suffragette cards, proclaiming 'We Want the Vote', and showing feisty women marching, or babies, cats and dogs holding up placards. Then there are anti-Suffragette cards. Basically, they're taking the piss. 'It's not a vote you want, it's a bloke!' shouts a cheeky youth to a Suffragette handing out leaflets. Many show henpecked husbands, down on their knees cleaning, warning what will happen to men if women get the vote.

I still keep an eye out for Suffragette stuff all the time – but the prices, my dears! Black-and-white postcards– of the Pankhursts and others, or of demonstrations and marches – which I used to pick up for £5, now cost

'QUEEN OF THE MOB'
Flyer showing Christabel Pankhurst, one of the heroes of the suffrage movement, who was imprisoned on several occasions. Her unflattering nickname was given to her by a hostile press.

£50–£80. If you can find them at all, that is. Even the comic ones, once around £2, are now £10. As for Suffragette letters, newspapers and leaflets, they now don't turn up nearly as often as they once did. I think they must be stashed away in feminist libraries and collections in Europe and the USA.

The other day, I bought a large 19th- and early 20th-century scrap album of Suffragette material. The album itself was handsome and expensive, solidly bound, all in leather, but now of course worn and faded. In fact it looked pretty tatty, which is why I got it for only £30. But inside, the cuttings were as pristine and clear as the day they had been stuck in. They consist principally of newspaper and magazine articles, plus cartoons, a lot of them from Punch, all relating to the Suffragette movement, its campaigns and meetings, and reflecting the arguments for and against women's suffrage. The scrap album covers the period from 1848 to 1917, starting much earlier than I expected.

The women's suffrage movement is generally dated from 1863, when the philosopher John Stuart Mill made a pledge to support women's suffrage when bidding to become an MP. The following year Barbara Bodichon, Emily Davies and others presented a petition, signed by 1499 women householders, to the House of Commons, demanding the vote. And got nowhere, needless to say.

Judging by these cuttings, the early stirrings of the Suffragette movement,

My wife's joined the Suffrage Movement. (I've suffered ever since!)

back in the 1840s and 1850s, were taken as a bit of a joke, a matter for mockery. The first cutting in the scrapbook purports to show The Women's Charter. It looks genuine at first, until you come on to the list of women's requirements: 'the honeymoon to last six months; all household expenses to be fixed by the woman, with an unlimited allowance for extras; the husband must smoke in the garden (if no garden, no smoke)'.

The cuttings have been stuck in, which to purists ruins their collectable value, but whoever collected them did at least have the sense to jot the exact dates, in pencil, at the top of the page. One of the problems with all scrapbooks, on whatever subject, is that people often don't date or give the source of their cuttings, imagining that they will always know where it came from. A hundred and fifty years later, it can become almost impossible.

Whole newspapers devoted to the Suffragette cause, such as *Women's Franchise*, *The Common Cause* and *Votes for Women*, are now hard to find. In good condition they can cost at least £30 each.

One of the great things about Suffragette memorabilia is that all the banners, posters, postcards, leaflets, newspapers, had real artistic merit. They used women's traditional skills in embroidery, velvet and silk, allied to the new technical ability of all the modern career women who were being trained in art colleges at the end of the 19th century. And in pottery factories (see China, pages 82–89).

The Suffragette movement is an important part of modern social and political history, as well as of the history of feminism. Its artefacts are well worth studying and collecting. And not just because the items are so pretty. Which really shouldn't matter, should it?

SPREADING THE WORD A Suffragette selling newspapers on a London street. Such journals are quite hard to come by these days.

MEN v WOMEN

Collectors come in all shapes, sizes, ages, races and classes, but are mostly male. I've never actually done a scientific survey. This is just an observation. I'm too busy, head down, waiting to push my way to the front of the jumbles when the doors open, to count heads.

But oft, when I pause, I do notice that almost all the punters around me, and the dealers, are scruffy old blokes, on their own. They always remind me of someone. Me, actually.

Likewise, when I go to Sotheby's or to Christie's, it's predominantly men. And at least 95 percent of the 100 or so stalls at the Bloomsbury postcard fairs are run by men. Women, as partners or daughters, are often there helping out, but they defer to the male figures, who usually run the business as well as owning the stall. The proportion of men, elbowing their way around, eager to spend their money, is about the same.

Books, stamps, ephemera, toys, tickets, magazines, programmes, pop music, films, football, tins, postcards – you name it, you'll find that there are very few women either buying or selling these items.

There are exceptions to this wild generalization. With Suffragette material, about half the collectors are women, along with most of the experts in the field. The subject, after all, is women. With vintage clothing and jewellery, dolls and dolls' houses, the collectors and dealers are also mainly female.

There are also a large number of women who collect and deal in china. I suppose that china, in all its forms, is a domestic item, traditionally bought and cleaned and cared for by women, so it's the sort of thing women go for, and know about already, if and when they get the collecting bug. I've also noticed quite a lot of women dealers in children's books, like the excellent shop 'Ripping Yarns' in Highgate, though I'd still guess that at least half of the collectors are men.

So, apart from these exceptions, that leaves the vast majority of collecting areas dominated by men, both as dealers and collectors. Why is this? Well, men, we are told, were the original hunter-gatherers, so it might go back to that. We tend to be more acquisitive and possessive than women. Men like status, showing off their belongings, and their knowledge, trying to outdo or impress their rivals. Having the best art collection is often a way for rich men to achieve this.

Men, traditionally, have had more money, with enough spare to spend on works of art and other objects. And also more time. Women's work, as we well know, is never done. They have little time for hobbies, certainly not. Men have usually also had more space – their own room, their library, or even just their shed – in which to display or play with their collections.

There is something in the male psyche that makes us become squirrels, collecting and hoarding things – as well as acquiring masses of useless information, and mastering the minutiae, the records and statistics, of any particular subject, if only to bore the pants off everyone else. But most of all, I honestly think women on the whole are just too sensible. Collecting, when you get right down to it, is a pretty silly thing to do ...

ies of India, The Arctic, The Amazon, Africa, America and Canada—All In...

THE NEW ADVENTURE

Nº 551 · MAY-21-193...

EVERY MONDAY · PRICE 2ᴰ

THE MONKEYS' CUP FINAL.—...

GET PART FOUR OF THE
**ADVENTURE
MAGIC MIDGET
MOVIE
FREE INSIDE**
AND
ANOTHER FOUR
ANIMAL PICTURES
PRINTED IN
FULL COLOURS

FIRST DAY COVER

MRS DESPARD · DAME MILLICENT FAWCETT · MRS PANKHURST

VOTES FOR
1918 WOMEN 1968

VOTES
FOR
WOMEN
1918-19...

1918-1968

50TH ANNIVERSARY of the SUFFRAGETTE MOVEMENT

VOTES FOR WOMEN · GIVE WOMEN THE VOTE

VOTES FOR WOMEN

"SUFFRAGETTES
TRY TO PETITION
KING GEORGE V AT
BUCKINGHAM PALACE 1914"

First Day of Issue

FIRST DAY OF ISSUE
29 MAY 1968
LONDON, E.C.

VOTES
FOR
WOMEN
1918-1968

9ᵈ

ABBOTT / HARRISON

L. Parker, Esq.,
"Joystead",
Crescent Rise,
Storrington,
Sussex

IDEAS, October 27, 1923.

HUGE PRIZES IN FOOTBALL AND OTHER COMPET...

Ideas

VOL. XXXVIII.—No. 973. [REGISTERED AS A NEWSPAPER] OCTOBER 2...

Joys & Pains of Collecting

So what's the joy in collecting? Why are so many people collectors? Equally, what are some of the nasty things that non-collectors say about us to explain away our obsession?

WORLD OF WONDER There is so much variety and interest in collecting, whatever your chosen specialism.

One in three people in North America and Europe are collectors, according to Professor Susan Pearce of the University of Leicester, past president of the Museums Association of Great Britain, who has written several studies of collecting (see page 149). Presumably she is excluding children from her estimate, which means there must be around 100 million people in North America and Europe alone who are currently collecting. And many of the remaining two-thirds can be assumed to have some sort of passive interest in collecting, judging by the millions who visit museums and exhibitions every year and tune into TV programmes like the *Antiques Roadshow*.

Professor Pearce and others have produced a great deal of academic research on the history of collecting, its place in ancient and medieval times, and the culture of collecting during Britain's age of imperial glory, when it formed part of the colonial urge to bring back the spoils of war and conquest.

As for me, I'm more concerned about today – trying to ponder why it is that ordinary people on the planet, from all walks of life, all ages and classes, become passionate about collecting. Mostly I'm trying to work out why on Earth I do it. If only to offer a half-decent explanation to my bemused wife when I come home with yet more rubbish – I mean treasures. I always call them treasures, whatever they are, and not even ironically.

Don't get me wrong – my wife loves galleries and museums and the *Antiques Roadshow*, and will often show a passing interest in a new item I've acquired, such as an early copy of *Votes for Women*. But she would never dream of going out and collecting anything herself. She hates clutter and litter of any kind. Her first instinct is always to chuck stuff out. I know where she gets it from. Her dad was just the same. When her mother died, I caught her father, not long afterwards, in the back garden, burning all his late wife's possessions – her clothes, letters, documents, papers. 'Don't burn all those, Arthur!' I cried, but it was too late.

I suppose the world divides into accumulators and chuckers-out. It appears to be inherited, and people rarely change as they go through life. Chuckers-out like to live clean and uncluttered lives. Accumulators accumulate. As such, it's hard to explain to the chuckers-out and non-collectors where the pleasures lie, but here goes: ten ways to describe and explain the Joys of Collecting:

1 HUNTER-GATHERING This instinct obviously springs from our ancient roots, but I still see this tendency in myself, and it's not just because of my first name. There is a delight in going out foraging, looking for treasures, or even scraps that might just turn out to be interesting. It takes cunning, patience and knowledge to bag the big one – just like hunting.

One of the huge pluses for me in having so many different collections is that when I go to Oxfam, or to a jumble or a car-boot sale, I will always find something I didn't know I was looking for and had no idea would be there. Thus I never come back home empty-handed, without a kill.

This hunt for objects may be more than just a male thing, the joy of going out on the prowl, to see what you can find. As the years have gone on, and I have accumulated so much stuff, I'm more conscious of the fact that the main joy was actually in the act of gathering itself. When I've got the object home, I often just dump it in a corner, or shove it in a box, telling myself I'll study it properly later, display it neatly, but often I never do. I just leave it there. That's when I realize that it was the business of tracking and killing the little beast and bringing it home, that took me out on the hunt, which is pretty stupid, and something I could never tell my wife.

108

2 POSSESSING Obviously the proper object of gathering is to have and to hold, otherwise why do it? Possession does give a great feeling, knowing you own something. I gloat and ogle, caress and fondle, feel smug and proud over a new-found treasure, often spinning out the pleasure for several days in order to truly savour my latest find. Being acquisitive seems to be a basic human urge. We're all squirrels at heart. And we like to exercise power and control over things that we own.

3 COMPLETION I don't think hunter-gatherers, back in their caves, experienced the thrill of completion, not in the sense that modern collectors do, though I'm sure when you'd killed all your enemies, wiped out all the nasties, that must have felt pretty good. I'm really talking about completing sets, runs and rows of objects, hunting down and then finally bagging that missing first edition, that programme you'd only read about, that plate you'd never seen till now, till at long last you have filled all the gaps.

Collectors often create their own gaps, just as they create their own hunt in the first place. They set them-selves goals that no one has asked them to achieve, or possibly ever thought of before. That's one of the delights, to feel you are creative, individual. When you've finally finished whatever task it was you set yourself to finish, you can tell yourself you've built up something unique. Then you look around and think, hmm, there must be another daft thing I can go after now.

4 KNOWLEDGE I would never have got to learn about the various different Suffragette organizations if I hadn't started collecting funny postcards about them. Likewise, I now find the history of football completely fascinating, but I'd probably never have bothered to start reading up about it if I hadn't been trying to date some old photographs and noticed that shin guards were being worn outside socks and thought, hmm, I wonder when that stopped? Knowing the provenance of your paintings, the maker's marks on your Sheffield silver, the potteries that made your coronation mugs, all these things collectors know, but almost certainly didn't until they started collecting. I like to tell myself all the time that I'm not a collector, I'm a social historian. Almost every collection has an educational element. Knowledge is good. And it makes you feel good.

STAN MATTHEWS, Stoke City F.C.   TOPICAL TIMES

5 ESCAPE I find all my collections a wonderful escape and distraction, as I did when I was a boy with asthma. When I'm out on the hunt, poking round the stalls, I tend to think of nothing else. Work worries or domestic annoyances vanish from my mind and time stands still.

Allied with escape is therapy. I'm amazed that Freud – a collector of antiquities himself – didn't advocate collecting as a means of easing psychological problems. Collecting soothes the troubled soul and eases mental tensions. And it keeps people off the streets, out of possible mischief. In fact, I'm surprised the government doesn't offer collecting on the NHS.

6 INVESTMENT Never collect to make money – only to acquire what interests you. Buying as an investment is a mug's game, as I know only too well from my experience with stamps. In many areas of collecting, prices see-saw, often because investors have muscled in, sometimes making a killing. A lot of men with money – though very rarely women – come into collecting when they read and hear about certain markets going up. In times of collapsing banks and poor rates from traditional sources of income, they decide collectables will be a good bet for a long- or short-term punt. This happens not only with art, but also with stamps, coins, first editions and even football memorabilia. Some of this investment is dodgy money; buying a collection can be a good way of laundering money. These rich-git collectors naturally spoil it for *real* collectors, the ones in it for life, and for fun, who suddenly find many items well out of their price range. On the other hand, it's nice to know that something you have

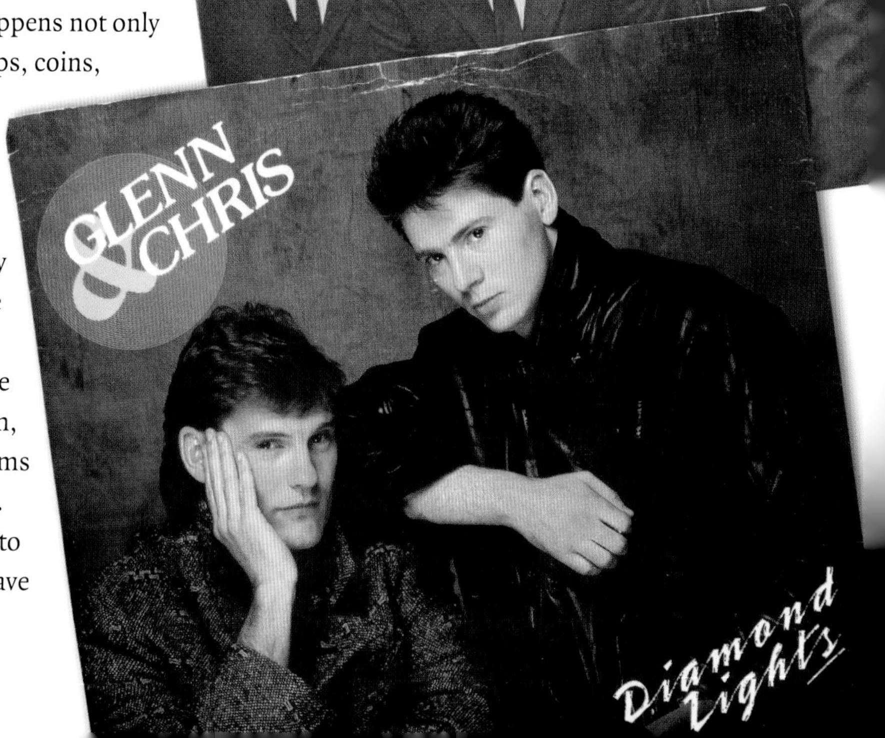

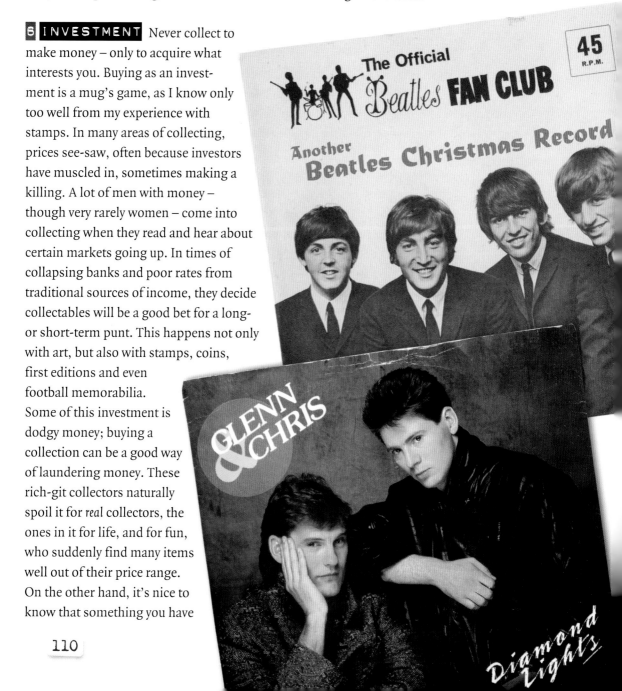

acquired out of personal interest, has, over the years, grown in value, though of course that wasn't the point, you keep telling yourself, piously.

If you buy good examples, look after them properly, then wait a while, you should always be able to at least get your money back. If you sell quickly, you're likely to lose, as the dealer who sold it to you at £10 will only pay £5 to buy it back. They've got to live, they bleat . . .

Most mainstream and popular collecting areas increase in value over the years, with or without the influence of outside investors. After all, there are millions of new people out there waiting to be re-born, to wake up in their middle years and think – golly! I must have those Cape Triangular stamps, that first edition of *Harry Potter*.

7 EXCITEMENT It's hard for non-collectors to believe, but I'm genuinely delighted when I find something I was looking for. Even more so when it's something I wasn't looking for, or didn't know existed, but which fits in exactly with an existing collection.

Wordsworth wrote that 'in getting and spending we lay waste our powers'. I disagree. I find it thrilling. Being by nature mean, I don't spend a lot on most items, and am always looking for bargains, quite happy with the worn and the foxed. And I don't consider it's a waste of my time or energy. We all need a break, an outlet, some pleasure and diversion in our little lives, and hopefully, now and again, a bit of harmless excitement.

My heart skips a beat when I come across an unconsidered trifle on a stall – unconsidered, so I hope, by the dealer, who doesn't appear to appreciate how unusual or rare it is, judging by its modest price, or how much I am lusting after it. I try to conceal my ardour, turning it over with heavy disinterest and mild contempt – 'hmm, bit missing here, badly torn, awful fading, what a shame, I might have been interested'. I then try to beat him down, on principle, even though I'm more than prepared to pay what he's asking. It's a game, after all. Is the excitement as great as love and sex and all that? Some people have suggested it is, likening the search for an object to going out on the pull. The first sight of the object of desire certainly sets the heart a-flutter like a first kiss.

8 SOCIAL LIFE The world of collecting, even the most obscure of objects, almost always turns out to have an infrastructure, an underground of like-minded people with their own little societies, magazines, meeting places, events, competitions, lectures, exhibitions, tours, holidays, parties,

SPIN-OFFS
My passion for the Beatles and football means that I collect pretty much everything associated with them. Records are a case in point: above, an Xmas record from the Beatles Fan Club; left, Spurs stars Hoddle and Waddle's venture into pop in 1987.

fun and feuds that can run forever and be endlessly entertaining. I was in a newsagent's in Belsize Park the other day and picked up some back copies of *The Enid Blyton Society Journal*; I hadn't even known of the Society's existence. The journal was erudite and informative, advertising events, meetings and lectures that brought people together from all over the world, united by their common interest. Gosh, what fun. I quite envied them.

Once you start frequenting fairs and get to know certain dealers, you begin to realize collecting generates a lot of human interaction. I find that dealers will readily share their friendship and experience, help you avoid stupid mistakes and listen to your hopes and desires (and throwing money at them on a regular basis helps, of course).

9 PERFECT FOR LONERS Equally, collecting is ideal for ungregarious people who are happy with their own company and don't want a communal experience, thank you very much.

If you take up football or rugby or tennis, you have by definition to interact with other people, otherwise you don't have a game. While collecting can give you a social circle, if you want it, you can easily pursue it all on your own, without meeting or talking to anyone else, in the privacy of your own room – and it's not against the law. You can pick your time, or frame of mind, to go out hunting or just to stay in, playing with your treasures, without frightening the horses. Collecting, then, attracts a lot of loners, who might

ANYTHING AND EVERYTHING
Items reflecting my magpie-like collecting habit: top to bottom; a Buck House garden party invitation; the front of John Lennon's card to me from India (see page 38), showing nationalist leader Subhas Chandra Bose; and an invoice from an old iron foundry in Cumbria.

EᴵᴵR

The Lord Chamberlain i.
commanded by Her Majesty to

Mr and Mrs Hunter Da

to a Garden Party at Buckingham
on Thursday, 16th July, 1981 from .

Uniform or Lounge Suit

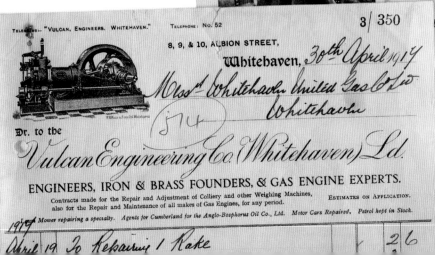

TELEGRAMS:— "VULCAN, ENGINEERS, WHITEHAVEN."   TELEPHONE: No. 52   3/350

8, 9, & 10, ALBION STREET,
Whitehaven, 30th April 1917

Mess. Whitehaven United Gas Co Ltd
Whitehaven

(514)

Dr. to the
Vulcan Engineering Co (Whitehaven) Ld.

ENGINEERS, IRON & BRASS FOUNDERS, & GAS ENGINE EXPERTS.

Contracts made for the Repair and Adjustment of Colliery and other Weighing Machines,   ESTIMATES ON APPLICATION.
also for the Repair and Maintenance of all makes of Gas Engines, for any period.
Mower repairing a specialty.   Agents for Cumberland for the Anglo-Bosphorus Oil Co., Ltd.   Motor Cars Repaired.   Petrol kept in Stock.

1917
April 19   To Repairing 1 Rake   2 6

appear outwardly sad, but inside are a bundle of enthusiasms. They just happen to be self-contained. So, always remember – you're never alone with a collection.

10 IDENTITY I collect, therefore I am. Extreme, obsessive collectors can get carried away by their own self-importance and erudition, coming to believe that their collections, their treasures, give them status and identity. This is particularly the case with very rich collectors, who wade in, gobble up all the Picassos or Damien Hirsts and think themselves world-beaters. Yet, in moderation, the feeling of many collectors that their hobby somehow sets them apart is no bad thing. There's nothing wrong with self-worth.

The Pains of Collecting

Then again, some non-collectors still wonder aloud what dreadful flaws or inadequacies drive us to do what we do. So, in the interests of fairness and balance, let's now address ten brickbats that have been flung at collecting:

1 TIME-CONSUMING Collecting takes up a lot of time and energy, which I could otherwise be spending with my grandchildren, fixing those shelves, clearing the garage, doing the garden ... yes, yes, do stop going on, I heard you the first time. I now try to set aside a certain part of the weekend for hunting down treasures or playing with them. The hunting normally takes place on Saturday mornings. Like pudding at the end of a meal, I save up playing with my treasures as a treat, after a hard working day down the word mines. So yes, there's no denying collecting takes up a lot of time.

2 EXPENSIVE We collectors all lie about how much we spend, even to ourselves, hoping to keep it secret from loved ones and in the end forget about own follies. I hate to think what I spend in a year. Whatever I confess now, treat with caution and suspicion. Never trust collectors to tell the truth.

Most Saturdays, I reckon to spend between £20 and £50 in cash. Every month I also get catalogues that tempt me to buy stuff I fancy, sight unseen. The monthly expenditure through those is about £100. And three or four times a year I go to a Big Fair, where I might spend £200. Then once a year, I usually bid at a big auction, at Sotheby's or Christies. God, it's mounting up. That must come to around £4000 a year. I could buy a decent secondhand car for that, or a luxury holiday in the West Indies. Potty, absolutely potty.

3 PRIDE AND VANITY Both these vices can be observed in most collectors. We take undue pride in our piddling finds, our little triumphs, our so-called exciting discoveries when no one else gives a damn. We feel smug in our obscure knowledge and expertise in useless areas. Mostly we're just impressing ourselves. Oh, and greed, that's another vice. Collectors are always hungry for more, desperate to be one up, to find and hug something others have not got or missed, just to have it to themselves. Pathetic, really.

4 SELFISHNESS While collecting can be sociable, it also tends to cut you off from the world in general, and from all those who don't share your own particular hobby horses. Collecting is very selfish and self-absorbing.

5 MADNESS Collectors can become obsessive or unhinged, as we say in philately. They start neglecting their partners, families and themselves, and display obsessive-compulsive behaviour. As with drugs, people may steal and lie to feed their collecting habit, desperate for the next fix. It's true that some collectors end up in the hands of psychiatrists, who offer them therapy and medication. But then plenty of non-collectors also see shrinks.

6 ANAL EROTICISM While collecting is a form of escape, taking your mind off your woes, your ill-health, and so on and so forth, clever people like therapists can't leave it there. They have to explain what we are *really* escaping from, and what it all means, deep down.

Some Freudian psychoanalysts see the act of collecting as being anally retentive. At least, that's what Professor Ernest Jones, biographer of Freud, appears to suggest in his work *Anal Erotic Character Traits* (1950). It all goes back to potty training, how we were disciplined and made obsessive about our motions. Looking at and admiring our files of collections today can be traced back to looking at and admiring our faeces, pleased with our productivity. Well, it's a theory . . .

7 MASTURBATORY If collecting's not anal, it could be masturbatory, according to some French philosophers. They see collecting as just another pursuit of solitary pleasures. No comment . . .

8 SEXUAL SUBLIMATION If, though, you are getting no pleasure out of it, solitary or otherwise, it could well be a substitute for the sex life you are *not* having. Collecting is your subliminal compensation. You are either running away from sex, or making up for no one offering you a good time, or even a horrible time. Collectors rarely admit this to themselves, being such guilty, nasty, shameful creatures, always in denial. Right, I think that just about covers sexual motivation.

114

9 `DEVIANT` As if all this subliminal sex, or lack of it, didn't make us unappealing enough characters, the charge of deviance has also been levelled at a certain species of collector. In her book *On Collecting*, Susan Pearce points the finger at some 50,000 collectors, mostly American, whose particular thing is Nazi memorabilia.

For sure, whenever I go to Camden Passage on a Saturday, I see lots of men milling around a basement area there that is filled with stalls special-

izing in militaria. They are after medals, badges, uniforms, documents, mainly from the Second World War. These inevitably include certain German/Nazi items, though I'm not sure they really make a beeline for these. But Prof. Pearce is of a different mind. In her view, 'we have to conclude that most of those who collect Nazi material now would have been Nazis then'. Her damning verdict is that 'the collector sees glamour in evil and wishes to identify with it through its relics'.

Then there's pornography, in particular sado-masochistic material. Usually called 'erotic literature', this has been collected by gentlemen for centuries, salted away in their libraries and examined in private. Recently, though, a museum in France put some of its spicier collections on show. Apparently, they turned out to be pretty tame by today's standards.

10 `UTTER POINTLESSNESS` Having finished the set, completed the task, the stuff often just lies there, ignored and forgotten, so what was the point? When you've gone, your wife/husband/partner or children will throw it out, give it to a jumble, let some unscrupuluous dealer come in and say 'load a rubbish, I'll give you tuppence for the lot'. Sadly, how very true.

WORLD CHAMPIONSHIP
JULES RIMET CUP

Final

ENGLAND v WEST GERMANY

SATURDAY · JULY 30 · 1966

EMPIRE STADIUM
WEMBLEY

SOUVENIR
PROGRAMME

PRICE
2/6

Football

My joint biggest collecting area, along with the Beatles, is football. My rebirth as a football collector came in the late afternoon of Saturday, 30 July 1966. When I got home I carefully put away the ticket for the historic game I'd just watched, plus the programme. This day might not be repeated, I thought to myself, not for some time, so I want to have proof that I was there. And indeed it hasn't: England doesn't look like winning the World Cup ever, ever, ever again – well, not in my lifetime, anyway.

It's always been normal for football fans to keep their programmes after a big game, but it was unusual to keep the ticket. After all, you're left with only part of the ticket, the counterfoil, as the other part gets taken by the man at the turnstile. Tickets don't contain much information anyway, usually just the date, the venue and the seat number.

TOP OF THE WORLD Left, right and below: Memorabilia from England's glory day, 30 July 1966. I'm proud to say that I was there when Bobby Moore lifted the cup …

For decades afterwards I never heard of other people collecting tickets. Dealers didn't advertise old tickets for sale, nor were they listed in catalogues. Then about five years ago they suddenly started appearing at auctions, at crazy prices. 1966 World Cup Final tickets like mine were being advertised for £150, while pre-war FA Cup Final tickets were going for around £1000.

Things have settled down a bit now, with more sensible prices, but it's an illustration of how the cost of football memorabilia – like Beatles stuff, like stamps, like almost anything really – can be influenced by outside investors coming in, attracted by a possible killing.

Collecting football stuff is a massive field, with lots of different specialists, dealers, magazines, societies, fairs and conferences. All the big auction houses, like Sotheby's and Christie's, have sporting

EMPIRE STADIUM
WEMBLEY

ENTER AT
K
TURNSTILES

WORLD CHAMPIONSHIP
1966
Jules Rimet Cup

FINAL TIE

ENTRANCE
36

ROW
9

SEAT
37

J.Burrows, SECRETARY.
THE FOOTBALL ASSOCIATION

SATURDAY JULY 30
KICK-OFF 3 p.m.

SOUTH STAND
£5
(SEE PLAN & CONDITIONS ON BACK)
TO BE RETAINED

(WORLD CUP WINNERS 1966)
ENGLAND

sales, in which football is the major element, as do dozens of local auctions all over the country. I often wonder why I bother collecting other subjects when football alone would have been enough to keep me happy for the rest of my life. It has depth, breadth, variety and richness, and covers a much longer timespan than the Beatles.

Football, as we know it today, began in 1863 with the foundation of the Football Association, after a meeting in a pub called the Freemason's Tavern near Lincoln's Inn in London. Crude foot and ball games, some of them pretty rough and brutal, had existed for centuries in many countries around the world, with different styles played in different places, but it was at this meeting that the game was properly codified. The rules were quickly adopted throughout Britain, and thereafter by the rest of the world. So hurrah for England – and Scotland, where a regulated form of the game was also played from early on. Britain gave football to the world, its laws and its language. Even today, the terms 'football, goal and penalty', give or take a few local pronunciations and spellings, can be heard wherever the game is played.

In his 2006 TV series *Twelve Books That Changed the World*, Melvyn Bragg devoted a whole programme to the *FA Book of Rules*. Bit of a liberty, really, calling it a book, as the original version was a handwritten list covering just a few pages. But I agree with him that it certainly was one of the most influential set of rules ever created. And it did, indeed, change the world.

The earliest known football memorabilia date from the early 1870s, after the introduction of the first international, between England and Scotland in 1870, and then the beginning of the annual FA Cup competition in 1872. The National Football

Tamen decido.

Schlagn wir jhn gleich noch eins so hoch/
Was nicht nauff soll/das bleibet doch.
B

Museum in Preston has what must be the world's earliest item of football memorabilia – the shirt worn by one of the players, Arnold Kirke-Smith of England, who played in that first international.

The Football Association was founded by ex-public schoolboys, Oxbridge and officer types, but within about 20 years the working classes were joining in. Professionalism became legal in 1885 – amateur gents had of course played for nothing – then in 1888 came the creation of the Football League.

EARLY KICK-ABOUT A 16th-century German print showing elegantly dressed gents playing a form of football.

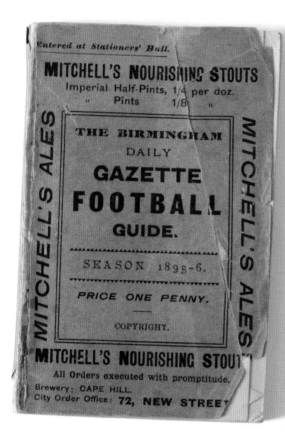

It's strange to realize that since football's foundation, the only games that teams had played had either been friendly matches or cup ties. At the outset there was no league system, with points for a win, and demotion for the duffers. It was only after the Football League's formation that football began to attract massive crowds, properly built stadiums, specialist manufacturers of football equipment and the beginning of a new breed of human being – football reporters.

One of my most prized football possessions is a run of the *Sporting Chronicle* from 3 July to 29 December 1888. The pages have all dried out, gone brittle and are in danger of falling to pieces, but the contents are still fascinating.

The period in question was of great historical significance, since it covered the world's first ever football league season. You can see the rules changing, as they went along. The season started off with a simple system of two points for a win – but after a couple of months, the League also decided to award one point for a draw.

Yet even in these embryonic stages of the organized game, what must be the first recorded instance of football hooliganism rears its head. 'Disgraceful scenes', screams a headline, had taken place at a Notts County v. Everton game. After a kicking incident between certain players, spectators invaded the pitch and set about the Everton team with sticks. Disgusting.

By the 1900s, a flood of football-related material was being pumped out, and it hasn't dried up since. Yes, we football collectors are fortunate. So much to learn about, so many artefacts to acquire.

STATE-OF-THE-ART KIT I don't collect shirts, shorts or caps but I am the proud owner of a pair of pre-war football boots. Printed on the undersole of these boots is the name 'Alex James', a famous Arsenal and Scotland player. Product endorsement didn't begin with David Beckham, or even with George Best in the 1960s. It's actually been going on for at least 80 years.

One major place of pilgrimage for all footer fans is the National Football Museum, which was founded in 2001. The museum has such a remarkable and comprehensive range of material that it will either inspire you or put you off collecting for life. Although the National Trust bought John Lennon's childhood home – 'Mendips', where he lived with his Aunt Mimi from 1945 to 1963 – and opened it to the public in 2003, there's still no National Beatles Museum. (Maybe there should be – just think of all the overseas visitors it would attract.) As for students of the Suffragette movement, the Women's Library in the East End of London is an excellent archive. But I can't think of any of my other collecting areas that is as well catered for as football.

Football Collecting

There's no end to the highways and byways you can wander down as a football memorabilia collector. But they're well-trodden, in the main. So popular is the game and everything to do with it that it's hard coming up with an esoteric area no one else has ventured into. Defunct Scottish clubs beginning with Q? Must be loads of them. Football socks tie-ups? Probably hundreds of people collecting those. Alex Ferguson's discarded chewing gum? Too late – examples of that have already been sold on eBay.

These, then, are my ten main areas of football collecting:

1 PROGRAMMES Programmes are the most numerous, longest established, easiest, generally cheapest (but in some cases dearest) football items to collect – and by far the most interesting. All footballing history is there.

The first products to be aimed specifically at football fans, programmes weren't intended as collectables but just to be leafed through during the match in question. Even so, people tended to retain them long after the game, for reference, for amusement, or as proof that they'd been there, to hand on to their children and grandchildren.

The earliest known ones date from the early 1870s and were little more than a team sheet, a single piece of card, perhaps

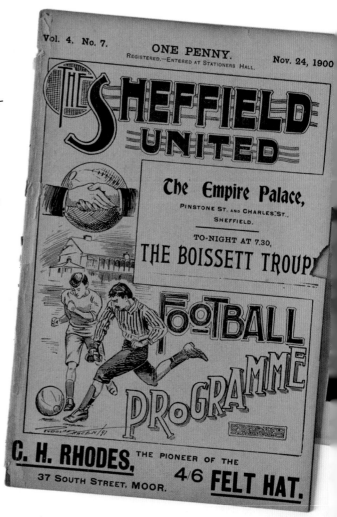

A football programme and magazine from the early 1900s. Goalie Jimmy Ashcroft, shown on the cover below right, was Arsenal's first England international, and was capped three times in 1906.

including forthcoming fixtures on the other side. They weren't sold, but were handed out to VIPs in the grandstand. Then some bright spark came up with the idea of selling advertising space on the back to defray the printing costs.

By the early 1900s, most programmes were being sold for one penny each, and had expanded to two or four pages. Having decided to charge, the clubs felt fans should get their money's worth, so they included news about the club and the players. By 1910, some programmes, like those produced by Aston Villa and Sheffield Wednesday, had grown to 12 or 16 pages. Chelsea's programmes contained jokes and cartoons, as well as club information.

Pre-First World War programmes are the most sought after, and generally command prices of £400–£500. Oddly, Sheffield United programmes of this period can be had for less than half that. What's going on? Were more printed, or has someone recently unearthed a cache of Sheffield Utd and is slowly leaking them into the market? In any event, I see a lot of them around. Prices for 1900s Arsenal programmes (in their Woolwich Arsenal days) are nearer £1000. For the early Cup Finals, expect to pay £10,000. The current record for a programme is £19,000 – for the Cup Final of 1889 between Preston North End and Wolverhampton Wanderers.

There's a surprising amount of information in programmes from the 1900s about the local economy and culture. They always contained lots of adverts from local businesses and for the Saturday evening music halls.

The star exhibit in my album of pre-1914 football programmes is one for a Walsall v. Grimsby game in 1897 (the oldest programme in my collection; see page 208). It's just a single piece of card, with the line-ups on one side, and two local adverts on the other. This happens to be my single most expensive programme. The price is in pencil, in code, to stop my wife from seeing how stupid I was. (OK, it cost me £395, but keep it quiet, eh?)

Part 2. Complete in 12 Parts. Published Fortnightly.

THE BOOK OF FOOTBALL 6D NET

ASHCROFT (The Woolwich Arsenal Goalkeeper)

Paper shortages during the First World War, and the Second for that matter, made programmes thin and weedy. But even in the 1920s and 1930s, they were often not as thick or as interesting as they had been in the early years of the century.

The logic of programme prices is often hard to fathom, for beginners anyway. You might think that very old programmes would be more expensive than later ones, and that ones from well-extablished clubs with the biggest fan bases, like Man Utd, Arsenal, Liverpool, Spurs, Celtic and Rangers, would be desirable. But in fact programmes from small clubs often fetch higher prices – for the simple fact that small clubs attracted fewer fans, and so fewer programmes were printed. For instance, I can buy a Spurs programme from the 1930s for £40, while one for Carlisle United, from the same period, will set me back £140. It's all a question of rarity.

Some of the most unusual programmes are the Liverpool–Everton joint programmes, issued from 1904 until the 1930s. Every Saturday, they shared exactly the same programme. If Liverpool's first team was at home, they would get the main coverage, while Everton's reserves, who would be playing the same day, but at nearby Goodison, filled the rest of the programme. Such a good idea. If only rival clubs from the same city could be as co-operative today.

I'm not so keen on modern programmes, even though they have grown glossy and fat, mostly with merchandizing and pointless stuff keeping in with the sponsors. Most Premiership clubs charge around £3, which is expensive, considering the quality and quantity of the editorial content. Give me the old ones any day. Even so, whenever I go to a game at Spurs, Arsenal or Carlisle United, I always keep the programme. In jumbles, I'll buy any old programme, from any club, even modern ones, if they're cheap enough –

THE FOOTBALL ASSOCIATION
INTERNATIONAL MATCH
Stadium Wembley
March 31ST 1928

ENGLAND v SCOTLAND

The valve with the wonderful Mullard P.M. Filament.
Mullard
THE·MASTER·VALVE

OFFICIAL PROGRAMME

PRICE SIXPENCE

PRODUCED & PUBLISHED BY FRED. E. BLOWER & CO, 132, HIGH ST, WATFORD

THE AULD ENEMY
England v. Scotland matches were the world's first internationals. They were such a major feature of my boyhood, as I stayed glued to the radio, desperate for Scotland to win. The Home Internationals came to an end in 1989, though there have been a couple of subsequent encounters, at Euro 1996 and Euro 2000.

Although I specialize in Spurs and Carlisle Utd programmes, I'm not averse to picking up old ones from other clubs at flea markets and car boot sales. These three come from the late 1950s and early 1960s.

say, 10p to 50p. If only I could keep hold of them for 100 years, I reckon I'd be onto a real winner.

But there are some programmes I'm prepared to spend serious money on. Spurs programmes, for instance. I've got examples dating back to 1910. Can't see me getting earlier ones, as the prices are now out of my range. Carlisle United is my second team, but I don't have as many of their programmes. They're thinner on the ground and rarely come on the market. So far I only go back to 1936, but I do have every programme, home and away, for that one glorious season, 1974–5, when CUFC was in the First Division. My collection includes a framed front page from Carlisle's *Evening News* on the day they got promoted, 4 May 1974. (By an amazing coincidence, there's also a photo of me on the front page, promoting a walking book about Hadrian's Wall that I'd just written.)

I also collect programmes for games between the old rivals, England and Scotland. I've got every England v. Scotland programme back to 1928. For return fixtures, I've got them back to 1927, but I'm missing 1931.

One oddity about football programmes is that they are a peculiarly British passion. Football has been followed just as avidly by the masses in most European and South American countries for almost as long as in Britain, yet the culture of programmes never caught on there. Many of the big foreign clubs, in places like Spain, never even got round to producing them for ordinary league matches until quite recently, so there's been no tradition of collecting them.

At one of the big national programme fairs last summer, I was surprised to see a German dealer with a stall – but it turned out he was mainly selling photos of British clubs that had played in Germany, or programmes from recent European Cup/Champions League games in Germany involving British teams. Programmes for regular German league games simply didn't exist before the war.

2 CIGARETTE CARDS I missed the heyday of cigarette cards, in the 1920s and 1930s, but they still appeal to me – only if they feature footballers or football teams, though. Collecting cigarette cards, of all sorts, is still a very popular hobby nowadays and there are clubs, magazines and guide-books to help you with the history and prices.

The idea originated in America, and they arrived in Britain in the 1890s. In those days, fags came in soft packs, so manufacturers put in blank pieces of card as stiffeners. Then someone hit upon the idea of printing on them, pretty pictures of flowers and the like, for people to collect. Cards became an important marketing tool in the battle for sales between the big tobacco

companies. Men and boys were particularly keen collectors, so they homed in on topics that appealed to them most, such as soldiers, heroes and sportsmen. Football became one of the most popular subjects and it's estimated that between 1900 and 1939 there were over 10,000 different cards with a football theme. In all, therefore, millions must have been printed.

Manufacturers produced special albums for people to stick their ciggie cards in and complete a set. What a mistake that was, at least where collecting is concerned. Today, no real collector wants stuck-in cards. It means you can't read all the words and information and the manufacturer's details on the back. Modern collectors use plastic pockets, so you can see both sides.

3 POSTCARDS Picture postcards, generally, enjoyed a boom in the 1900s, when new printing methods brought down prices and reduced postage rates.

You could buy postcards with good quality team photos of every professional club in England and Scotland. These days, prices for the well-known clubs have gone crazy, with people asking £80 for a little postcard of a Man Utd or Spurs team photo from this period.

I gave up, when I discovered these prices. Instead I decided to concentrate on unknown, local clubs. For it wasn't just the big teams who appeared on postcards. From the 1900s to the 1930s, everyone who ever put on a strip, played in any sort of team in a vaguely organized

TO MY VALENTINE

A FOOTBALL ENTHUSIAST
YOU SHOUT ALL DAY ON SATURDAY,
AND COME HOME BLACK AND BLUE;
ALL SPLASHED WITH MUD FROM HEAD TO FOOT—
I'LL NEVER MARRY YOU.

FISCAL FOOTBALL

P.V.B

A Foul. John Bull Fouled by Foreign Team. Joe to the Rescue!

Different types of
postcard from my
collection. I love the
old team photos: you
can see the pride
players felt, being
part of a team. Even
though some sides
look as if they are
playing for the ragged
school, or have just
finished a shift at the
pit, they're still deter-
mined to hold their
heads up and look
like winners.

league, lined up once a season in their clean kit for their traditional team shot, whether or not they'd won a little pot. All the players, plus friends and supporters, would buy postcards to send to each other, with little messages reporting last week's score, or who they were playing next week. Often, if it was a girlfriend or auntie, they'd put a ring round their own face, and maybe add the names of the other players, plus a few jokey remarks about them.

I like to study the strips, to see if they had string at the neck or proper collars, examine the shin guards and boots, and observe how they changed over the years. I like to think I can now date most of the teams, even if I don't know their names, just by their strips. But sometimes there is a date, with a ball between the captain's feet painted with '1909–10', or whatever, plus the club's initials, and perhaps a record of the league title or trophy they've just won. I love the players' proud, smiling, innocent young faces, often with some older, gnarled faces of people in the background holding a towel or perhaps a bucket. Pre-First World War ones are poignant: you know that many of these lads would later have perished in the trenches.

I now have so many of these postcards of unknown teams, over 300, bought for between £1 and £5 each, that I have subdivided them into categories, which is what daft collectors do, trying to bring order and sense into what is an irrational compulsion. One section, for example, consists of military teams. The clue is that the coach or someone in the background will be wearing some sort of uniform. Then I have a section marked 'Unusual Line-ups'. It's my own, loose definition, covering all manner of odd poses, when for example the whole team is standing in a straight line on the goal-mouth or deliberately lounging at strange angles. Public-school teams favoured poses like this, possibly to show what amusing or superior chaps they were. The normal configuration for team photos was – and remains – two lines, with five players sitting at the front and six standing at the back, or alternatively three rows, with two of the smaller players sitting on the ground at the front.

You can tell public-school or upper-class clubs among these old, unknown teams by their high-quality, immaculate strips, or by the top hats and long coats sported by their club officials. A view of cloisters or an ornate doorway behind is also a giveaway.

Another extensive subdivision is comic footer cards, which includes old Xmas and birthday cards with a football theme. I only have a few foreign footer postcards, from Russia, France, Germany and Holland. They don't seem to have produced so many on the continent. Or I haven't tracked them down yet. As a football collector, one's work is never done.

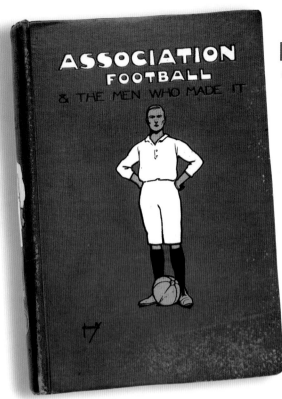

4 BOOKS Football books started to appear just a few years after the FA had been formed. FA Secretary Charles Alcock, who thought up the idea of the FA Cup, produced what is generally considered the first proper football book. Entitled *Our Winter Game*, it's 139 pages long and was published in 1874.

The three best early football books – actually, in my opinion, still the three best of all time – came out around the turn of the century. The upper classes were still running football then, and they knew how to write prettily, as well as shelling out for good photographs and using decent-quality leather for the bindings. The results were the sort of books that any gentlemen would not be ashamed to have in his library.

Famous Footballers, edited by Alcock and Hill in 1895, came out initially as a series, a part-work, before being bound together in a large-format, lush hardback with stunning photographs. The quality is amazing, far better than anything done today. (Except perhaps for the modern 'Opus' series of sporting books, but they retail at £3000 – £4000 each.)

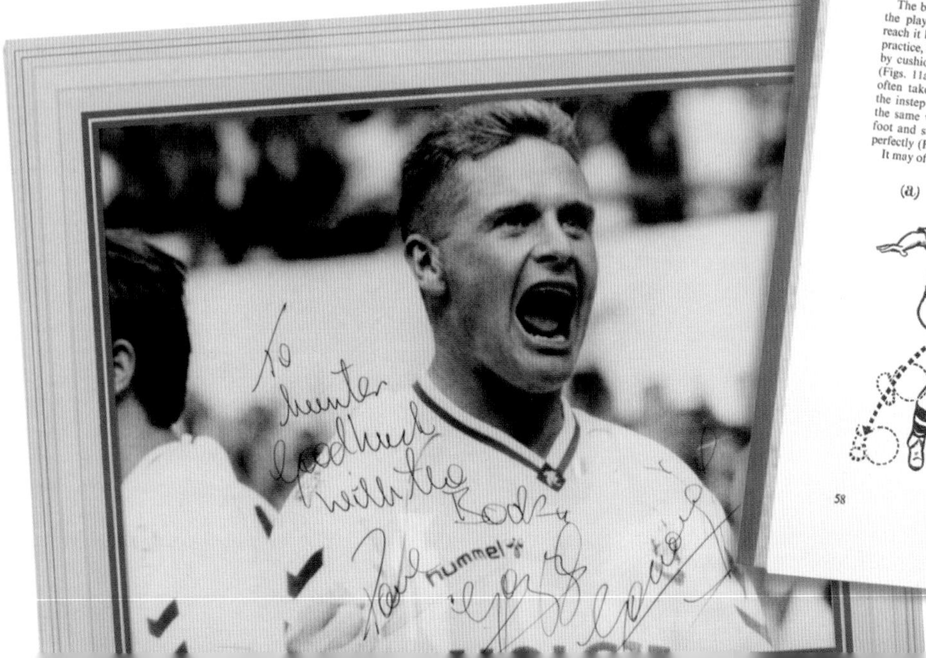

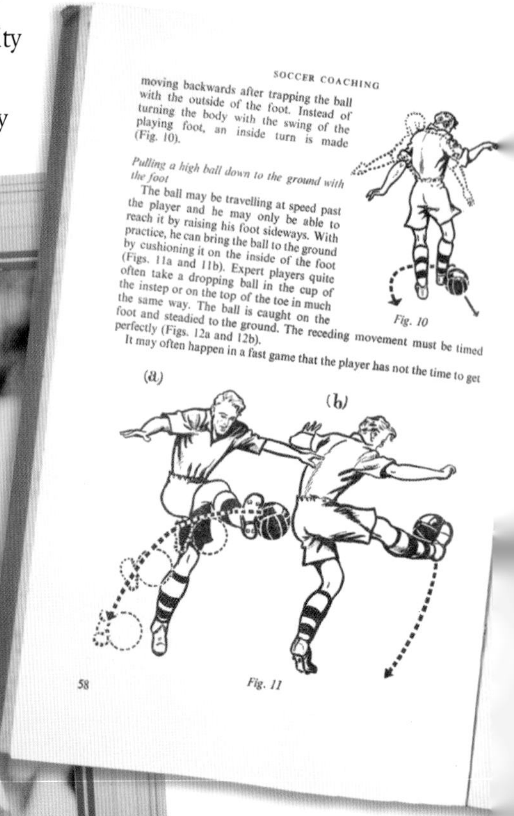

SOCCER COACHING

moving backwards after trapping the ball with the outside of the foot. Instead of turning the body with the swing of the playing foot, an inside turn is made (Fig. 10).

Pulling a high ball down to the ground with the foot

The ball may be travelling at speed past the player and he may only be able to reach it by raising his foot sideways. With practice, he can bring the ball to the ground by cushioning it on the inside of the foot (Figs. 11a and 11b). Expert players quite often take a dropping ball in the cup of the instep or on the top of the toe in much the same way. The ball is caught on the foot and steadied to the ground. The receding movement must be timed perfectly (Figs. 12a and 12b).

It may often happen in a fast game that the player has not the time to get

Fig. 10

(a)

(b)

58

Fig. 11

The *Book of Football*, 1905, also first came out as a part-work. The photographs are not quite as remarkable, but there is more writing and information, with contributions by the leading football experts of the day. The third book, *Association Football and the Men Who Made It* by Gibson and Pickford, was published in four volumes. They have distinctive blue covers with a lone figure in white football kit, a ball at his feet. All three titles are regarded as the classic football books. They come up for sale fairly regularly at the major auction houses, usually priced around the £350–£500 mark, depending on condition.

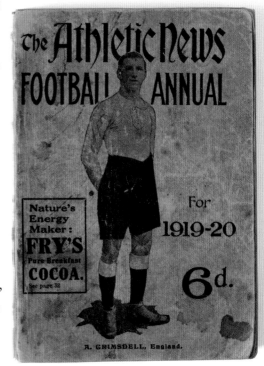

In the 1920s and 1930s, by which time football had become the game for the unwashed masses, football publications were cheaper, flimsier and not as well written.

Ghosted biographies of star players became popular in the 1930s, but they too were pretty thin, weedy, little more than a cut-and-paste job. They contained nothing controversial or revelatory, not until fairly recently at least. It was in the 1990s that players began to confess to drink and drug problems, depression, dirty tricks and bad behaviour. Which of course surprised us all.

5 ANNUALS The first football annuals came on the market in 1868, when our friend Charles Alcock edited the *The Football Annual*. The football annuals issued by *Athletic News*, considered amongst the best, began in 1887 and continue to this day as the *News of the World* annual.

Football annuals are not to be confused with boys' annuals – the large-format, comic-style picture books that usually came out at Xmas. Football annuals were published at the start of each new

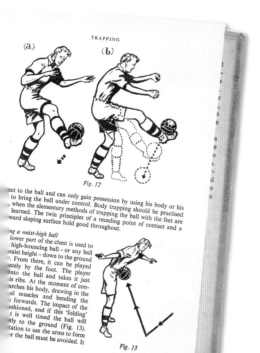

TRAPPING
(a) (b)

Fig. 12

...eet to the ball and can only gain possession by using his body or his
... to bring the ball under control. Body trapping should be practised
... when the elementary methods of trapping the ball with the feet are
learned. The twin principles of a receding point of contact and a
...ward sloping surface hold good throughout.

...ng a waist-high ball
... lower part of the chest is used to
... high-bouncing ball – or any ball
...waist height – down to the ground
... From there, it can be played
...ately by the foot. The player
...into the ball and takes it just
...is ribs. At the moment of con-
...arches his body, drawing in the
...al muscles and bending the
... forwards. The impact of the
...ushioned, and if this 'folding'
...t is well timed the ball will
...tly to the ground (Fig. 13).
...ation to use the arms to form
...r the ball must be avoided. It

Fig. 13

59

season and were small, fat paperbacks, sometimes up to 1000 pages long, absolutely crammed with information, all about the season just gone and the one ahead. Most newspapers, both national and provincial, produced one, together with large department stores like Gamages, which sold football merchandising, and Littlewood and Vernons football pools. They are a mine of information, loved by all anoraks.

The oldest football annual I have in my collection is one for the 1895–6 season, issued by the *Birmingham Daily Gazette* (see page 119). It is 130 pages long, and originally cost just one penny. I paid £70 for it in 2006, which was a bargain. *Athletic News* annuals from the 1900s, which were bigger and better quality, currently cost twice that much, if you can find them at all.

I now have about 200 annuals, covering every year from 1906 to 1956. And yes, I often look things up, and am amused to see that the same old moans were raised even then at the start of every new season – about the transfer market being out of control, about football as we know it being ruined by money, about the FA being such a shambles, etc., etc. I also love the old adverts for football boots and shirts, as endorsed by famous players, most of whom swear that it was Bovril what helped them win the FA Cup.

6 BOYS' ANNUALS By which I mean books with titles like the *Bumper Book of Football*, or *Champion Football Stories for Boys*, which combined famous football events with stories, jokes and cartoons. Most of them had full-colour illustrations of football scenes with great artwork and typography, showing wonder goals being scored or goalkeepers making brilliant saves.

In the fictional stories, the setting is almost always a public school, which most young readers in the 1920s and 1930s had absolutely no first-hand knowledge of. Even in the 1940s and 1950s, in the comics I loved, such as the *Wizard* and *Hotspur*, this was still the

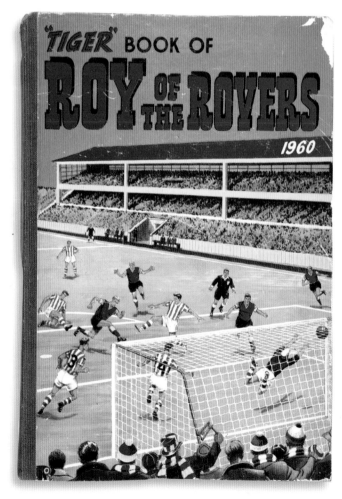

Special Article by George Wilson, England and Sheffield Wednesday Centre-Half, Inside!

The BOYS' REALM

The Sports Paper For Young Men

1½d

No. 137. Vol. VI. (New Series.)   November 12th, 1921.

THE SCHOOLBOY INTERNATIONAL.

A Stirring Story of Football Pluck, Introducing the Famous Blue Crusaders.   By ARTHUR S. HARDY.

STIRRING STUFF
The Boys' Realm, which ran from 1902 to 1926, served up tales of sporting prowess and empire-building derring-do to its young readers.

ROY UNLEASHES A ROCKET Roy Race, star striker for Melchester Rovers, enthralled genera-tions of football-mad kids. He began life in *Tiger* magazine in 1954, but soon proved so popular that special hardback annuals featuring him were published.

case. The trend continues to this very day. The millions of readers of *Harry Potter* around the world have had no experience whatsoever of an English boarding school, but it continues to have great appeal as a fantasy setting.

7 NEWSPAPERS AND MAGAZINES I mentioned – nay, boasted about – my *Sporting Chronicles* from 1888, but I have some even earlier papers from the 1870s containing reports on or illustrations of football games, alongside racing, boxing and cricket. By the 1900s, there were scores of dedi-cated football magazines and papers, which then continued to proliferate. At present, I have about 500 examples in my collection, divided roughly chronologically.

The first large box file contains news-papers and magazines from the 1880s to the outbreak of the First World War. The second box, marked 'Between the Wars', covers the 1920s and 1930s. I also have a separate box devoted to 'Football Fiction', covering boys' mags and football comics from the 1920s to the 1960s. Plus two boxes of post-war football mags and papers, for the 1940s and 1950s and the 1960s and 1970s respectively. I also have some later material, but I haven't got round to sorting it out.

8 FOOTBALL IN ART I'd love to have a proper collection of paintings on a football theme. Over the years, quite a few famous painters, including Picasso, have been inspired by football scenes or motifs. What I really covet is the picture *Going to the Match*, painted by L.S. Lowry in 1953. It shows crowds converging on Bolton Wanderers' old ground, Burnden Park. It was last up for sale in 1999, so in theory I could have bought it. All I needed was £1.9 million. That's what the Professional Footballers' Assoc-iation paid for it, making it the most expensive football-related item ever.

I do have a very nice untitled football scene painted by Alfred Daniels in 1969 and a signed screenprint from 1991 by Peter Blake, entitled F *for Foot-ball*. I've also got some attractive football-themed fruit wrappers, cigar labels and other bits of packaging. These can be had quite cheaply at ephemera fairs. Posters, especially for World Cups, are far dearer. I only have one football poster, for Valencia FC against an English invitation side in 1929.

There are many examples of china and crockery, statues and ornaments with a football theme, produced by well-known artists or firms. They are surprisingly expensive, but then many people regard them as precious *objets d'art* in their own right. I wish I had some, but on the whole I shy away from fragile or bulky objects. They take up took much room, might get broken and, worst of all, need dusting.

I don't collect football medals, which is another specialized area. Won by famous players on big occasions, medals command huge prices: Alan Ball's 1966 World Cup medal was sold at Christie's for £164,000 in 2005.

Nor do I have any football shirts, signed or otherwise. I suspect many of the autographs are dodgy, and the history of the shirts dubious, plus I wouldn't know where to keep or display them. Not in my room. Have you seen the state of it?

I always prefer objects I can read, which have some content. And where football is concerned, I have plenty of those to be going on with, thank you.

9 TOYS AND GAMES Football-related toys and games came on the market from very early on, as toy manufacturers sought to cash in on the craze for the game. In many cases, all they had to do was stick a football image on a kite, a ball or hoop – and bingo, it was a football toy.

ACTION FIGURINES
These plastic models of the England squad for the Italia '90 World Cup tournament featured star players of the time like John Barnes, Chris Waddle and Gary Lineker. Mind you, you'd be hard pressed to recognize many of them …

Actual football games, which you could play and make believe were the real thing, took a bit longer to appear. Manufacturers grappled with the problem of how to accommodate 22 individual figures on a kitchen table, and the mechanics of how to score a goal. Blow Football solved these problems very simply, if not very satisfactorily. There were also games involving mechanical players, with strings and levers, some of which were most ingenious, but they proved expensive to produce and never caught on in the mass market.

Until the advent of videos and computer games, the most successful footer game was 'Subbuteo', which first appeared in 1947. The name comes from the Latin name for the hobby hawk (*Falco subbuteo*). Its inventor, Peter Adolph of Tunbridge Wells, was an avid bird watcher and thought this would make a good pun on the word 'hobby'. To date, it's estimated that some 500 million Subbuteo sets have been sold, in over 50 countries.

PLAY UP! Baines cards were originally sold in packs of six. The craze reached its height just after the First World War, when an amazing 13.5 million cards were sold across the North of England and Scotland.

10 BAINES CARDS

Football stickers, collected by little boys, were not invented by Panini in the 1960s but actually began 80 years earlier. From 1887 to c.1920 the Bradford firm of J. Baines Ltd. produced sets of little cards in different shapes – circles, hearts, diamonds, shields – showing club colours, players and slogans. The slogans were either exhortations – 'Play Up Oldham', 'Now's Your Chance Manchester', 'Well Dribbled Everton', 'Bradford to the Front' – or congratulations like 'Cardiff Take the Cake' and 'Well Won Hull'.

Which was presumably what chaps on the terraces shouted in those days. So different from the rude cries we hear today, like 'Who's The Wanker in the Black?'

Boys paid a few pennies for a set, and then swapped them, just as they did with Esso World Cup coins in 1970 or today with Panini and the other stickers that always appear at World Cup time.

Modern footer stickers are cheap and crude compared with Baines cards, which were little works of art, beautifully drawn and coloured. For his screenprint, *F for Football*, Peter Blake drew heavily on Baines cards as his inspiration.

A lot of no fewer than 277 Baines cards came up for auction at Christie's in 1998, at a guide price of £600. Two mad-keen collectors were so eager to

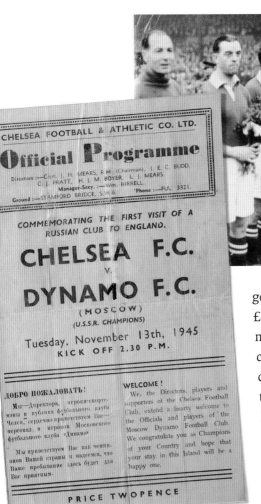

get hold of them that they went for
£12,000. Today, a really pretty one in good
nick can fetch £40. Tattier, simpler ones
cost nearer £10. I have about 30 in my
collection, mostly fairly dog-eared, but
they make me smile. They certainly knew
how to cater to young footer fans in the
old days.

Moscow Dynamo

One of my earliest ever football memories was of the arrival of Moscow Dynamo
in Britain in 1945. They played four games – drawing with Chelsea 3–3,
hammering Cardiff City 10–1, drawing with Glasgow Rangers 2–2 and
beating Arsenal 4–3. The Arsenal game took place at White Hart Lane, home
of Spurs, because Highbury was still being used as a prisoner-of-war camp.

A little while ago, I made a bid for all four of those Moscow Dynamo
1945 programmes at a Sotheby's sale – I got them and to my surprise and
delight they came with a little album made by a boy in Glasgow aged about
11 at the time, who had been fascinated by the Russians, cutting out all the
reports of their games and sticking them in a school exercise book. Just as I
had done.

Women's Football

Women's football is one of the world's fastest-growing sports, especially in
the USA, China, Germany, France and Norway. In the UK, it's big in colleges
and schools, especially in primaries. FIFA now reckons that in a couple of

years, more women will be playing footer round the globe than men. By heck.

Many people are unaware that women's football in Britain has a long and rich tradition. The British Ladies' Football Club was formed in London in 1895 with Lady Florence Dixie, daughter of the Marquess of Queensbury, as President. Secretary and Captain was Miss Nettie J. Honeyball, a name that sounds as if she should have been in a James Bond movie. I have a photo of her in full gear, with voluminous knickerbockers and massive shin pads, worn over her socks, as all players did in those days.

Women's football, like men's, was played mainly by the middle and upper classes in the early years. Only later did the workers join in – and then took over. When the First World War broke out, around one million women moved into munitions factories, replacing men who had gone to the front. The factory girls often had a kick-around in their break, against the young apprentices or older men. This led to the formation of all-women factory teams, one of the most successful being Dick, Kerr Ladies' FC from Preston. I used to think this was named after someone called Dick Kerr, but it actually stood for a Mr Dick and a Mr Kerr, who founded the factory. On 26 December 1920, they broke the record – which still stands today – for a women's game in the UK, when 53,000 turned out to watch them take on

St Helen's Ladies at Goodison Park, home of Everton FC.

Then, in 1921, the rotten old FA decided to ban women's games. They hinted darkly at the fiddling of expenses – as if that wasn't rife in the men's game – but the real reason was medical. They believed football would harm women's bodies, making them incapable of bearing children. They couldn't actually stop them playing, only ban them from using grounds affiliated to the FA. In 1971, the FA saw sense and officially recognized women's football at last.

Many magazines and books of the period featured articles and stories about women playing football, as it captured the imagination of the whole country. Women footballers also appeared on saucy seaside postcards and humorous drawings. The targets of the humour were pretty easy and obvious, with blokes hoping to meet a 'fast forward' or offering to swap shirts after a game . . .

THE COW.

Thank you, pretty cow, that made
Pleasant milk to soak my bread,
Every day and every night,
Warm, and fresh, and sweet, and white.

Do not chew the hemlock rank,
Growing on the weedy bank;
But the yellow cowslips eat;
They perhaps will make it sweet.

Where the purple violet grows,
Where the bubbling water flows,
Where the grass is fresh and fine,
Pretty cow, go there and dine.

Twelve,
the Bell.

13, 14. Thirteen, Fourteen,
Maids are courting.

the daisies, white and red,
mamma has often said
may gather them instead.

uch I hope we always may
ry dear mamma obey,
ind whatever she may say.

A BOOK

ILLUSTRATED BY

KATE GREENAWAY

FREDERICK WARNE & CO.

COLD MEAT
And How To
DISGUISE IT

Books

I don't think I've laughed aloud and enjoyed books as much as I did as when I was young. Now I seem to read mostly for work, rather than pure pleasure, though books for work can often turn out to be pleasurable. My wife reads a new novel every day – goodness knows where she finds the time – but on the other hand she doesn't watch football on TV. If there are three live games on a Saturday or a Sunday, it means I can be watching, slumped, for up to six hours at a time. It's not easy.

A MISCELLANY OF BOOKS
Some tomes from my eclectic book collection. From top to bottom: Poems by Jane Taylor (1783–1824) from *Little Ann,* illustrated by Kate Greenaway; illustrations from Walter Crane's *The Buckle My Shoe Picture Book* (1910); and the marvellously bluntly titled *Cold Meat and How to Disguise It* (1904).

The books I loved most as a boy were the *Just William* books. Now and again, in the local library, you'd find a couple on the shelves that you hadn't read, so you'd hide one, either for yourself or a friend, in a special place for next time, thinking no-one was watching. The librarians all wore buns and rimless specs, that's my memory of them, and while sitting at their desks, busy filing tickets, you'd think they couldn't possibly see you, but they could, out of the corner of their eye, and the moment you left, they'd put the books back in the correct place.

I can still smell the public library in Carlisle, the polish and disinfectant, feel the hush and holiness of the place. Even in the children's library, you felt intimidated and overawed. 'Flying up' to the big library was a rite of passage, like going up from the Cubs to the Scouts, a mark of impending adulthood.

I also loved all the *Biggles* books but didn't care for *Worrals of the WAAF,* who was Captain W.E. Johns' Biggles-esque heroine, unless I was really stuck. Nor was I a great fan of Enid Blyton, though we read her books at school. The stories were quite nice, I suppose, but a bit soppy and precious with no jokes, no fun, not like the blessed *Just William* books.

It's strange that I loved *Just William* so much – as did every boy I knew, and lots of girls too – as his life was so remote and different from mine. He lived somewhere in the Home Counties, wherever that was, way down South, in a big house with a conservatory, staff and tennis parties. But he was in a gang, that was the big thing, and saw himself as an individual, against grown-ups and authority. He was fond of plots and plans (which usually went awry), spoke not very grammatically, got blamed for everything, and was always scruffy, with his socks round his ankles. All this appealed to boys everywhere, regardless of class.

I was never sure if Richmal Crompton was a man or a woman, as the first name was so strange, or if she was alive or dead, not that it mattered to me. Authors were mysterious figures, not part of our world. I'd never met a writer, or someone who made their living by writing of any sort. No author came to our school to give talks, the way they seem to do all the time these days. But I suppose that was to be expected, living in an out-of-the-way place like Carlisle.

All the while, I never knew that we actually had a real writer living in our midst in Carlisle, whose work I listened to on the radio. He went by the name of 'Romany', and he gave nature talks on *Children's Hour* on the BBC. His real name was the Reverend George Bramwell Evans and he was a Methodist minister. If only I'd realized, I could have got his autograph.

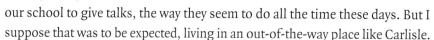

Meeting my Childhood Heroes

As a grown-up, supposedly, and working as a journalist on *The Sunday Times*, one of the things I did in my early years was try to track down and interview some of the authors I'd loved as a boy. Pure self-indulgence, of course.

I failed to get an interview with Enid Blyton. She was born in 1897 and died in 1968, and in the early 1960s she was still going strong. Librarians of the time had not yet turned against her, but I think she just didn't like publicity or enquiries about her personal life. Or perhaps she was simply too busy. In her lifetime she published 600 books, which is phenomenal. In one year, 1951, no fewer than 36 Enid Blyton titles appeared.

Nor did I manage to get Richmal Crompton (1890–1969), who died about the same time as Blyton. Her output was not as prolific, though she did write 40 books for adults – none of which is remembered today – as well as her 42 *Just William* books.

But I did persuade Captain W.E. Johns, who was born in 1893, to give

CREATOR OF 'BIGGLES' Above: Captain W.E. Johns, pictured at his London flat in 1960, had been an RAF flying instructor in the First World War, so his exciting *Biggles* tales of a daring flying ace were based on first-hand experience.

IRREPRESSIBLY FUNNY Frank Richards, a.k.a. Charles Hamilton, meets some young fans of his books. A 1958 *Time* magazine profile described him as 'a wispy, monkish little man who wears a black skull-cap and translates Horace'. I found him great fun.

me an interview. He too died in 1968, so he was in his seventies when I met him. I've tried to find a copy of the interview, which a Johns' fan wrote to me about recently, saying he'd read about it, but I can't locate it. As far as I can remember, he was living in a big red-brick mansion block somewhere in West London, possibly near the river. He was very pleasant, but a bit cagey about what sort of captain he had really been.

I had a much jollier time meeting Frank Richards, the author of the *Billy Bunter* books. He died in 1961, so I was lucky to catch him. Richards was born in 1876, real name Charles Hamilton, and wrote millions of words of school stories, under various names, such as Martin Clifford, Owen Conquest and Ralph Redway. He was best known for his contributions to the *Gem* and the *Magnet*. These were very popular pre-war comics, before my time, and were most loved by the generation before me, but I still often read old copies.

By the time I interviewed him, Richards was living in a semi in the suburbs, perhaps Kent or Surrey (awful how one's memory goes!) in what appeared to be reduced circumstances. This despite the fact that he had had a hundred or so books and around 5000 stories published. But I do remember how full of fun and life he was, even in his eighties. He insisted on giving me, for no reason I can remember, a copy of the old Dixieland jazz classic 'Won't You Come Home Bill Bailey', which he had translated into Latin. He'd typed it out, not very well, and insisted on reading it out to me aloud. He laughed all the way through, delighted by his own cleverness and silliness.

vember, 1959

WON'T YOU COME HOME, BILL BAILEY?

Aestivo die sub caelo claro,
    Uxor maerebat,
    Namque carebat
Absente marito,
    Ignavum quem
    Illa quidem
Iratissima calcitraverat ex domo.
    Sola manebat, -
    Et cito plorat,
Quod procul est homo. -
    Namque virum amat,
    Et saepe exclamat:

    CHO.

"Nonne vis umquam revenire domum?"
    [Semper audimus eam!]
"Debita tota solvam, coquam cibum,
    Fateor culpam meam,
Noctis memento qua te ejeci domo,
    Tibi et dedi nummum nullum,
Fuit culpa,
Nimis aspera,
    Imploro ut redeas domum!

The Golden Age of Book Design

As a born-again collector, especially when I started to write my own children's books, I began a collection of children's books, mainly by authors whose works I'd avidly devoured as a child.

To make up for the disappointment of not meeting Enid Blyton or Richmal Crompton in real life, I bought signed letters from them, to go with my collection of their first editions. I don't have many Blytons, but there is a very active Enid Blyton Society. I have more *Just William* books, even a first edition of the very first one, published in 1922, but alas it hasn't got a cover. The later *Just Williams* are easier and cheaper to find, as the print-runs were much larger than the early editions. In *William and the Pop Singers* (1965), the blurb on the fly-leaf says that more than 7 million *Just William* books had already been sold, and lists all the many languages into which they had been translated.

I also have a good collection of *Biggles* firsts. Once again, the early ones, from 1932 on, are hardest to find, as are copies with decent dust jackets. It's vital with these children's books to make sure they are notjust first editions, but issued by their main publishers – Newnes in the case of *Just William* –

and not by reprint or special-edition publishers like Dean & Son.

A good dust jacket is vital, and can double or even increase tenfold the value of a first edition, but is a nonsense in a way as the book, and the words inside, are just the same, regardless of the state of the cover. As collectors well know, though, there's not much logic in collecting.

Having started with favourite books from my own childhood, I moved on to looking out for examples of classic children's books, especially by famous illustrators and artists. Many of these didn't have separate jackets like a modern hardback book, but their hard covers were themselves lavishly decorated and sometimes extremely colourful, with great lettering and design, little works of art in themselves.

I now have quite a few books by famous late 19th-century illustrators such as Randolph Caldecott and Walter Crane, the two I like best. I've also kept some copies of books by modern illustrators that my own children enjoyed, such as John Burningham and Maurice Sendak. I also have about 50 Victorian books that I've never read and never will read, having bought them purely for their covers. They looked so attractive, examples of the sort of ornate book design we will never see again.

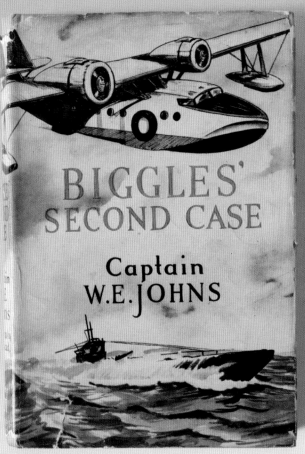

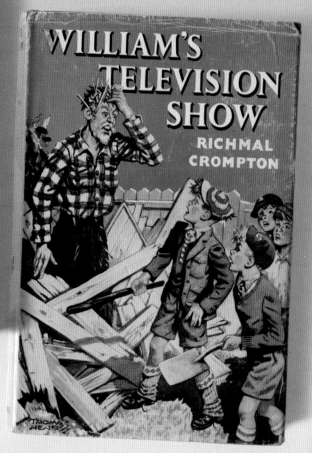

Our Bookshelves

Over the decades, my wife and I have constantly rearranged our bookshelves, which I suppose is what most people do, or at least tell themselves they'll get round to. But while my dear wife regularly conducts a cull of her books, to keep the total number in check, my collection just seems to grow bigger and bigger. I've been forced to double-stack books, so you can't see what's on the shelves behind.

There are two areas of the house where my wife keeps her books. In her office, where she does her writing, she has a very good collection of women's books – books by and about women. Downstairs, in our main living room, she keeps her novels, all arranged very neatly, in alphabetical order. Some of them are quite desirable now, as she's had them so long and has always made a point of reading first novels, before their authors become famous. For example, she's got a first edition of John Fowles' *The Collector* (1963), which I have tried to bag for my room, as I love the title, but she won't let me have it.

In one corner downstairs, I am allowed five shelves on which I keep my collection of topographical books. They were well arranged at one time, with London on one shelf, the rest of the UK on another, then the Rest of the World on top. But now they've got a bit messed up. I should do a cull.

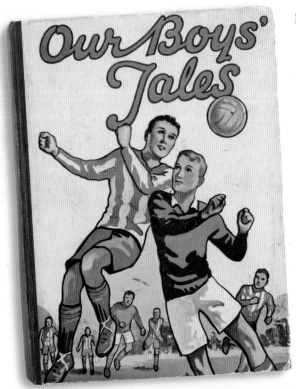

In my room – well, where to begin? Either side of the fireplace I have ten shelves, floor to ceiling. On the left-hand side are my Beatles books, on the right Football, my two main book-collecting areas. At the other end of the room, I have more football titles, the choicer older ones, plus my children's books and also biographies.

Upstairs, in a spare room, is my collection of Robert Louis Stevenson first editions. I bought them when I was writing a biography of him. I won't do another book about him, so I don't need them, but I'm not selling or giving them away. They're a collection, after all.

Beatrix Potter Books

One of the things I admire about Beatrix Potter was how smart she was commercially. Something you wouldn't gather from the recent Renée Zellweger film, *Miss Potter* (2006), where she appears unconcerned and innocent about things like royalties.

Yet as early as 1903, just a year after the publication of her first book, *Peter Rabbit*, she was registering a Peter Rabbit doll at the Patent Office and had hawked it round the big department stores, like *Harrods*. She also created Peter Rabbit wallpaper, which was taken on by Sanderson. We tend to think the merchandizing of animal characters began with Walt Disney and Mickey Mouse, but Miss P was actually years ahead.

I'm delighted that she loved Herdwick sheep, becoming a breeder and judge, a passion that took over the second half of her life. I am surrounded by them when we're in our Lakeland home in Loweswater, most of them scrawny and raggety-taggle, but ever so hardy. They can survive for up to six weeks when the ground is covered by snow, so it is claimed, by sucking the oil out of their own wool. And I love the fact that she gave all her fortune and thousands of acres to the National Trust. Oh yes, and her books – they're pretty good as well.

I began collecting BP stuff almost 20 years ago, as a result of writing a book about her. That's how my collections usually start. I convince myself it will be vital research, just to give myself another excuse to go round the stalls, fairs and dealers.

I managed in those days to pick up about ten first editions for little more than £40 each. Now the prices have gone crazy, thanks to the millions of devoted Potter fans in the USA and Japan. A first edition of *Peter Rabbit* – which I don't have – is now worth £50,000, but it has to be a privately printed one, before Frederick Warne took over as publisher.

It takes experience to be sure of first editions. For a start, the date of publication must be on the title page, under the publisher's name. If there are illustrations on the endpapers, which only

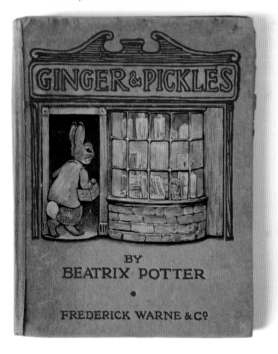

FIRST EDITION
You can tell by the shape of my *Ginger and Pickles* that it must be an early copy. Another clue is the publisher's name – 'Frederick Warne & Co'. If it says 'Frederick Warne & Co Ltd', you know it's later than 1919. That's when the firm got into financial problems and became a limited company.

appeared later, then obviously you haven't got a first edition. It can be awfully hard being a collector. You need to keep your wits about you.

My best BP treasures are three handwritten letters to the Secretary of the Loweswater Show in 1935, about her Herdwick entries. You might miss them if you didn't recognize 'H.B. Heelis', her married name (she married Hawkshead solicitor William Heelis in 1913). But her address is the vital clue – Hill Top Farm, now the major pilgrimage site for all BP worshippers.

Funny Book Titles

On our tenth wedding anniversary, a long time ago, but in the same country, I gave my wife a copy of *How To Be Happy Though Married*. I bought it in a secondhand bookshop in Hampstead, before they all turned into estate agents or coffee bars. It's a beautifully bound hardback with embossed gold and silver lettering, published by Fisher Unwin in 1889. There are 28 chapters instructing Victorians on such diverse subjects as 'The Choice of A Wife', 'The Management of Servants', 'What is the Use of a Child?', 'Politeness at Home', and 'Making the Best of a Bad Matrimonial Bargain'. We had it on the mantelpiece in our bedroom for years, but now, after 48 years of marriage, I keep it on a shelf in my room, part of my collection of Odd Titles.

I look for books with odd titles all the time, but they're hard to find, as bookshops don't have sections dedicated to them. And anyway, one person's odd title is another person's ordinary one. Titles also take on different nuances of meaning over time.

For example, *Games to Play with Your Pussy*, published in Massachusetts in 1885 was about cats, obviously. *Shag The Pony*, published by the Catholic Truth Society in 1952, concerned a pony called Shag. *Enid Blyton's Gay Story Book*, published by Hodder and Stoughton in 1946, was not about gays, evidently – not in 1946.

Nor is *Queer Cousin Claude* about, er, queer people in the modern sense. It was written by Brenda Girvin and published by George Allen & Co. in 1912. My copy has a presentation plate at the beginning, saying it was given as a Sunday School prize by the Primitive Methodist Church, Wandsworth Bridge Road, for regular and punctual attendance. Chapter headings

CURIOUSER AND CURIOUSER
Two splendidly offbeat titles of books I've acquired. Other gems of this ilk include *Invisible Dick* by Frank Topham, and *Correctly English in Hundred Days*, by the Correctly English Society.

include 'Pent-up Feelings', 'Uphill Work', 'The Dangerous Stock Whip', 'A Treat in Store', 'Pleasure and Pain', 'A Pair of Wranglers', and 'A Change of Feeling'. Once you start playing this game, you can snigger at almost anything.

Under my own rules, the oddness or humour of the book titles in my Odd Titles collection must be unintentional. Take the titles of the following scientific and erudite works, deadly serious to the authors, but cheap amusement for cheap people like me: *Fish I Have Known* (1905), *How to Test Your Own Urine at Home* (1935) and *Masturbation in the American Catholic Church* (1984). In *Fish Who Answer the Phone* (1937), the fish don't actually pick up the 'phone and answer it. The book describes an experiment by a Russian biologist to see if fish can hear by constantly having a telephone ringing nearby. Answer – yes, they can.

PORCINE DOODLES Some very different sketches of pigs, scribbled and signed by famous people in the 1940s. From one of the odder books in my Odd Titles collection.

I was attracted to *Seeing the Way to Heaven by the Use of Eye, Ear and Heart* – published in London by Pickering & Inglis – purely because of the length of the title and the pretty lettering, but I'm still not sure what it's about. It appears to be a book of religious instruction, using tricks and stories. But the illustrations are excellent.

I recently bought a copy of *Famous People's Pigs*, published by Forum Press in 1943. It turned out to be a book of drawings of pigs, done blindfold by famous people of the day, including George Bernard Shaw, Sybil Thorndike and Arthur Conan Doyle. A handwriting expert then analyzed their efforts, drawing conclusions about their personalities. All proceeds from the book went to the wartime Famine Relief Fund. I'm surprised the idea hasn't been copied since. So much more imaginative as a charity book than today's boring celebs and their boring fave dishes. And a brilliant title.

My friend Michael Moon, who has a bookshop in Whitehaven, has a book called *The Resistance of Piles to Penetration* – which is not a medical book but about construction and civil engineering. He also swears he has a book called *Sixteen Hands Between My Legs* but can never find it when I'm in his shop. It's about riding horses.

COLLECTING BOOKS

By which I don't mean acquiring and keeping them — but books about collecting. The obvious sort are books about individual collecting hobbies. Shire Books, for example, has published scores of books on different things people collect, mostly of the 'bygones' variety.

They include old bottles, farm tools, horseshoes, bobbins, lace, samplers, buttonhooks, glass, clay tobacco pipes, dolls' houses, fans, fire grates, magic lanterns, old gramophones, sewing machines, toys, telephones, pen-knives, post-cards, playing cards, pewter, rocking horses, spectacles, spoons, toy trains, walking sticks, and loads more, so check on their website to see if they cover your collecting hobby. They're booklets, really, reasonably priced and well illustrated.

The bigger collecting hobbies — bigger both in size as well as importance and history — such as furniture, china, antiques and paintings, tend to have larger and more serious books written about them, glossy and expensive. A lot of them are basically reference books, some of them very old, and now collectors' items in themselves.

But there's a third definition of Collecting Books — and that is books about the subject of collecting itself, rather than about individual collections. I didn't know such books existed until the last year or so — because they are aimed at academics, not collectors. Funny that. We are the subject of their research and wisdom, but most of us are blithely unaware that there are all these clever people out there who are obsessed by us, and make a living by lecturing and holding conferences — all about us. I feel quite proud, though humble.

Many of these academics, scholars and curators are attached to traditional museums and specialize in Greek, Roman and other antiquities. Thanks

to Freud, the psychoanalysts later waded in, trying to work out what makes us tick. Then came the sociologists and philosophers, giving us their ha'porth. They are big in Europe and the US, not so much in the UK. Between them, these writers have produced hundreds of books on the phenomenon of collecting. Most of their efforts, alas, I have found pretty unreadable. Their main concern seems to be with impressing each other.

I remember at university having to spend a term studying economics — and not under-standing a word of it. I didn't blame my own stupidity. I put it down to academics' gift for disguising the obvious with pseudoscientific

language and jargon. Sociologists do much the same. So while reading most academic studies about collecting, I am constantly thinking, what are they on about?

Having bought this book, you won't of course need another book on collecting, ever again. But here are six books about the subject of collecting which I can recommend to any collector who has ever wondered: What am I doing? What's it all about?

In Flagrante Collecto by Marilynn Gelfman Karp (Abrahams). This is my fave amongst collecting books written by an academic – a personal account, full of insight, wisdom and amusement. I like the title – 'caught in the act of collecting' – though others might find it cutesy. It's a huge, wrist-tiring, heavily illustrated book, a joy all the way through. Ms Karp is Professor of Art in the Steinhardt School at New York University, and is on the board of several worthy bodies, but she is also a mad-keen collector herself. Some of her passions even I find dopey, such as ice-cream cartons, whoopee cushions, and crêpe paper. The range of her book is enormous, from proper works of art and antiquities to everyday, trivial objects. A lot of these are American, from the 1940s and 1950s, when she was growing up, and are unfamiliar to Brits or Europeans, but we had similar objects and crazes. Her strength is that while she has an academic mind and training, she is trying to explain and make sense for the general reader. Best of all, it's a personal book, drawing on her own life and her own collections.

Cultures of Collecting edited by John Elsner and Roger Cardinal (Reaktion Books). A collection of essays by academics and experts from the UK, US and Europe, including the Frenchman Jean Baudrillard, the enfant terrible of collecting studies. I got lost in a few of the essays, some of which are easier to read than others. There is a

revealing interview with Robert Opie, creator of the Museum of Packaging; a piece on Freud and his collections; and a surprisingly interesting essay on a very corny subject – picture postcards of Paris – by Professor Naomi Schor.

On Collecting by Professor Susan Pearce of Leicester University (Routledge). Prof. Pearce is a leading expert on collecting and curating. While some of her language is heavy going, she's useful on the history and different periods of collecting (see also pages 98–99).

The Encyclopaedia of Ephemera by Maurice Rickards (British Library). The author was an academic at the University of Reading, specializing in Ephemera Studies. His style is straightforward and informative with over 500 entries, covering playing cards to phone cards, train tickets to cheese wrappers. Fascinating, if you don't know much about them. With topics I like to think I do know about, though, such as football programmes, his info is a bit thin.

Men and Collectors by Brian Jenner (New Holland Publishers). Not remotely academic, but it does give some insights into the range of daft things that people like me, and probably you, collect. Each chapter features a man – all unknown to me, but clearly real blokes – and his collection. Traffic cones, beer mats, lawnmowers, bean tins, blow lamps, slide rules, and airline sick bags. You name it, it's here.

Error World by Simon Garfield (Faber and Faber). Poor title, but ignore that. It focuses on one collecting hobby, stamps, and one particular aspect of it, stamp errors. It's also about the nature of the collecting obsession, all the phases we go through, and also Simon's own life, including the collapse of his marriage – which is related to his stamp bug. A warning to us all. Very well written, can be enjoyed by collectors and non-collectors – which can't be said about all collecting books. *Error World* does for stamps and collecting what Nick Hornby's *Fever Pitch* did for football.

THE ESTIMABLE MR OPIE Robert Opie, collector *par excellence* of packaging, in his museum when it was based in Gloucester (it later moved to London). The collection's 500,000 or so items tell the fascinating story of Britain's consumer society.

Toys & Games

I never really fancied being a dealer myself, although most dealers start off as collectors. Just imagine having to listen to people like me, wittering on about their treasures, while you're stuck behind your stall, unable to budge, wishing they'd either buy something or bugger off.

I go to the Bloomsbury Postcard and Collectors' Fair, held in the Royal National Hotel, most months that I'm in London. There are usually about 100 stalls, so there's lots of fun to be had. It's always chocka, so you have to push to get served, which means you hear all the punters in front, twittering away.

'What's your best price?' is what you hear most. Poor dealers, having to restrain themselves from saying: 'Can't you read, you dum-dum, it's in pencil on the back, that is my price, what is it you can't understand about money?'

'I used to have loads of those,' is the second most common thing you hear, 'only mine were in blue/better nick/overprinted/first editions/mint condition/the rare French acetate/signed by the author; the whole Cup Final team; John Lennon's auntie; Hitler himself.'

I do it myself when I see someone selling some Dinky toys, the sort I used to have, the ones kids used to give me when I was at school, which they had stolen from Woolies. I wish I'd kept all the toys and games I owned as a kid. That said, I didn't have many of them. I spent my time filling home-made scrapbooks with treasures torn from *Pink 'Uns* or picked up from the gutter. That was how I came to collect fag packets, sticking the fronts in my album. 'Sweet Afton', that was my favourite. Lovely design.

But I did have some card games, plus Ludo, Snakes and Ladders, and Bagatelle. All gone. I blame my mother. So now, when I'm wandering round the stalls, I like to pick up old games, as memories of times past.

Footie Games and Lotto

Naturally, I have quite a few football games, but I keep them as part of my football collection (see pages 114–135).

One thing about having so many different collections is how to categorize and arrange them, as they overlap so much. It means I'm constantly thinking: now, did I file Somerset Maugham's cheque under 'Cheques' or 'Writers'? And what about my Spurs cheque? Where the hell have I put that? Blow Football: did I put that with Assorted Toys and Games or on my Football shelves?

I don't actually play with the games, or even open the boxes, except for some of the pre-war football games. With their metal or enamel figures and proper metal goalposts, they look very attractive set out on a shelf or table-top, as if a game is about to begin. Only trouble is, the figures fall over easily, and they attract dust. Not that I care about dust. I haven't time to do dusting, and I don't like other people touching my treasures.

I buy old games in their original boxes, pre-war if possible, if the artwork on the box looks nice, or if the cards inside are decorative. I have two sets of Piktee, for instance. This was a card game based on football with very complicated rules. Never played it, though. I'm a collector, after all; don't want to wear things out.

Lotto, which features a happy 1930s family playing the game round a table, can also be called 'House', according to the box. I think I remember it being called 'Housey Housey'. Today, it's known universally as 'Bingo'. And that's what you should be shouting out, if you find any old games in your attic, or even better, an old Dinky toy still in its box.

A Game of Chance

Lotto is one of the games now played in the National Lottery, run by Camelot. Buying lottery tickets is not normally looked upon as a game, but it is, actually – a game of chance, with a much longer history than I ever imagined when I first became interested in the subject.

I bought a ticket for the first day of Britain's National Lottery on Saturday, 19 November 1994. I don't put money on horses or on the pools, and I refuse to buy raffle tickets or bet on things like whether it will be a White Christmas. I've always said you make your own luck in life – and

PLENTY OF PUFF
Before Subbuteo came on the scene, blow football was a popular table-top football game. This is a nice old set of mine, dating from the 1930s.

HAPPY FAMILIES
Lotto may no longer
be played in British
households, but
Bingo is an abiding
national obsession,
with lots of old
cinemas converted
to Bingo halls in the
1970s and 80s, and
many people now
playing the game
online.

anyway, I had my best bit of luck when I met my wife, tra-la.

The birth of the National Lottery was an historic day, the culmination of years of campaigning and planning, and it's turned out to be a huge success. No government, unless it has a total brainstorm, will ever stop our National Lottery, not while they're making billions from it. I can see John Major reaching the Pearly Gates and being asked: 'So, you were the one who brought in the Lottery, but what else did you do as prime minister?'

The only reason I bought a ticket that day was not to win – which of course I didn't – but as a piece of memorabilia. The ticket clearly states 'First Day Issue', which is reassuring. I also kept lottery leaflets and other bits issued during those first few exciting months. And excitement really was at fever pitch, particularly among the tabloids. They cleared the front pages every week when there was a big win. The Sun went so far as to create a full-time Lottery correspondent called Lenny Lottery. Up till then, he had been Aidan McGurran, a graduate in politics and history from Manchester University, but the Sun's news desk persuaded him to change his name by deed poll.

I wrote a book about the Lottery, following the lives of ten jackpot winners over the year after their win, observing the changes they'd gone through. There was a myth, still prevalent, that a big win always ends in tears, with family splits and a downward spiral of 'spend, spend, spend'. This is not the case. By any reckoning, over 90 percent of Lottery winners are far happier a year after their win than they were before. It's a compensatory myth, which people like to believe to make up for not winning.

A Brief History of the Lottery

The original meaning of a lottery was something drawn by lots, which goes back to the Bible, when Moses divided up the land of Israel. The Romans used lotteries as public spectacles, giving away slaves or villas during feasts or public events.

The idea of selling lottery tickets with the chance of cash prizes didn't arrive until the 15th century. Immediately, lotteries became entirely financially driven, with the organizers – public or private bodies – aiming to skim off some profit, and the punters hoping to win a few quid. In France, Germany and Italy they were used by town authorities to raise money to repair walls or equip armies.

The first lottery in Britain was drawn in the 1560s, during the reign of Elizabeth I. Lotteries were held until 1826, except for a gap of ten years between 1699 and 1709 when they were banned. The government used them to raise funds for building projects such as Westminster Bridge and the British Museum and for financing the colonization of Virginia. The tickets were expensive, at one time costing £10 apiece, to

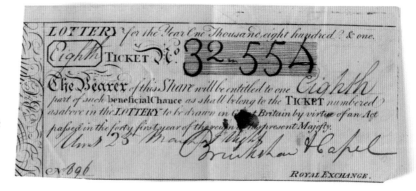

deter the poor from squandering money, but they were often split into smaller shares, so less well-off people could take part.

There were always allegations of fiddles, involving the results either being fixed or most of the profits being siphoned off by the middlemen with the government ending up with little. There was also opposition to lotteries on religious grounds, from those who considered that all forms of gambling were wicked. This is one of the reasons why, until very recently, several states in the USA continued to ban lotteries. In Britain, William Wilberforce, while campaigning to abolish the slave trade, also fought to have lotteries banned. They came to an end in the 1820s after a massive fraud, when someone made off with all the prize money.

One factor in the rebirth of our National Lottery in 1994 – apart obviously from greed on all sides, and changing attitudes towards gambling generally – was that the advent of computer technology made fiddles far less likely. At least, there hasn't been one so far.

It was only when I started to collect modern lottery memorabilia that I discovered just what huge national events lotteries were in the 18th and 19th

IN IT TO WIN IT Lottery memorabilia from the early 19th century. In the 1820s, the prizes were huge – four annual lotteries at £20,000 – equivalent to several millions today. Lotteries were promoted with flyers, filled with funny verses and amusing drawings, which were given away to the public in the hope that they would be persuaded to buy tickets.

centuries. The winning draw was made in grand style, with music, firework displays and processions, usually at the Guildhall in London from where the Lottery was administered.

Plays and songs and ballads were written and performed to cash in on lottery mania. The writer Henry Fielding even wrote a satirical play, *The Lottery*, first performed at Drury Lane in January 1732. Some of its verses still sound pretty modern:

> *A Lottery is a taxation*
> *Upon all the Fools in Creation*
> *And Heaven be prais'd*
> *It is easily rais'd.*

I have one old lottery flyer showing a sexy-looking black woman dancing, inviting 'Your London Girls with roguish trip' to buy a ticket because, well, you could really be on a winner:

> *And when you a Prize have gain'd*
> *Thousands, Ten or Twenty,*
> *I'll be bound, there'll soon be found*
> *Suitors for you plenty.*

Posters for the lottery would detail all 'the additional and superior advantages', listing all the prize monies given out in the previous draw.

When it was about to be outlawed, in 1826, the posters made a special effort to whip up public interest before it was all over: 'By the Positive Order of Parliament, this is the very Last Lottery but One that can ever be drawn in England.'

Last year, at an auction in Carlisle, I bought a bundle of lottery tickets and documents issued in 1801 to a Mr R. Thorpe of Alnwick. The ticket was an eighth share, but it doesn't say what it cost. There's an accompanying letter, from the Royal Exchange, saying that this ticket, numbered 32 55A, had drawn a blank. But in another letter, referring to another lottery ticket, Mr Thorpe had won a prize of £50. Lucky old Thorpy. Let's hope there was dancing in the streets of Alnwick ...

First of the Regency.

State Lottery

WILL BE DRAWN ON

His Majesty's Birth-Day,

4th JUNE, 1811,

AND CONTAINS

60 Capital Prizes

Being SIXTEEN MORE than in last Lottery.

SCHEME.

4	of	£20,000	are	£80,000
24		1,000		24,000
32		500		16,000
60		50		3,000
1,000		25		25,000
1,000		20		20,000
2,000		16		32,000
20,000 Tickets.				£200,000

TICKETS and SHARES are Selling by

BISH,

4, CORNHILL,

And 9, CHARING-CROSS,

Who sold Two Prizes of £20,000 in the last Lottery, also Two Prizes of £20,000 in the Lottery before, and Seven Prizes of £20,000 in the last 15 Months.

Evans Ruffy, Printers, 29, Budge Row, London.

THE INDEPENDENT

TUESDAY 7 OCTOBER 1986 · 5p · No 1 · Published in London

'Missile tube blast sank Soviet sub'

By Mark Urban
Defence Correspondent

SUBMARINE design experts said last night that an explosion in a missile launch tube caused the damage which sank the stricken Soviet Yankee class submarine in the Atlantic Ocean.

According to one, the force of the blast — caused by missile fuel rather than warheads — was such that it would have blown all of the access hatches, and may well have "split the whole tube".

The Yankee-I class submarine carries 16 SSN-6 ballistic missiles. The tubes in which they are held are extremely strong, being designed to cope with the forces involved in launching missiles under water. At least one of the liquid-fuelled missiles exploded, following a fire during maintenance.

This allowed water to rush into the rest of the submarine. It is not known whether the explosion happened before or after the submarine surfaced on Saturday night.

After it surfaced the crew were able to assess the damage, which included a gaping hole, and water without affecting sea-keeping qualities.

But the blast was so strong that it weakened the whole missile section, which flooded in heavy seas...

Soviet merchant ships took most of the 120-strong crew off the boat. Some sailors stayed on board, trying to get back the fair-ing over the missile section so that they could patch the hull.

The Soviet merchant vessel Krasnogvardeisk took the submarine in tow on Sunday. The Pentagon believed the boat was out of danger because the Yankee class have great inbuilt buoyancy — all 16 launch tubes can be full of water...

Baker to set up 10 city colleges

By Colin Hughes
Political Correspondent

PLANS TO create between 10 and 12 city technical colleges, funded jointly by government grant and private industrial sponsorship, will be announced today by Kenneth Baker, Secretary of State for Education.

INSIDE

James Fenton gives a goat to the rebels. Page 10

■ Bundesbank chief to see Thatcher
■ Pound falls to all-time low

Conservatives try to halt sterling slide

By Sarah Hogg and Andrew Marr

THERE WILL be no pre-election spending spree, Norman Tebbit, the Conservative Party chairman, promised...

A GLANCE AT PUNCH

THE HOTSPUR

THE MECHANISED MOUNTIES GET THEIR MA...

EVERY THURSDAY   No. 672—SEPT. 24th, 1949   PRICE

OZ

2'6

theological striptease

PRIVATE EYE

Vol I No 1   Friday 25th October   Price 6d

CHURCHILL CULT NEXT FOR PARTY AXE?

contents

Harold Throbson interviews Sir John Feelgood (see Arts)

Arts (see Belmondo)

Film Man Dead (see Press)

YOU'VE BEEN SOLD A DUMMY — of what we hope, after further experiment, will be a weekly newspaper to appear regularly in the New Year.

...Butler for Gambia?

by Pravdaman Edouvard Khrankschov

Papers, Mags & Comics

I assume, without any proof, that many collectors start a collection because they have some direct or indirect connection with the objects in question. It might be something associated with their childhood and growing up, a place or experience or pleasure, or alternatively something to do with their working life. Supposing, of course, that you have a propensity to collect in the first place.

ALL OUR YESTERDAYS
I'm a great fan of first editions of British newspapers, comics and satirical magazines. Oddly perhaps, the most valuable of all of these is the unassuming first issue of *Private Eye*, from October 1961.

If I had become a doctor – and people have often said I have doctor's hands – I might well have collected scalpels. As a barrister, I possibly would have looked out for old wigs. As a carpenter, I would definitely have collected old tools; I think they look terrific. But for all of my working life, I have been shifting words, as a journalist and then a full-time book writer. A lot of my collections have come out of the subject of a specific book, and my research on it, which I've then carried on long after the book was published. But from the outset, I've always been interested in old newspapers and magazines, produced by the trade I like to think I know best.

I used to buy them indiscriminately – any old paper that was cheap enough, preferably pre-war. I would always read them from cover to cover before putting them in my 'Old Newspapers' drawer, imagining the dramas behind their faded pages. However turgid the prose, grey the layout, unsensational the prose, I knew there had been screams and shouts in the newsroom that day as the news editor organized his troops, battles for space between rival departments, small private moments of joy as a hack saw his or her own words in print, even though they hadn't got their own by-line. But after a few days, even those working at the paper had forgotten who had written what.

I went for artistic-looking old newspapers – both national and regional –

with nice lettering and layout, or with interesting adverts. When I started collecting, I was particularly keen to track down papers from areas I knew most about, like London or the Lake District. Having got hold of some issues of the *St Pancras Chronicle* from the 1930s, I was amused to see that they contained adverts for shops and businesses in Kentish Town that were still going in the 1960s when we arrived here. The Forum, for example, today a well-known music venue, has changed its name over the years, but in 1937 it was a cinema. Illustrations of the Forum show clearly that it got its name from its mock-Roman colonnaded frontage.

I never collected wartime papers, or royal anniversary papers, or those associated with big events, like the death of President John F. Kennedy. It seemed too obvious. A lot of people did, and today you see them on stalls all over the country, great bundles of them, a godsend for TV researchers working on yet another Kennedy or Princess Diana documentary, who are looking for cheap images or authentic contemporary items.

The original owners of these newspapers were not in all likelihood habitual collectors, but ordinary people who kept them simply as a record of important events or interesting times. The stuff that they held on to was, eventually, chucked out by their children – hence all those piles at car boot sales.

My grandmother had a small collection of Royal stuff, picture books of the princesses, bought through the *Daily Express*. I had to wash my hands before being allowed to read them. With their gold covers, they seemed so precious and rare at the time, but millions of people had copies of them and today they lie gathering dust on the back shelves of secondhand bookshops.

For a while, I specialized in newspapers from 1936, the year of my birth, and then when friends and relations had birthdays coming up, I looked for papers and mags from their birth year, to give as presents. At one time, there

DOMESTIC COMPENDIUM
First edition of *Enquire Within* magazine, October 1890. It was a spin-off from a Victorian 'how-to' book, first published in 1856.

UNFREE PRESS
I bought 20 copies of wartime editions of the *Guernsey Evening Press*, for just 50p each, when I visited the island. They're full of propaganda stories claiming Britain was losing the war, and adverts for German films at the local cinemas. The classified ads, or so I fondly imagined, must have contained messages in code …

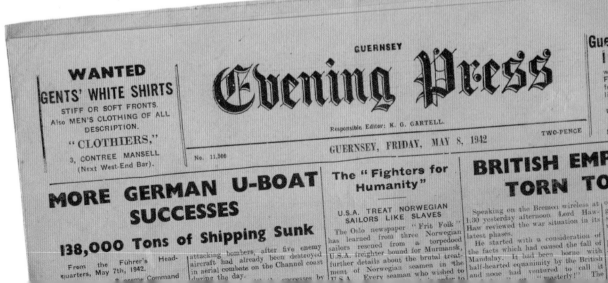

was a great trade in copies of *The Times* from the exact day of your birth, which sold for about £15 each. You rarely see them now. I knew one of the dealers in this market when it first began, who bought thousands and thousands of old papers from libraries having a clear-out. It took him about ten years to realize what a mistake he'd made. He was selling original copies that he could never replace. He then went into repro versions.

I once went on a trip to Guernsey, in 1988, and was surprised to find in a secondhand shop a bundle of wartime issues of the local paper, the *Guernsey Evening Press*. I knew the Germans had occupied the Channel Islands during the war, the only part of the UK they had taken over, but I hadn't been aware that local newspapers continued to come out, in English, censored by the German authorities (see below left and page 94).

Odd Number Ones

I eventually lighted on a speciality – first editions. This area still excites me, and I'm adding to it all the time, though prices of the good stuff are going up all the time and the real treasures are now well out of my range.

I began collecting first editions about 20 years ago when I found I had bought by chance a first edition of *Picture Post* – dated 1 October 1938. The dealer, I think, hadn't been aware of it, as I got it for only £5. I then decided to look out for other first editions of newspapers and mags.

I now have about 100. A lot of them are long-dead papers, which only survived for a few years, or perhaps decades. I find it sad, reading the proud, hopeful messages in their first editorials, boasting about the gap they are filling, the long-felt need they are providing for, how they will change the face of journalism, etc. Now they are all gone, and almost entirely forgotten. There were so many bright newcomers that appeared from the 1890s to the 1920s – where did they all get the money from, the staff, the resources? Many of them had such odd specialities you wonder how they thought they would ever survive.

The *Invalid*, for example, which first appeared in October 1905, and was aimed at people in the 'Hygiene, Treatment, Nursing, Diet, Health Resorts'

trade, ran a front-page story on 'The Consumptive Poor of England'.
I wonder how many copies of that issue were sold.

Volume 1, Number 1 of *The Clerk* came out in January 1908 and had a
special article inside by G. Bernard Shaw, quite a coup. Reading the small
print, I see that it was the organ of the National Union of Clerks, so perhaps
it had a tied audience. *Clubland*, which first appeared in May 1910, was about
the world of the London clubs, a small but presumably affluent market.

Enquire Within, a title now used by a radio programme, first came out on
11 October 1890, and was aimed at women, covering 'housekeeping, fashions, health, cookery, law, fancy work, literature, etc.'. A pretty broad sweep,
so it should have done well. It had adverts on the cover and, inside, a feature
on 'Piano Drapery'. This was not to hide your piano's bare legs – yes, the
prudish Victorians actually did this – but to drape the back of it, making it a
decorative object in itself rather than just a plain bit of wood. Jolly good idea.

The first issue of *Feathered Life*, 21 January 1903, also had adverts on the
front, mainly for poultry incubators and chicken coops. If I was a poultry
farmer, I would definitely be on the lookout for back numbers today.

Famous Firsts

I also have Number Ones of publications that are still well known. One of
the most interesting aspects of collecting these is to see how the first issue
of a famous publication looked then, compared to how it looks today.
Totally different, is often the answer. Especially with our national newspapers.

I have quite a few, including a first issue of the *Daily Mail*, from 4 May
1896. My copy is in quite good nick. So is my *Daily Mirror*, born 2 November
1903, and my *Daily Herald*, which first appeared on 15 April 1912. I see I've
got three copies of the first *Picture Post* – which is a clue that it might not be
mega-valuable – and also the first edition of *Illustrated*, from 4 March 1939.
I've also got a first of *Private Eye*, which began on 25 October 1961, and of *Oz*,
dated February 1967, plus the first *Girl*, from 2 November 1951.

Now, look at those eight titles I've just listed above, and guess which one
might be considered the most desirable? The *Daily Mail* and *Daily Mirror*,
despite being over 100 years old, and therefore potentially valuable, are actually quite common and cheap – a first edition costs between £10 and £20.
It pays to know about newspaper history, then you realize that millions of
first editions of those nationals were printed, because they were part of big
groups. Same with *Picture Post*.

If I had to sell all of them, the one I'm sure would fetch most would
be *Private Eye*. That's because only a handful were printed, probably on
someone's mum's kitchen table. I got it for free about 20 years ago, well, in

THE PIONEERING
PICTURE POST
Photojournalism
didn't exist in Britain
until the advent of
the weekly *Picture
Post* in 1938. Its
circulation reached
almost 2 million in
war years, but it later
tailed off, and the
publication finally
closed in 1957. Its
documentary photo
archive, the Hulton
Picture Library,
remains an invalu-
able historical
resource.

PICTURE POST

October 1, 1938

No. 1.

80 PAGES

HULTON'S NATIONAL WEEKLY

OCTOBER 1, 1938

Vol. 1. No. 1

3D

the sense that I swapped it for a Penny Black with a friend, Christopher Matthew. He'd suddenly found a little dusty pile of them in a drawer, given to him years earlier when he was supposed to sell them at his Oxford college. But he never did. Today, one could set you back £4000. That's what the *Eye*'s current editor Ian Hislop told me – but even he hasn't got one.

Comics

First editions of comics in good nick are very hard to come by – most comics get torn and worn by little hands. A *Dandy* dated 4 December 1937 sold for £20,000 while a *Beano* from 30 July 1938 fetched £12,000. I don't own either, alas; I only have them as repros. It shows you the scarcity value of something if someone has gone to the trouble of reprinting or reproducing it, all those years later.

My best first edition of a comic is *Hotspur*, from 2 September 1933. I paid £100 for it in 2007 from a dealer in Cockermouth – the most I've ever shelled out for an old newspaper, magazine or comic.

I still buy any old comics I come across, even if they are not number ones. I love old *Wizards*, *Hotspurs*, *Rovers*, *Adventures* and *Champions* from the 1940s and 1950s, the ones I used to read so avidly at the time – and of course never kept.

My time at *Punch*

I worked on *Punch* for ten years. Well, not on the staff as such – I wrote a weekly column, 'Father's Day'. One of the greatest honours in my life came, after about five years, when the then-editor, the late and great Alan Coren, invited me to join the 'Punch Table'. It was like being a member of a very exclusive club. You didn't have to pay, but got a slap-up lunch with excellent food, wine and company every Friday. Once elected to the Table, you could just turn up, for ever.

There was a real table, an enormous mahogany thing on which famous contributors such as the novelist William Makepeace Thackeray had scratched their initials. We all sat round it, guzzling away, plus one or two VIP guests whom Alan had invited each time.

While working for *Punch*, I bought dozens of old copies as I browsed charity shops and stalls. You see copies everywhere, all over Britain and the old Empire, cluttering up shelves in secondhand bookshops, either single copies or bound volumes, going for a pound or two. Most probably they came from the nation's dental waiting rooms. It's a shame that people aren't more interested in them, as they are full of good writing, clever jokes and well-drawn cartoons and illustrations (though, admittedly, a lot of the jokes and references are lost on the modern reader). *Punch* was always pretty topical, so it's a good source for period costumes, motor cars, furniture, slang and other aspects of the time. I also look out for other *Punch* memorabilia, including ornaments and diaries.

I eventually managed to acquire a first issue of *Punch* – for 11 July 1841. It's a bit of a cheat as it's in a bound volume for that year, but it's still the first-ever copy.

Punch has been dead since 2002, alas, which I never expected to happen, given that it had been such a vital part of British life for so long. I often wonder what happened to the famous Table. At the end of the meal, they used to hand round the cigars, special *Punch* cigars. I usually took one, even though I've never smoked.

A memory of times past.

BOY'S OWN PAPERS I used to devour all these old comics eagerly, with their tales of derring-do and great sporting feats. But I never kept any of my old ones, and have had to build up my collection from scratch.

The Lake District

I said in an earlier chapter that the Beatles and Football were my two main collections, but that's when I'm living in London. For the last 20 years, we have lived half of each year, roughly from May to October, in the Lake District, in a small hamlet called Loweswater.

It's not a holiday home, certainly not, and I'm incensed when people ask me 'enjoying your holidays?' We both work up there, each in our own little work room, carrying on much as we do every day in London. Only the views are better. We both originally came from Carlisle, so we look upon ourselves as Cumbrians, not 'off-comers', as outsiders are normally called. Technically, I'm not a native, having been born in Scotland, but as I first moved over the border when I was four, I've always claimed residential rights. My wife, though, is a true Cumbrian, going back generations.

I'm here now in Loweswater, as I write, and as I look around the house I see I have far more shelves and space filled with my Lake District collections than I have in London devoted to my Beatles and Football collections combined. That's because a great deal of it consists of books about Lakeland ...

One room contains all my Lakeland guidebooks, whole runs

of the well-known popular guidebooks, such as *Black's, Ward Lock, Baddeley, Brabant,* which ran from the 1860s to the eve of the last war, in pretty much identical formats. They got updated almost every year and must have sold millions. Their illustrations were excellent, including fold-out maps, which you rarely get these days. Too expensive and complicated, apparently.

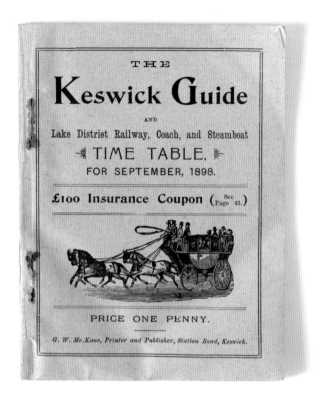

These mass-produced early Lakeland guidebooks, in their various editions, can still be picked up all over the Lake District for £5–£10 or so. Outside Lakeland, in London or the Deep South, you can get them for £2. This is one of the anomalies of topographical collection. Outside the region in question, stuff is always cheaper, if you can find it, because it's less well recognized, and so attracts fewer browsers and buyers. In the region itself, local shops specialize in their immediate area, and have more books, in better condition, but they put prices up accordingly, since it is their main source of income.

I also have some early copies of the classic Lake District Guides, which tend to be expensive, both inside and outside Lakeland, because most dealers know they are of antiquarian interest. They also happen to be of literary as well as historic interest.

History of Lakeland Guides

Until the middle of the 18th century, outsiders never visited the Lakes. The population at large, if they ever thought about the Lakes, had curiously medieval notions of a land of monsters and falling rocks, wild beasts and frightening legends. Adventurous gentlemen went to the Alps for scenery, but around 1770 – the year that Wordsworth was born – guidebooks and writings about the Lakes started to appear and it soon became fashionable to explore Britain's own wild areas, such as Scotland, Wales and the Lakes.

Thomas Gray, the poet (his most famous work is *Elegy written in a Country Church-yard*), published his *Journal* of his visit to the Lakes in 1775 and did much to improve the image of Lakeland tourism, presenting it as a sensitive and lyrical experience, but the first of the guidebooks proper, and for decades by far the most successful, was by a Jesuit Father, Thomas West,

The first visitors to
the Lakes saw them-
selves as explorers,
witnessing terrifying
sights and braving
impassable moun-
tains, but the ex-
plorers soon gave
way to tourists.
The first published
account of a tourist
visit to the Lakes was
by a Dr Brown in
1770, in the form of a
letter to a friend, and
concentrated mainly
on Keswick.

who published his *Guide to the Lakes* in 1778. West's *Guide* sold in enormous numbers and ran to several editions (ten by 1812). Wordsworth knew it well. He was very fond of guidebooks, which were his main light reading.

After West, the other big-selling and highly influential early guidebook was by another cleric, the Rev. William Gilpin. His book was called *Observations, relative chiefly to Picturesque Beauty, made in the year 1772, on several parts of England; particularly the Mountains and Lakes of Cumberland and Westmorland*. It was first published in two volumes in 1786. I know the full title because I bought a copy 30 years ago, price £30, at auction at Phillips in London.

They're exceedingly handsome volumes, with hand-coloured aquatints of idealized Lakeland settings. The whole object of Gilpin, and his followers, was to find the *Picturesque*, defined by Gilpin himself as 'that kind of beauty which is agreeable in a picture'. Everything in the *Observations* is described in strictly visual terms: Gilpin indicates whether views should be painted or sketched in pencil, and lays down hard-and-fast rules for what was and was

BLACK'S

PICTURESQUE GUIDE

TO THE

ENGLISH LAKES

INCLUDING

THE GEOLOGY OF THE DISTRICT
BY JOHN PHILLIPS, M.A. LL.D. F.R.S. F.G.S.
LATE PROFESSOR OF GEOLOGY IN THE UNIVERSITY OF OXFORD

OUTLINE MOUNTAIN VIEWS BY MR. FLINTOFT
ILLUSTRATIONS BY BIRKET FOSTER

NINETEENTH EDITION

EDINBURGH
ADAM AND CHARLES BLACK
1879

not a picturesque scene. He categorized mountains according to their form and shape, their light and shade, stating whether they would make a good background to a painting or not.

This passion for the Picturesque – which Coleridge poked fun at and Wordsworth and De Quincey argued about – was at its height at the turn of the 18th century. Visitors would come to the Lakes, armed with guidebooks like Gilpin's, and head for the 'stations' – the places he had decreed were the best vantage points – where they would admire the view, usually with a piece of kit known as a 'Claude glass', and then perhaps get out their painting materials, or pencils if Gilpin had said that the scene could be better captured in pencil. A Claude glass (named after the 17th-century French painter Claude Lorrain, celebrated for his pastoral scenes) was a special mirror for admiring the landscape and most guidebooks of the time expected you to use one. You turned your back on the view and peered into the mirror over your shoulder, getting the sort of framed, perfectly shaped view that the experts had described. Today we have photography.

Wordsworth, for all that he moaned about the tourists, in the end did more than anyone else to draw them in. In 1810 he wrote, anonymously, an introduction to a collection of drawings of Lakeland by a Norfolk vicar – a copy of which I own. Later, encouraged by his sister Dorothy, because they needed the money, he turned it into a guidebook, which first appeared under his own name in the 1820s.

Wordsworth's *Guide to the Lakes*, in its many editions, became a bestseller and made him better known to many people than his poems. It was Matthew Arnold who first told the story about the clergyman who asked Wordsworth if he'd written anything else – apart from his *Guide to the Lakes*. The story has passed down through the decades and become legend, but it is probably based on fact. Wordsworth's poems never sold all that well, but his *Guide* still sells today in a facsimile edition published by Oxford University Press.

Hotel Leaflets

I've always collected old letterheads, from Lakeland hotels and shops and businesses, because they are so pretty. Also, since so many of the views and images and names can still be recognized today, we can enjoy tut-tutting about how everything has changed, and going on about how things were better in ye olden times, and how they knew about service and politeness back then ...

Actually, I don't say such things, as I believe people on the whole are far better off nowadays. But it is true to say that in the past local small businesses (even modest little shops), took a great deal of pride in how they presented themselves. Their letterheads, brochures and leaflets showed such care in their design, lettering and choice of illustrations.

Hotel leaflets were often little booklets, with a cover and a photograph, giving several pages of description of the hotel's attractions plus the wonders of the local area. I have about 50 Lakeland hotel brochures from the 1930s, all beautifully produced and presented. The ones I find of most interest are those from my local area, around Loweswater and Buttermere. Most of the hotels still exist, though not necessarily under the same name.

The leaflet for the Victoria Golf Hotel in Buttermere – now called The Bridge – is crammed with information. The Resident Proprietor at the time, who signed his name at the end, was Nicholas Size, who was a fairly well-known Lakeland writer. His brochure boasts of electric light, hot-running water in all bedrooms and 'the only Petrol Pump for six miles'. His best bedroom was the Thomas Carlyle bedroom. For 15/- a day you got to sleep in Carlyle's actual bed. The sales pitch then goes on to the question of dress code:

A STAY IN THE LAKES The style of old Lakeland hotel leaflets is generally very traditional, with a nice snap of the hotel, mountains behind, and simple lettering, but some leaflets attempted to catch the fashion of the day. This one, for Rigg's Hotel in Windermere, shows the influence of 1930s Art Deco design. Very tasteful.

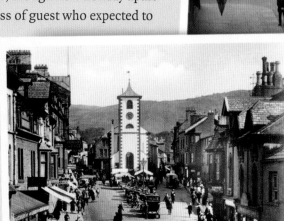

Out of consideration for climbers, the wearing of Evening Dress is discouraged in this hotel; jewellery is out of place. Visitors are recommended to bring old clothes and heavy boots or 'Uskide' shoes as mountain air makes them feel younger.

The most surprising thing to me was that the hotel had a golf course with nine holes, some up to 400 yards in length. I must have been visiting Buttermere for 40 years, and know this hotel well, yet I never knew it once had its own golf course. There's absolutely no sign of it today.

Scale Hill Hotel in Loweswater – still there, though now holiday apartments – was perhaps catering for a higher class of guest who expected to dress up each evening for dinner, which was normal in most hotels with any pretensions in the 1930s. Its brochure offers accommodation for servants at 10/6 a day for room and board, as opposed to 15/6 per day 'pension rates' for their masters. Hotels elsewhere in the Lakes, such as the Windermere Hydro, offered an Orchestra and Dancing every night.

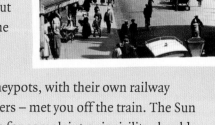

Hotel brochures always boasted about electricity and such luxuries as fires in the rooms – which would typically cost you 2/6 for the day or 1/- for the evening. In Keswick and Windermere, the main honeypots, with their own railway stations, hotel 'Boots' – bellboys or porters – met you off the train. The Sun Hotel at Coniston advises that 'any cause for complaint or incivility should be reported personally to the Proprietors'.

Lakeland Postcards

Lakeland postcards are a big specialist area. As with postcards elsewhere, huge numbers were produced during that crazy first decade of the 20th century, when every village and street seemed to have its own set of cards. In the Lake District millions of visitors arrived every year, all of them desperate to send a postcard home.

When I first started collecting Lakeland postcards, 20 or so years ago, I bought everything. Then slowly I started organizing them into different albums – Waterfalls, Tarns, Lakes, Mountains, Villages and Towns; Literary Figures and Literary Houses; Castles, Famous Buildings, Churches.

I soon gave up on churches. They are always among the cheapest postcards to buy. Nobody wants them. I think it's partly that churches always

HUGH AND BINGO
1930s postcard of the novelist Hugh Walpole (1884–1931) and his dog Bingo. Walpole lived in a large house, Brackenburn, on the slopes of Catbells, overlooking Derwentwater. His grave is in St John's churchyard in Keswick.

170

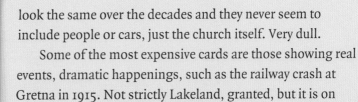

look the same over the decades and they never seem to include people or cars, just the church itself. Very dull.

Some of the most expensive cards are those showing real events, dramatic happenings, such as the railway crash at Gretna in 1915. Not strictly Lakeland, granted, but it is on the Border, so it is nearly in Cumbria.

My postcard collection includes the work of some classic Lakeland photographers, often produced or published by themselves or firms they worked for. Two names to look out for are the Abrahams and Maysons.

Odds and Sods

All around our Loweswater home, I have other Lakeland collections – too many to list, or even keep track of. In the front hall I have framed my choicer examples of cheques issued by Dead Cumbrian Banks. I've collected these to remind me, and visitors, of just how many different banks there were in the old days, not just in Cumbria, but everywhere.

In the bathroom I have some old scenes of lakes, steamers and buildings, in their original frames, just as they were when they used to hang in railway carriages. You have to be of a certain age, say over 50, to remember the days when you didn't have open coaches but separate compartments in each coach, with a corridor down the side. At the back of each bench-type seat were framed views of the region where the trains mainly ran. Students started pinching them for their rooms, so the railway companies took to screwing the frames down securely. They were sold off by British Rail in the end, with all the other bits of railway stock, at their warehouse behind Euston. I managed to buy ten that showed Lakeland scenery.

On shelves I have folders and boxes, containing Lakeland posters, leaflets, tickets, timetables, maps and also autographs and letters from eminent Lakeland personalities. Naturally, I have a collection of Carlisle United memorabilia that I keep here, in Loweswater, not down in London with my general football stuff. I also have some three-dimensional objects, such as pieces of quartz. Crystal, I like to call them, but they're really just lumps of rock picked up from disused Cumbrian mines.

Recently I've been finding pig iron, or what I think is pig iron, in the field beside the house. Funny-shaped bits

PAST TIMES
Postcard views of Cockermouth (above) and Keswick (left). It's fascinating to see Lakeland towns and villages as they used to be, with hikers and climbers in their old-style clothes.

HUGH WALPOLE & HIS DOG BINGO

of molten rock, at any rate. Lead used to be mined locally in open-cast mines. What I'd found was the slag left over after the rock had been heated to extract the lead. They still have a heavy lead content, so make good paperweights. My wife thinks they look horrible. I tell her they are a vital part of Cumbrian mining history.

Mining is a huge and fascinating subject in its own right, with lots of collectors, books, societies, and museums, but I've told her not to worry. I'm not getting into that. Got enough to be getting on with. Such as AW ...

'AW'

When I picked up my first Wainwright book in the mid-1970s – *The Northern Fells*, the fifth in his *Pictorial Guides to the Lakeland Fells* – I thought A. Wainwright must be long dead, perhaps an eccentric Victorian who had insisted on having his little guidebooks written and drawn in his own copperplate hand, exactly as he had created them, without an ounce of printer's type. There were no biographical notes on the cover, or an author pic, or even any clue to his first name.

I thought I'd discovered him for myself, until I realized that there was already a modest cult. Fell walkers boasted they'd got all the Wain-

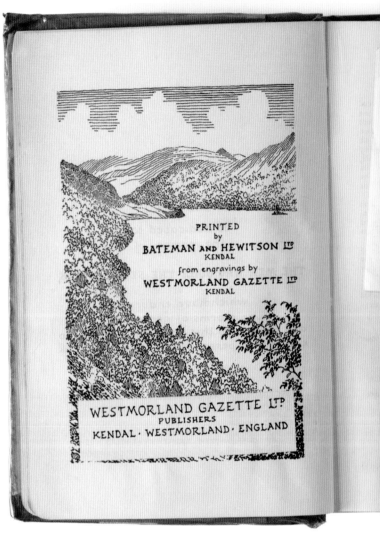

wrights and referred to him as 'AW', which was how he signed himself off at the end of each book. I never realized that he was alive and well, born in Blackburn in 1907, and working not far away in Kendal, where he was the Borough Treasurer. He'd self-published his first guide in 1955, not wanting any London publisher mucking up his words and layout.

I met him at his home in 1978, when I was writing a book on walking in Lakeland. He imposed the condition that I didn't write about him in a newspaper. I bought two of his drawings, which his wife Betty was taking to an

THE WONDER OF WAINWRIGHT
I instantly became a Wainwright fan. They're not just expert walking books, but also little works of art in themselves, worth keeping and cherishing.

exhibition. They cost £10 each. I was just about to write out a cheque to AW when she stopped me. She asked me to make it payable it to 'Animal Rescue, Cumbria'. I never knew, and nor did his readers, that he was giving away all of his book earnings, which by then were considerable, to an animal charity.

In 1985, the *Westmorland Gazette*, which had taken over the publishing of the *Guides*, realized that the millionth copy was about to be sold. Wainwright had, hitherto, kept himself to himself. He had not done signing sessions or attended literary lunches. Nor had his publisher done any advertising, marketing or PR. However, to mark this remarkable milestone, AW was talked into agreeing that whoever bought the millionth copy would win, amongst other things, the prize of dining with him. But next day he woke up and thought, 'What have I done? I don't want to eat with a total stranger.' The millionth copy, secretly marked, never turned up. I suspect AW himself tracked it down, bought it and destroyed it.

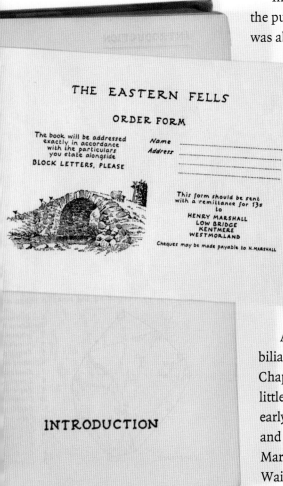

Amongst my 100 or so pieces of Wainwright memorabilia, I have the notice that was put up in the window of Chaplin's bookshop in Keswick (now gone) announcing the little prize – and all his first editions. First editions of the early guides are easy to spot – they were printed by Bateman and Hewitson of Kendal and published by Henry Marshall. Marshall was the Kendal Librarian, a work colleague of Wainwright's. I've got a flyer that was produced for his very first book, *The Eastern Fells*. It's interesting because it states that the name of this new author is – Alfred Wainwright. Then he thought better of it. In the published book, and in all the 50 or so that followed, he styled himself simply 'A. Wainwright'.

AW died in 1991 and for years was remembered mainly by his existing fans, but now he has a massive new following, thanks to The Wainwright Society, some hugely popular TV programmes and the urge of so many walkers to climb the 214 Lakeland fells now known as the 'Wainwrights'. Naturally, first or early editions of all his books, plus his drawings, are highly desirable, though still not hugely expensive. Wainwright, after all, is for lovers of Lakeland, not nasty investors.

Postcards

While stamps are the undisputed aristocrats of the collecting world, postcards remain something of a Cinderella. Collecting them has traditionally been looked down on as amateurish and naïve – a flibbertigibbet of a pastime.

And yet I suspect that there are more households with old postcards lying around than old stamps. It doesn't mean to say that someone is consciously collecting the postcards, just that they haven't got round to throwing them out. I suppose they hang on to them for memory's sake or for the pretty picture, to remind them of someone or just to fill a space on the mantelpiece.

For instance, my wife, the famous non-collector (well, famous in our house, at least) keeps a little silver display rack in the kitchen with a nice postcard propped up in it. Just the one, mind. Every week or so she changes it, depending on what has dropped through our letterbox.

It's usually an attractive repro of some painting by a well-known artist. She's not interested in the stamp, the postmark, where the postcard is from or who sent it – just the image. Checking the current one, I see it's by Gwen John, but then she is one of her faves. I'm not sure what she does with the

"IS THIS WEMBLEY?"
"NO IT'S THURSDAY!"
"SO AM I—LET'S HAVE A DRINK!"

WEMBLEY STADIUM

A 'BAMFORTH' COMIC

MANY AND VARIED Examples from my eclectic postcard collection. In the early 20th century, manufacturers rushed to produce cards for every sort of location and occasion, from national monuments to the parish pump, from the religious to the rude. They came plain and coloured, simple or decorated, in silks and embroidery, flat or pop-up. Some cards had pockets, bits stuck on, could be opened to reveal another card or perhaps, like a concertina, fall open to show a whole string of different views.

old cards when they get demoted. Slings them out, I assume, as I never see them again. Then again, her father Arthur, the arch-burner and chucker-out, did soften somewhat in his later years and started to keep all the picture postcards his grandchildren sent him from exotic places he had never visited. As he hadn't been anywhere – only going abroad once in his entire life, to visit us in Malta – his choice was pretty wide. Especially when the grandchildren all started spending their gap years in places like Papua New Guinea. When I discovered he was doing this, I bought him a large album, into which he ceremonially stuck each card. But they stayed there for one year only. Every New Year, he cleared them all out and started again.

He turned the pages of the album in odd moments, when there was no racing on the telly. It amused and amazed him to see all the places his grandchildren had been and how the world had shrunk, but I think he really looked on them as a status symbol. He'd show them off to visitors – nurses and carers, the gas man and meter readers – proof that he had so many grandchildren who had done well and seen the world, and that they cared about him.

It's amazing really, in this internet age, that postcard-sending survives at all – but it does, if not to the same extent as in the past. People still send cards from their holidays, as proof that they were there, showing off their good times, but also out of an inherited tradition. This is what you do, and have always done, when you're on your hols.

Yet it's often a drag in a foreign country, tracking down postcards, getting a stamp, working out the postal system and locating a postbox.

Not to mention that the card will probably arrive weeks, if not months, after you've come back. If at all. An e-mail or text message would be instant.

A postcard, though, is a tangible, physical object, with lots to enjoy and study on both sides. There's the stamp, for a start, and the postmark, even before you come to look at the picture. Postcards are public property. The postie can read it, if he or she likes, seeing where you've been and enjoying your lame jokes. At the same time, there's something personal about post-cards. Every one is unique, never to be replicated with quite the same scribbles or postmarks. Unlike e-mails, the same one isn't sent simultaneously to all recipients.

WE 'RE PRACTISING ECONOMY AS ALL OF US SHOULD DO WE DO WITHOUT THE LIGHT AND MAKE THE ONE CHAIR DO FOR TWO !

Economie:—Nous nous passons de lumière et un fauteuil nous suffit pour deux.

Postcards can sometimes be intensely private. They have long been used by lovers to convey hidden messages or to signal certain arrangements. They might look all innocent and above board, but a secret, pre-arranged code may be concealed in the way the stamp is stuck on, be it at a certain angle or even upside down. And even where no clandestine affair is involved, postcards are human, intimate. The sender has physically touched them. Until the advent of self-adhesive stamps, you knew that your loved one's lips had caressed them. They were sending you their DNA, not just their fond wishes.

All my children, and now my grandchildren, send postcards from their holidays. They've followed the tradition. It's also good for their handwriting, discipline and imagination. I send them postcards when I'm away, too, even from a day trip, though my handwriting is rubbish and no one can read it.

I still keep a postcard that our son Jake sent from his first-ever school trip. His class had gone to Belgium and he promised to send a card as soon as he arrived. Naturally, we were eager to hear about his journey, what the dormitory was like, and the food, and how he was getting on. In the event, his card didn't arrive until a week after he'd got back. And all it contained was five words – 'I am in Belgium, Jake', which wasn't exactly enlightening. But somehow I still treasure it.

History

Postcards were a European creation, the first official one being printed in Austria in 1869. They became a huge industry in France and by the end of the century, it's estimated that more than 30,000 people in that country were employed producing postcards.

The mass-market boom in Britain started in the late 1890s when, as in Europe, two advances happened around the same time. Improvements in photography and lithographic printing meant picture postcards could be produced cheaply in vast numbers. Secondly, various changes in Post Office regulations introduced a low rate of just a halfpenny for postcards. The illustration took up one side while the other side was divided in two – one half for the address, the other for the message.

Postcards generally sold for one penny each, or cheaper if you bought them in sets. They were available from all kinds of shops, as well as from vending machines on railway station platforms. In the year 1900, 419 million postcards were posted in Britain. By 1914, it had grown to over 800 million.

It was a genuinely national craze, with people from all classes and ages sending each other postcards practically every day. Before long, people started to keep their favourite ones, sticking them in special albums. Postcard-collecting seems to have begun almost from the outset, according to an article in a London magazine, *The Standard*, in 1899:

The illustrated postcard craze, like the influenza, has spread to these islands from the continent, where it has been raging with considerable severity. Young ladies who have escaped the philatelic infection or wearied of collecting Christmas cards, have been known to fill albums with missives of this kind received from friends abroad.

Interesting that collecting postcards was seen as a feminine hobby while stamps were for boys and men. The influx of cards from abroad was accelerated by the number of World Fairs and Expositions held in the USA and in Europe around the turn of the century, such as the Paris *Exposition Universelle* of 1900, which attracted 51 million visitors. You could buy postcards of the Eiffel Tower and post them there and then. People would buy dozens to send to all their friends.

It became relatively cheap to create your own postcards, with your own image, just by going into a High Street photographic studio, possibly with your wife and children, deciding on a pose and a background of your choice, usually one that was a social class up from your actual one. The studio would run off a few hundred thick, glossy cards for you to send off to impress your relatives and friends. It means that the choice of what types and categories of postcards to collect is enormous – far more varied even than with stamps.

In her book *In Flagrante Collecto* (see pages 148–9) Professor Marilyn Karp describes how she has in her postcard collection categories of cards depicting 'Leaps of Faith', both literal and metaphorical, and also 'Exaggerations', by which she means photos of larger-than-life vegetables. Some of her categories I didn't quite understand, but they were awfully clever.

My postcard categories are a bit simpler, such as 'Angry Seas'. I thought that was dead clever, when I first started to look out for them, but now I've amassed about 50 of them, I'm beginning to realize that it's a pretty boring speciality. An angry sea at Brighton looks very much like an angry sea at Bournemouth. In fact I'm sure the manufacturers use the same photograph of a monster wave, but crop it differently and stick a different place-name underneath. My collection of 'Seaside Piers' is more interesting as the architecture and attractions have greater variety.

As a generalization, the most desirable and expensive postcards are those with real photographs – not drawings or hand-coloured chocolate-box views – which show real places, people, objects (especially motor cars and trains) and events, such as disasters or national celebrations. I know with my Suffragette collection that any postcards showing one of the leaders or a demonstration can cost up to £100. In football, any team or players or crowd scene pre-1900 will cost a small fortune – as long as it's a real photo, not a cartoon.

The big advantage of postcards, as opposed to postage stamps, is that they reflect social history, capturing people and events of the day, and displaying images that were better quality than anything in the newspapers. They were cheap, portable, easily collectable, a perfect size to preserve and cherish – that's why so many of them have survived for well over 100 years in surprisingly good condition. Stamps are too small, too detailed, too subtle for the non-expert to appreciate, while paintings are too big, and too expensive for the ordinary person. Postcards, in truth, are the perfect collectables.

"POOR MAN ! AND HAVE YOU BEEN WOUNDED AT THE FRONT ?"
"NO, MA'AM ——— AT THE BACK!"

OFF SIDE !   OFF SIDE !

"'ERE, WHY DONT YER
REFEREE: — I C-C-CANT —

"I want to see something tasty in silk knickers."
"Certainly, Sir. Miss Jones, will you step this way!"

I SAY, I SAY, I SAY! Examples of Donald McGill's work. An amazing 350 million McGill cards are estimated to have been produced in his lifetime.

YER WHISTLE?"
SWALLERED IT!!"

Donald McGill

Saucy postcards have a long history in Britain, along with suggestive music-hall comedians and risqué songs with double-entendres. The postcards often featured brassy, big-busted women with meek little henpecked husbands, or sexy young flirty girls being eyed up by respectable older married men, or waitresses and shop assistants inadvertently making suggestive remarks.

You had to pay to hear fruity music-hall jokes, and knew roughly what to expect, but saucy postcards were on full public view. Anyone could see them, including innocent children or vicars who happened to be passing by. So right from the beginning of the postcard boom in the 1900s, some people were intent on outlawing the ruder ones. One of my all-time heroes, Canon Hardwicke Drummond Rawnsley (1851–1920), co-founder of the National Trust and one of the earliest environmental campaigners, was convinced that vulgar postcards were a corrupting influence. He spoke out against them in 1910 at the Public Morals Conference and wrote to chief constables and town councils the length and breadth of the country, urging them to set up local censorship committees.

One of the most prolific and gifted of postcard artists was Donald McGill, a Londoner with a Scottish ancestry, who was born in 1875. At the age of 16, after an accident playing rugby, he lost a foot and was fitted with an artificial limb. He trained as an engineering draughtsman and didn't move into drawing picture postcards until he was almost 30. In the early days, he earned only six shillings a drawing. And even at the height of his popularity – before, during and after the last war – he was not well paid. It was the postcard manufacturers who made the big profits.

Despite having his work praised by the writer George Orwell – who saw it as folk art that blew 'a chorus of raspberries' at the prissy authorities – McGill eventually fell foul of the moral censors. In July 1954, in Lincoln, he was prosecuted for alleged obscenity. Rather cravenly, his publishers persuaded him to plead guilty and he was fined £50. Today, original examples of his work can sell for thousands of pounds. Sadly, I don't own any, just several hundred of the postcard reproductions.

During the First World War McGill produced a lot of military cards, usually showing weary Tommies, plus loads of harmless, sentimental ones featuring children, which Canon Rawnsley no doubt enjoyed. One shows a little girl praying by her bedside with a dog pulling at her nightdress: 'Please Lord, excuse me a minute while I kick Fido.' He reworked it several times and by 1962, when he died, that one card had sold 3½ million copies.

But McGill will be best remembered for his rude ones: 'There's a vicar at the window sponging his Aspidistra,' says one haughty-looking woman to another. 'Horrid Man,' replies her friend, 'he ought to do that in his bathroom.' Or how about this one? 'Do you keep stationery,' says a male customer to a pretty girl in a bookshop. 'Well, I wriggle about sometimes,' she replies.

All pretty innocent, really, compared with the kind of stuff that's readily available on the internet today.

Topographical Cards

Postcards showing familiar places are amongst the most popular and obvious to collect. There's something really appealing about suddenly spotting a landmark, natural or man-made, on an old postcard and then noticing how the surroundings have (or haven't, as the case may be) changed radically over the intervening years. As I mentioned with my Lakeland cards (see pages 172–3), I like best the ones that show people of the period.

While idly gazing over piles of assorted tat on a crowded table, looking for nothing in particular, I can instantly spot a Lake District card – which invariably turns out to be one I've got – or a Hampstead Heath or Highgate card. These are my two main topographical collections.

I tried to specialize, to keep things slightly under control, and so I started looking for postcards of the North London street where we live. So far, I've amassed the princely total of one. Not surprising I suppose. It's not a well-known street, not very long, and with no significant buildings

On Parliament Hill, Highgate

5024. HIGH STREET, HAMPSTEAD

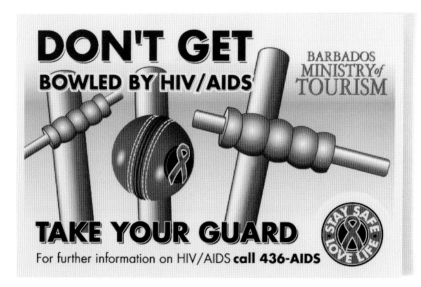

DON'T GET BOWLED BY HIV/AIDS

BARBADOS MINISTRY *of* TOURISM

TAKE YOUR GUARD

For further information on HIV/AIDS **call 436-AIDS**

STAY SAFE LOVE LIFE

or notable occupants. Well, not until recently, at least. The postmark reveals that it dates from 1904. But the fact that there is a card of our road at all shows that in those early days, every street everywhere – and everyone – stood a chance of being immortalized for posterity on a postcard, long before Google Street View.

Free Postcards

I'm always on the lookout for bargains and getting something free is the best bargain of all, so I was delighted when, about ten years or so ago, free postcards started appearing on racks in restaurants, cinemas, shops and elsewhere. They started by simply promoting, say, a shop or caff. Now you see whole racks of them, for all sorts of goods and services, from new books to new films, not always connected with the place where you picked them up.

I was surprised at first, as running off glossy, full-colour postcards seemed too expensive a business just to give them away. I do it myself, but then I'm a rich, wildly generous person. We have pretty postcards showing our London and Lakeland houses, which I use for correspondence if I deem the recipient worthy. I usually get 1000 printed, which works out now at about 20p each. But then I worked out that if a business is producing thousands, it'd be much cheaper. I also assume that, in terms of their total advertising and marketing budget, a few publicity postcards cost nothing.

One new trend is for these free postcards to be used to send messages or exhortations as part of some worthy government or NGO-sponsored campaign. The authorities use them to raise awareness, impart helpful information such as helpline 'phone numbers or just raise their own profile and let us see what they are doing with our money.

My favourite free postcard so far is one I picked up in Barbados – part of an HIV/AIDS campaign there. By using a reference to the favourite sport of the West Indies, they hoped to make it a bestseller. No, that's not the right word. Free things can't be bestsellers. Let's say 'very popular' – popular enough, at least, to be picked up and kept by a passing and very mean postcard collector . . .

LAMBETH BATHS,

WESTMINSTER ROAD,
(ENTRANCE FROM THE NEW CUT.)

BY REQUEST OF THE COMMITTEE OF THE

LADIES' SANITARY ASSOCIATION,

ROBERT DRUITT, ESQ.,

WILL DELIVER A LECTURE,

ON

"DRINK,"

ON

TUESDAY EVENING, Jan. 20th, 1863, at 8 o'clock,

AT THE ABOVE PLACE.

JOHN MACGREGOR, ESQ.

WILL PRESIDE.

The Working Classes are earnestly invited to attend. ADMISSION FREE.

GARDINER AND SON, Printers, 20, Princes Street, Cavendish Square.

Aggie Grey

HOTEL ▪ WESTERN SAMOA

JOHN WILLAN,

Bull & Mouth Inn, Bull & Mouth Street.

COACH

Carriage - - - - 3 - 4

Porterage - - - - — 3

1811   11 July 11   3 10

Portsmouth, Portsea, Gosport, and Isle of Wight Coaches, DAILY.

Morning at 7, Afternoon at 5.

Brighton Royal Mail every Evening.

Porter.

BIBA

PRINTED PAPER RATE

Inland
½
Stamp

to
JONATHAN CAPE LTD.
Publishers
THIRTY BEDFORD SQUARE
LONDON, W.C. 1

Name and address only to be written here, in
BLOCK CAPITALS please

If you are interested in any particular type
of book kindly state the nature here

from   Name   Address

NOTICE

THIS FOOTPATH

IS CLOSED

ON ACCOUNT OF

FOOT & MOUTH DISEAS

By Order of the Minister of Agriculture Fisheries & Food

Ephemera

At root, we're all ephemeral, transient, just passing through, for today only, mere mortals, all doomed, the end is nigh … Then again, we're all well aware of that, so the obvious response is to start collecting now, before it's too late. It'll give you something to do, until the final whistle blows.

RUBBISH OR SOCIAL HISTORY?
Left: The weird and wonderful world of collecting (mis)leads you into amassing all sorts of strange stuff that other people might discard, like Biba bags, publishers' cards and Foot and Mouth notices. A friend of mine even used to collect airline sick bags (unused) – until his cleaning lady threw them out.

The word 'ephemera' comes from the Greek – from *epi-* meaning 'near' or 'close to' and *hemera* meaning 'day'. In its restricted, scientific sense, it denotes the mayfly genus – insects that hatch, live and die within 24 hours. In a more general, metaphorical sense, it means something passing, which won't last, hardly worth much or bothering about, here today, gone tomorrow, something discarded and left to blow in the wind.

Collectors use the word in a much more specific sense. The most widely accepted definition was formulated by Maurice Rickards of the Centre for Ephemera Studies at the University of Reading, author of the classic study *The Encyclopaedia of Ephemera*, published by the British Library in 2000. (See page 149; he died in 1998, before it was completed.) Rickards' definition was short and simple: 'Minor transient documents of everyday life.' Not bad, though some collectors would defend their ephemera as being neither transient nor minor. 'Documents' is a good word, though, because it suggests printed paper matter, and ephemera does tend on the whole to be paper.

My own definition – and all collectors are allowed to define their own collections – would have to include the free element. To me, ephemera covers those objects that have never had a monetary value in themselves, nor were produced to be collected. So I don't include football programmes as ephemera, which Mr Rickards did. You had to pay for them, and they were quickly seen as souvenirs. So football programmes, to me, come under football memorabilia, not ephemera.

But I would describe football tickets as ephemera – or any sort of tickets, for that matter, for buses, trains, the theatre or whatever – as they had no intrinsic monetary value. You paid for a ticket, but in itself it was worthless once you had gained entry, so usually it was thrown away. A cigar label or cheese label can be counted as ephemera, too, because although it was part of something that had to be paid for, it was the packaging, the free bit which came with it, and was also normally thrown away.

Cigarette cards, according to my definition, have to be regarded as ephemera, even though you had to shell out for the cigarettes. By the same token, so must cigarette packets. Or indeed tokens themselves, come to think of it. All that kind of stuff always came absolutely free.

Magpie collectors like me, who have lots of collections, usually spread their ephemera around. Under football, they will have odd bits of inconsequential stuff, such as tickets, flyers, labels with football themes. Among their Beatles treasures, they'll have bubblegum cards and wrappers. In this book, I have included lottery tickets and leaflets under Toys and Games, but I could just as easily have put them under Ephemera, which is what they were.

So what's the point of ephemera? Their content, being in the main free, is never as important as a proper, paid-for, printed document, like a newspaper or book. They tend to be skittish, flimsy, slight, easily torn or lost. There's not a lot of reading in them or on them.

A broom label, for example, isn't going to give you much insight into domestic life or even brooms. They're just, well, labels. People do collect broom labels, by the way, especially American ones produced between 1890 and 1910, because they were pretty and highly decorative, showing not just women sweeping but steamboats and locomotives.

Their nice colours and striking designs are probably their main attraction, but they were also interesting typographically, as you can see the changing styles and fashions in mass-produced printing. Now and then, ephemera may contain some fairly interesting content – on prices, manufacturers, addresses. Historians might not pay them much heed, but they can serve as useful illustrations or footnotes to a particular period.

Anyway, here's some of the stuff I count as ephemera. To some people they might be total rubbish. Others might consider them little treasures.

Tax Discs

That's what I and most other people call them, but technically speaking they are 'motor vehicle licences'. You need them to drive or park a car on the road and they are issued by the DVLA in Swansea – probably the hardest organization, anywhere in the world, to make contact with on the telephone. Try it – you'll die before you get through.

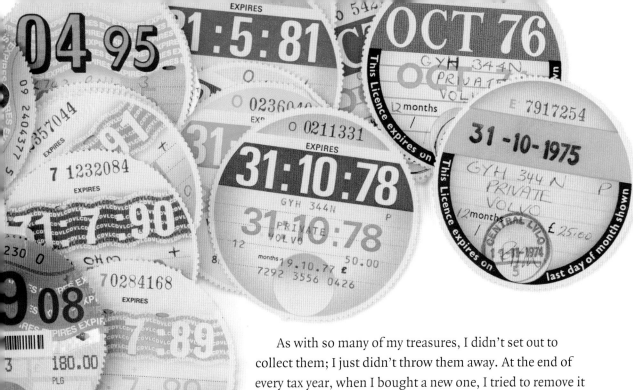

As with so many of my treasures, I didn't set out to collect them; I just didn't throw them away. At the end of every tax year, when I bought a new one, I tried to remove it from its perforations ever so carefully, though there's invariably one corner that gets torn or spoiled. Every year, I look upon it as one of my annual achievements, if I can produce a perfect disc. Then you have to fold it the right way to insert it into the round plastic holder on your car window – having first, of course, removed the old one. Hope you're following all this. Most people immediately throw the old one away, but for over 30 years, I haven't done so.

Why not? I don't really know. Partly I'm thinking, huh, I've spent a fortune on this flimsy bit of cheap paper, or on what it represents, so I'm loath to just throw it away. I also quite like the colours, which change from year to year. But mainly I collect them because I collect them. Once I'd started, back in 1975, I couldn't just stop, now could I?

What's interesting is that in all these years they haven't changed in size, shape, contents or the basic colours. Well, maybe the lettering has grown slightly more modern, and in the last few years they've added fancy watermarking and a small silver strip, presumably for security reasons. But basically, they've remained the same for over 30 years. You can't say the same for most other official documents. Governments often go mad on makeovers, spending millions on new logos and designs when they're not necessary.

But there is one big change since I started collecting them 33 years ago. The cost, my God, the cost. I paid only £25 in 1975 to tax my car which, now I look at the disc, I see was a Volvo. Today I've got a Jaguar, 11 years old. Its tax disc cost me £185. Talk about inflation.

UNHAPPY MOTORING We all grind our teeth about having to buy ever more costly tax discs to keep our vehicles on the road. But at least I get another collection out of this official extortion racket.

Telegrams

Telegrams first appeared in the 1840s and were connected with the railways, run by them as a sort of sideline. They had introduced electrically transferred messages for their own internal use before they began offering the service to the public.

Separate telegraphic companies grew up in the 1850s and 1860s and took over the service. In the USA, there were scores of rival companies, including Western Union and the American Telegraph Company. Cable and Wireless, founded in England in 1929, expanded all over the world.

In Britain, the service was nationalized in 1974, after which all telegraphic services were run by the Post Office. Telegram boys, in their neat uniform, on their bikes and then motorbikes, were a familiar and usually welcome sight all over Britain for many decades. Now, telegrams have all gone, finally killed off by the boring old internet.

POST HASTE

Two examples of old telegrams from my collection. Mistakes could always occur in the transmission: a woman who thought her son was walking in Scotland once got this alarming cable: 'Headed for Russia, hiking through Persia'. It should have read: 'Headed for Ross-shire, hiking through Perthshire.'

Foot and Mouth Notices

I have a collection of Foot and Mouth memorabilia, which I began in 2001. We were at our Lakeland home at the time and the whole area was being devastated. As I walked around (until they stopped you doing so) I spotted all these different notices – from the National Park, the National Trust, Cumbria County Council and the Ministry of Agriculture. As the disease got more serious, the notices grew heavier, sterner, with convoluted legalese. Farming mags, like *Farmers' Guardian*, even produced special ones for their readers to use. Some farmers wrote their own. I found them all fascinating.

I asked my farming neighbours, when all this is over, can I have your notices? Of course, they said, thinking I was barmy. I also went into Carlisle, to the local Ministry of Agriculture office, and said don't throw anything out, I'll have it. One farmer friend offered me a 10-minute government video he'd been sent, telling him how to disinfect his farm. 'Er, no thanks,' I said. 'Very kind. But I'm just collecting paper memorabilia.' One has to draw the line.

I didn't get any items from the 2007 outbreak in the South of England, but I hope someone did. It's a vital bit of social and agricultural history.

Funny Notices

One advantage of ephemera is that it's easy to store. The bits and pieces are usually fairly small, so you can just shove them in drawers and boxes and forget about them until you decide what to do with them. If anything.

They can also be amusing, which you can't say about all collections. For many years now I've kept an eye out for what I call funny notices. They come in two forms. There's the kind that are amusing because they are funny-peculiar, old and dated, with quaint wording or illustrations. That's what attracted John Lennon to an old circus poster that he had in front of him when he wrote the song 'For the Benefit of Mr Kite, there will be a show tonight, on trampoline!' on the *Sergeant Pepper* album.

I have a postcard of an old notice that used to hang in Kentish Town Baths (I hope it's still there, when the Baths, closed at the moment, re-open). It tells patrons to kindly refrain from things like petting – and I should think so too – with nice little drawings, in case you're not sure what petting is. It makes me smile to look at it.

I also have an 1863 notice from Lambeth Baths (see page 182), announcing that the Ladies' Sanitary Association is holding a lecture

STOP!
FOOT & MOUTH DISEASE

It is now unlawful to use this path (possible penalty £5,000)

All footpaths and bridleways across fells, other farmland and through woodland are now closed to public use. Foot and Mouth is a contagious disease which threatens the way of life of everyone in rural communities.

For further information, please telephone 0845 6014068

FARMING TODAY
The Foot and Mouth outbreaks hit hill farmers in Cumbria hard. Left: a Penrith farmer and his wife watch their flock go for slaughter.

on 'DRINK: The Working Classes are earnestly invited to attend. Admission free.'

Then there are those notices that are meant to be funny, taking the piss out of some current event or person. In the 1900s a lot of anti-Suffragette material came into this category: 'Great Salvage Sale – Bargains in Women: A few Suffragettes just arrived from Pentonville; A good collection of Tarts, Old Sports, Relics, none over 99 . . . some with wooden legs, who can speak 5 languages, 7 when they have been indulging, would suit a cabman. All goods delivered free, packed in Sawdust' (see page 100).

Around the same period, printers issued 'funeral cards', with black edgings, sold after big football games which mocked the team that had just got beaten. 'Farewell dear old Everton, No more pots for you . . .' They'd create two different versions to cater for either outcome.

In the 1980s, spoof kidney donor cards were circulated mocking prime minister Mrs Thatcher (see above). And if you found yourself in prison, there was a similar one advising that you would not like to be visited by Lord Longford. A period piece already. But still well worth keeping . . .

Cheques

Cheques are much older than either stamps or postcards – the first one in Britain being issued in 1659 – and they have a fascinating past. They are not just part of banking history, but also of Quaker history, for many of our modern banks, such as Barclays and Lloyd's, were founded by the Society of Friends. And old cheques are so pretty, far more so than stamps, with lovely vignettes, nice engravings and interesting typefaces.

I didn't know any of this 20 years ago when, at a car boot sale, I bought an 1897 cheque paid out to Gladstone, and signed by him on the back. That's when I got the idea of collecting cheques signed by famous people.

I bought myself a big album, stuck the Gladstone cheque in, and proceeded to look out for dealers in cheques. I've always been surprised, when chancing upon a new madness, to discover a support network I never knew existed. With cheques, I'm still looking. So far, my album contains only five cheques – signed by Ramsay MacDonald, Somerset Maugham, Lord Tennyson and Saul Bellow. In 1992, I briefly thought I'd come across a fellow collector. I went to interview the entrepreneur Alan Sugar in his

My fave cheque is actually in my Football Collection. It's a 1929 Spurs cheque, paid out for gate expenses, and is huge – about four times the size of a modern cheque. It includes a great football scene and a fancy scroll. Note also the cockerel. Over 9 feet high, and made of copper, it perched on the West Stand from 1909, and became the symbol of Spurs. Right: A Maryport and Carlisle Railway Company cheque from 1912.

Brentwood office. On his wall, I noticed some framed cheques. On examination, I found they were all paid by him to the Inland Revenue, including one dated 27.3.1989 for £48,231,250. Amazing. Just shows you how well he was doing. But they were a sign of his fury, not evidence of any collecting bug.

I suppose the main reason for the lack of a specialist cheques fraternity is that they're absorbed into other collections. If you collect literary autographs, you'll come across cheques signed by literary figures at autograph fairs.

Stolen Stationery

Stolen might give the wrong impression, as obviously I wouldn't dream of stealing anything. 'Liberated Stationery' might be a better way of putting it. Or simply 'Free Stationery'. I paid nothing for it and it was lying there, free for guests and customers to use. The fact that I didn't actually use it there and then, which presumably was the intention, is irrelevant really. I like to think that I was complimenting the institution in question.

I keep such items in an album entitled 'My Life in Stationery'. Poncey title, really, considering that all it consists of is blank pieces of headed notepaper gathered from various places I have visited. But compared with some of my collections, still shoved in drawers, or lying in corners, it's well organized and arranged and has a certain logic to it.

It shouldn't be confused with my various albums of letters written and signed by famous people, though many of them are on headed notepaper. And it's different again from my Vignettes, which is what I call my collection of prettily headed 19th-century business notepaper and bills, mainly from shops. No, the whole point about 'My Life in Stationery' is that that's precisely what it is – unused bits of stationery, with nothing written on them. They fall into two categories: stationery from newspapers and magazines I once worked for; and from hotels and places I have visited. Hence the 'My Life' bit.

It all started when I found I'd kept some *Sunday Times* notepaper from 1960, the year I joined the staff. At that time, the paper was based in Kemsley House, 200 Grays Inn Road, and its phone number was TERminus 1234 – later becoming 837 1234. As I also used to write for *Punch*, I kept some pretty little postcards from its years at 23–27 Tudor Street. I thought *Punch* would be around forever, but it folded. So I'm pleased I have those cards today.

I've also kept various sheets of notepaper from hotels around the world, such as Aggie Grey's in Samoa, a place well known in the Pacific, where I stayed while I was researching a book about Robert Louis Stevenson, and from Riley's Hotel in Botswana, where our daughter once lived. These are places I'll probably never visit again, and they have their own memories. I like looking at the typefaces, seeing the changes in style over the last 40 years, and how 'phone numbers have altered and postcodes been introduced.

I also have a few pieces of political stationery. My sheet of White House notepaper was given to me while I was in Washington DC in the 1970s, visiting a friend who was an economic adviser. The Deputy Prime Minister's notepaper is more recent, from 2008 in fact, when I was helping John Prescott

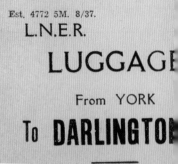

Est. 4772 5M. 8/37.
L.N.E.R.
LUGGAGE
From YORK
To DARLINGTON

SEATS OF POWER Inveterate hoarder of free ephemera that I am, I was pleased to get hold of genuine headed notepaper from John Prescott's office and from the White House.

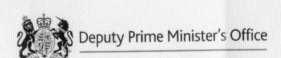

Deputy Prime Minister's Office

26 Whitehall
London
SW1A 2WH

Tel: 020 7944 8615
Fax: 020 7944 8618

From Joan Hammell
Chief of Staff

THE WHITE HOUSE
WASHINGTON

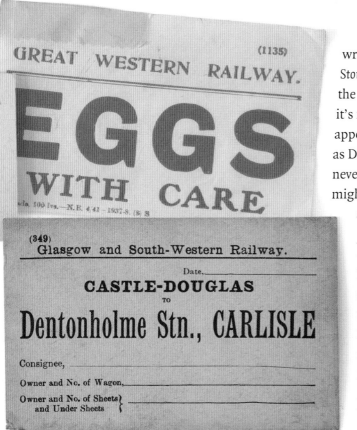

GREAT WESTERN RAILWAY.   (1135)

EGGS
WITH CARE

(349)
Glasgow and South-Western Railway.

Date,

CASTLE-DOUGLAS
TO

Dentonholme Stn., CARLISLE

Consignee,

Owner and No. of Wagon,

Owner and No. of Sheets
and Under Sheets

HANDLE WITH CARE Luggage labels for goods carried by long-defunct railway companies.

write his autobiography: *Prezza – My Story: Pulling No Punches*. But although the stationery didn't have his name on, it's now obsolete: no successor was appointed when Prescott stepped down as DPM in June 2007. And there might never be one again. So, my stationery might be rubbish, but some of it has already become historic rubbish . . .

Railwayana

Railway memorabilia is a huge subject on its own, and shouldn't really be lumped in with ephemera. I have some old examples of railway material, including old lamps and metal signposts for long-dead railway companies, such as the Great Western or North Eastern, but most of my railway stuff is ephemeral – luggage labels, notices, bills, invoices, timetables, posters. I collect them mainly for the old companies, especially ones from the North.

Other Ephemera

For some reason I've got a little collection of 1930s publishers' trade cards, – pre-printed, with the publisher's name and address on one side and on the other a list of their latest books, which you could send off for by filling in your name and address. They weren't pre-paid, though; you had to buy your own stamp. Publishers have always been canny. They were given away or stuck inside books, so if you liked what you were reading, you might be tempted to buy other books from the same source. I bought them because a lot of those publishers are still with us today, trading under the same names, even if they are now part of conglomerates, such as Jonathan Cape, or Hodder and Stoughton. Some are still independent – Faber and Faber, for example – and are based in the same area of London as when they started out.

I do have one piece of ephemera I'm very fond of which isn't printed on paper. This is a small plastic bag, about the size of a postcard, which came from Biba, a famous trendy 1960s and early 1970s boutique founded by the designer Barbara Hulanicki. The bag was free – hence it's ephemera – but I also have a pair of purple, knee-high Biba boots, bought by my wife.

COLLECTING FOR FREE

One of the many joys of collecting is that you don't have to wait till the shops open. No need to depend on dealers, fairs, stalls, auctions, car boots, jumbles or charity shops, either. Nor do you even have to spend a penny.

Let's test the truth of that statement right now. I'm off for a walk. I open my front door and there are three rubber bands, discarded by our postie. They use them to tie up bundles of letters for houses that get lots of mail. As we do, being ever so popular. We're also allergic to e-mails, text messages and even, in the case of my dear wife, to answering the 'phone. Old-fashioned post is the only way to gain access to Casa Davies.

The posties just seem to drop the rubber bands, instead of re-using them. Whoever has the contract to supply rubber bands to the Royal Mail is clearly onto a winner. Two are the usual browny-red colour, got loads of those, but – ah! here's an orange one. Never seen that before. I'll keep it for my collection. Perhaps I can swap the others, not that I know anyone who collects rubber bands. But there will be someone, no question.

Two cigarette butts in the gutter. I think not, ugh, I've always hated the smell of cigarettes, but there are Americans who collect butts, according to Professor Marilynn Karp in her book *In Flagrante Collecto*. No sign of any interesting fag packets. As a boy, these were one of my first collections. I'd still pick them up now, if they looked interesting or unusual.

Next, a discarded parking fine, still in its plastic sleeve, thrown away in disgust by some furious driver. Should I take it? I collect tax discs, but not parking fines. If I did, I'm sure an unused, mint example must be quite desirable. Better leave it. Said furious driver might think twice and come back for it.

Hanging on a gate I find a single glove, brown, woolly, with that Nike flash thing on the back. I try it on. Fits like a glove, ha, ha! Someone has found it on the pavement and put it in a prominent spot

in case the owner returns. I put it in my pocket. It will add to my collection of odd gloves, some of which I wear. When people say to me 'You're wearing odd gloves' I express surprise, as if I didn't know, then say 'I've got another pair, exactly the same, at home.'

Further along our street, on a front wall, there is a large cardboard box full of junk. This is what people seem to do round here. Instead of dragging stuff to the jumble or charity shops, they leave it on their front wall, sometimes with a sign saying 'Please Help Yourself'. It's always gone by the next day. It contains odd bits of wood of different lengths, all clean and new. What a waste! I do hope they find a home. A kettle, probably not working. Some damp copies of *National Geographic*. Children's toys, chipped plates, some football magazines. I pick them out, but I don't really want to carry them on my walk. Hey, this looks good, though – at the bottom there's some ancient weighing scales, black cast iron, with brass pans. Keep still, my little heart. Probably broken, but no, they're in excellent nick, just lacking any weights, but who cares about that? Perfect for my kitchenalia collection which is rather modest so far – in fact it only consists of a butter churn and an old glass and wooden dolly, the sort women used for scrubbing clothes.

Should I leave them to pick up on the way back? No, someone else will find them. So I gather them up, along with the football mags, and hurry home. I don't want to go back inside, as my wife will wonder why I'm back so early from my walk, so I hide them behind our dustbins.

At last I reach the Heath, where at the entrance I find a ticket for a concert at the Forum, probably dropped by some kid from one of the local schools. Oh good, I can put it with old local

du MAURIER
FILTERED FOR PERFECTION

THE CIGARETTE WITH THE EXCLUSIVE **FILTER**

newspapers – or start a new collection called Forumania.

On the Heath, as usual, lots of trees are deco-rated with cries of anguish and distress for Lost Dogs and Cats. Twenty years ago, these notices were handwritten, usually with pathetic drawings of the lost pet. Now they're big and glossy, computer-generated, with excellent colour photos. These simple notices chart changes in lifestyles, language and design. Some of the pleadings are intense and emotional. Some childlike and sad. Most give mobile numbers, but not addresses. Too dangerous, I suppose. Many promise unspecified rewards.

I wonder if Elizabeth Barrett Browning put up notices on trees in Regent's Park when her dog Flush got lost in the 1840s? He was kidnapped by a gang of roughs from the East End who were going around stealing pets. They extorted five guineas for Flush's return, a large sum in 1844. Didn't do much good, though. Flush got stolen again. By then the ransom money had gone up to seven guineas.

Further on, I see some more of the same notices for Lost Pets, so I take one. Well, it was hanging loose. I will start collecting them.

Never too late. Then I spot a lottery ticket, out of date, not a winner I presume, and pocket it. On a seat by the boating pond is a shopping list: 'Aubergines, dolcelatte, Indy, Oil of Olay, evening primrose, Tate Mod, Rupert, Asilone tablets.' Well, it is Hampstead Heath. Not quite the sort of list I'd find in Cockermouth Main Street. Asilone is for stomachs, after eating too much dolcelatte, but the tablet form has practically disappeared. Perhaps it's an old list, some woman clearing out her handbag … Why do I think that? Could be a gay man. Lots on the Heath.

On the way home, I find a red plastic bottle, rather bashed in. I think it must have contained some sort of alcopop. Sixth-formers, after their exams, have been having late-night drinking parties on the Heath. Interesting shape, not a brand I recognize. Maybe I should send it to Robert Opie for his Museum of Advertising and Packaging in Notting Hill. Or maybe not; he's probably got it.

At our front door I spot something dumped behind the dustbin. The scales! I'd forgotten about them. My heart skips a beat, all over again. Twice blessed, all on one short walk …

CARLISLE CASTLE

THE MAGAZINE OF THE DURHAM CAS...

castel...

Durham Bank. £5.

No. C/W 298

Promise to pay the Bearer on demand FIVE POUNDS value received C/W 298

Durham

For Jonathan Backhouse & Co.

Five Pounds.

Palatinate

ROMAN WALL

Evening Chronicle

London Office: Kemsley House, W.C.1

KEMSLEY HOUSE, MANCHESTER 4
(P.O. BOX 200)

HW/SC   July 25, 1958.

Mr. Edward Hunter Davies,
28, Caird Avenue,
Carlisle.

Dear Mr. Davies,

We are now able to offer you an appointment
on the Evening Chronicle reporting staff on the lines
discussed with you by Mr. J.P.Goulden, Managing
Editor and Mr. J.W. Fraser of our London executive
staff.

It is understood that the appointment
will be, in the first instance, for a probationary
period of six months at the conclusion of which,
subject to our mutual agreement, you will be required

Hunter Davies

HERE WE GO, ROUND
THE MULBERRY BUSH

Best Wishes to You Both

Hunter Davies,
9, Heath Villas,
Vale of Health,
Hampstead
LONDON N.W.3.

IL-MEJDA TAL-GORDAN
WIED IL-GHASRI
GOZO, MALTA G.C.

Mrs. Hunter Davies

OFFICE STAMP

23   45

HUNTER DAVIES
EDITOR
THE SUNDAY TIMES MAGAZINE

to a Garden Party at Buckingham Palace
on Tuesday, 14th July, 1981 from 4 to 6 p.m.

81274 4.10 GULLIVER TS 17

FORSTER 180 RICHARDSON STREET CARLISLE

GIRL 2 PR 8 POUNDS 3-1/2 OUNCES BOTH

...SHINA LOVE - HUNTER

TUFNELL PARK   60p

TUFNELL PARK   60p

6071

DAVIES OR BALAIA
HOTEL ALGARVE AL
ALBUFEIRA
ALGARVE AL
PORTUGAL

Morning Dress, Uniform or Lounge Suit

Tottenham Hotspur
Company

Admit Bearer to
PRESS B...

ON

NAME Hunter Davies
The Times

HUNTER DAVIES
PHILATELIC CORRESPONDENT

THE SUNDAY TIMES
P.O. BOX X
200 GRAY'S INN ROAD
LONDON, WC1X 8EZ

FINAL FAREWELL, MARCH 1

Feb 16, 1984

You are invited to champagne in the Look
suite, room 416, 5th floor, Sunday Times,
at 6 pm on Thursday, March 1, 1984........

Yes, you thought I'd left ages ago, but no, I've been
on the strength, if only just. Too many people seem to
have slipped away too quietly in the last few years,
so I thought I'd go with a slight pop. Afterall, I joined
the company in 1958, and the ST staff in 1960, so now
I'm officially going. I'd like to say a fond farewell
to all those I've known and loved, tra la . I'm trying
to contact some of those I worked with over the years,
from Atticus to Look, Scene to the Mag, as well as
those stalwarts still hard atit, just to join me for
a drink. I hope you'll come. Let me know if you can...

Hunter :)

FATHER'S DAY

FLOOK
by TROG

HUNTER DAVIES
Advance bookings

HUNTER DAVIES
BRITISH PARTICIPANT
IN THE LITERARY
ROUND TABLE

Collecting Myself

I got the idea of collecting myself from the artist Peter Blake. About 20 years ago I went to see him in his studio, and he turned out to be a great collector of the sort of things I collect, such as Beatles memorabilia (he designed the famous cover for *Sergeant Pepper's Lonely Hearts Club Band* in 1967) and football stuff. He also had something he called the 'Museum of Myself'.

It was a framed collection of personal objects that had to do with his own life. They were artistically arranged and beautifully framed. Some of the objects were three-dimensional, so the frame was actually more like a display case. When I got home, I tried displaying some similar stuff from my own life, but I couldn't mount them as well. So I just stuck to flat things, like postcards, labels, envelopes and photos. It's still on the hall wall. I often hear visitors sniggering as they pass.

Glancing at it again, I see I used some original materials – such as a real 1891 £5 note. This was issued by the Durham Bank and I put it in the frame not because I was interested in banking or money but to represent where I was a student, as it has on it a nice vignette of Durham Cathedral. *Palatinate* was the name of the Durham student paper I edited, where I first got the idea of becoming a journalist. Since then, I've actually written a column on money for about 10 years, so the banknote's turned out to be more relevant than I realized.

MEMENTOES OF ME My Museum of Myself – a ragbag of bits and pieces that have to do with different phases of my life. Yes, of course it's completely self-regarding and appallingly self-obsessed and really only of interest to me – but that's just what it's meant to be. Right: a long-defunct passport.

Carlisle features at the top – in the form of a British Rail luggage label – as that was where I was brought up, and also other places from my life, such as Manchester, where I first started work on the *Evening Chronicle*, the Maltese island of Gozo, where we lived for six months, and a Portuguese beach, where we spent our summer hols with the children for 20 years. Plus there's a snap of our London house under snow, as it was when we first saw it in 1963.

There are items relating to the subjects of various books I've written, including Hadrian's Wall, Spurs and The Beatles, and to my work on *The Sunday Times*. I've also included some paragraphs from my first-ever book, a novel called *Here We Go Round the Mulberry Bush*.

The telegram is real – sent to my in-laws on the day our first child, Caitlin, was born in 1964, announcing her safe arrival and the fact that she weighed a healthy 8 lbs 3½ oz. I suppose I should give it to Caitlin herself now.

I like to think most grown-ups in the world, whatever their situation, keep hold of old family photos and mementoes, especially of their loved ones. It seems a natural human reaction. How often do you see on the news pathetic survivors in war-torn, devastated, earthquake-hit, flood-inundated, terrorist-attacked houses and villages clutching crumpled family photographs? I believe we should cherish such things. You can't expect children themselves to do it, yet there will come a time, when they are grown up, when they'll want to know where they came from.

As a collector, I suppose I have taken it more seriously than normal people – deliberately keeping and collating all sorts of personal stuff. When I first created my little Museum of Myself, there were several bulkier objects I couldn't fit in, so I put them in a big box file

TINY TOT A page from 'My Record Book', which charts my first year of life. The cover gives my full name as 'Edward Hunter Davies' – which I usually deny. From birth, I was always called 'Hunter'. I didn't realize it was my second name until I was about 11, when the school nurse came to inspect us for nits and called for 'Edward' to step forward. I sniggered and looked round, wondering which poor sod had such a soppy name.

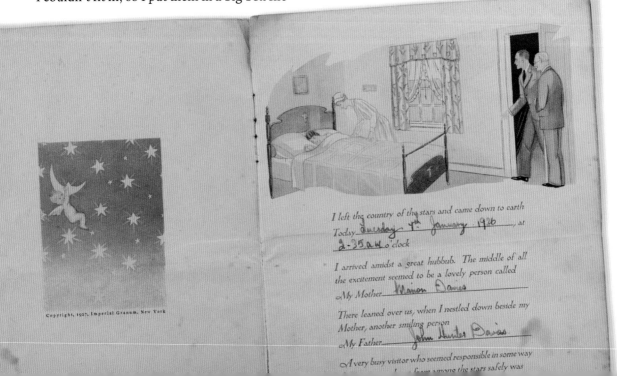

I left the country of the stars and came down to earth
Today ~~Thursday~~ 1ˢᵗ January 1936 , at
2·35 a.m o'clock

I arrived amidst a great hubbub. The middle of all the excitement seemed to be a lovely person called
My Mother___Marion Davies

There leaned over us, when I nestled down beside my Mother, another smiling person
My Father___John Hunter Davies

A very busy visitor who seemed responsible in some way from among the stars safely was

Copyright, 1927, Imperial Granum, New York

Playing with my daughter Caitlin at the London house in 1968, when she was 4 years old.

entitled 'My Life, Number One' – in case I decided to keep going, and needed further volumes. I'm now on 'My Life, Number 5,' which takes me roughly up to the 1980s.

We're all obliged to hang on to certain things as we go through life, even those of us who don't call ourselves collectors: important documents such as our birth certificate, passport and driving licence, for example. On the other hand, no one is likely to ask to see your Baptismal Certificate or your Baby Record Book. But should it ever happen, I'm ready. I have both, along with dozens more such objects, in 'My Life, Number One', which covers my life up to the age of 18. It includes my National Identity Card, which I see was issued in 1940, when I was four. I never realized they had been given out to children.

I still have my reports from all the schools I attended, in Dumfries and Carlisle, and also records and certificates from Durham University. I've even kept the first letters I got from newspapers and magazines – mostly refusals – in response to my submissions of stories and articles. In 1957, however, I see that I was paid £4 by the *Daily Express* and then in 1959 six guineas by *The Guardian*. Naturally, I've kept touching memorabilia from my dear wife, mementoes of our wedding in 1960 – and then a 1961 list of possible names for children, should we ever have any. One of the girls' names I favoured was Morag. I can still hear my wife protesting as I made her put it down on the list. She's always had better handwriting than me.

My mother kept a record of my early life, but I had no idea she had done so until she died. 'My Record Book' records my first year, with my weights, month by month, the first day I smiled, the first day I sat up, ahhh. On the inside page it says 'Copyright, 1927, Imperial Granum, New York'. I wonder

Edward Hunter Davies of University College

HAVING COMPLIED WITH ALL THE CONDITIONS
REQUIRED BY THE UNIVERSITY, HAS BEEN
ADMITTED TO THE DEGREE OF BACHELOR OF ARTS
*Thaving been placed in the Second Division, the subjects of examination
being Ancient History, Geography and Modern History .•*

G. M. Trevelyan
CHANCELLOR

Em.Betterson
REGISTRAR

DATE 5th July 1957

Left: My degree certificate from Durham University, where I graduated in 1957. Below: early breakthrough – *The Guardian* accepted an article of mine in 1959 for the princely sum of 6 guineas.

where she got it from? It's prettily illustrated, very American and frankly a bit mawkish. One line reads: 'There leaned over us, when I nestled down beside my Mother, another smiling person, My Father . . .' You had to fill in his name in the blank space. I hope my parents weren't leaning too near me; they both smoked, which was the reason, my grandmother always claimed, why I got asthma.

In turn, I kept all the trivia from my own children's lives, their swimming certificates and little drawings. I've still got them, what's more – they're not bleedin' interested. But they will be one day, mark my words.

Domestic Bliss

One of the things I wish I had done, all those years ago, was keep a proper record of our domestic life when we moved into this house in 1963. I would love to have a scrap of every piece of wallpaper we have ever used, a square of every carpet, an example of every tile and a photo of every room as it was in the beginning and then every time we made a change. I have kept a lot, but I wish I'd started earlier.

THE MANCHESTER GUARDIAN

GUARDIAN BUILDING
MANCHESTER 2
BLAckfriars 2345

11th January 1959

Dear Sir,

We shall be glad to accept your article

Ships like Swans

and offer you a fee of _____six_____ guineas. This, in default of alternative arrangements, would give us full world serial rights for four months from publication, after which all rights in the article would be yours.

Yours very truly,

for the Editor,

You don't realize it at the time – when you fancy you're making bold, individual, personal decisions – that you are actually a creature of your times, and that even if you're not slavishly following the herd, you're still influenced by it. Getting rid of old-fashioned open fireplaces, sanding and sealing the floorboards, going mad on Laura Ashley wallpaper, just like millions of other families and households around the same period. Then fashions change. After a decade or so, we suddenly hankered after a real fireplace, so we called in the very same builders who had ripped out the old ones to restore two of them to full working order, with old grates.

The main reason why I didn't keep meticulous records back then was that we didn't imagine we'd still be here, 47 years later. We thought we were just passing through. We'd been living in a flat in Hampstead, paying a rent of six guineas a week, in an absolutely stunning location in the Vale of Health – stunning to look at, though it brought on my asthma as our bedroom overlooked the pond and in the winter especially there was always a nasty, moisty mist that seeped into our bedroom.

PRIME LOCATION An Edwardian postcard of the Vale of Health pond on Hampstead Heath. A singularly misnamed place: the dank atmosphere played hell with my asthma when we lived there.

7644   Vale of Health & Pond, Hampstead.

We wanted to stay in Hampstead, but after three years of saving hard, we still couldn't afford anything there. Houses in roads we liked, such as Flask Walk and Christ Church Hill, were around the £7500 mark. The most we could afford was £5000 and that was based on saving £1500, with us both working, my wife as a teacher, me as a journalist, and on getting a mortgage of £3500, three times my salary, which was the most they would allow you to borrow in those days, the wise and prudent chaps. We drew a circle round the Heath and decided our best bet was to try the less desirable Kentish

Town side, across Highgate Road. So we started looking in what was then called Parliament Hill Fields. You still see that name on the buses, but local estate agents – who never existed, locally, in the 1960s – have now rechristened it Dartmouth Park.

In December 1962 we found a house we liked, though we couldn't see much of the garden as it was under snow. The house, which appeared to have been empty for some time, was three storeys but the top floor was let to a protected tenant. She was an elderly woman, we were told, staying with relations in America and might never return – which turned out to be a fib. I haggled the price down to £5000. It did, after all, have a sitting tenant and was in pretty bad nick.

Then, at the last minute, the mortgage collapsed. The company we had been saving with suddenly said 'oh sorry, we are not lending now on Victorian houses, nothing earlier than 1900'. Our house, as the deeds later revealed, was 1860s. Our offer had been accepted, so I had to rush around to find another lender. We finally got a 25-year mortgage from Norwich Union. I still have the estate agent's details from 1962, issued by Jennings and Samson, a local firm that's still going. This sheet is nowhere near as posh or glossy as modern estate agents' bumph – just a single page of cheap paper listing ten properties in our price range in or around the NW5 area.

I see our tenant was paying a controlled rent of 32/6d a week for her three rooms. It describes the house as 'attractive' with a 'pleasant garden at the rear' but it gives away the property's true condition by stating it would 'suit the discriminating buyer who is desirous of carrying out repairs and redecorations to his own requirements'. Most of the other nine houses listed also had sitting tenants, paying modest rents. They ranged from Camden Town to Muswell Hill, but alas the exact addresses are not given – only the street names or just the general area, like Tufnell Park. I made a note that the Camden Town house was in Arlington Road. Today, that would cost about £2 million. And all the rest would be worth at least a million.

I found a local builder, J.P. Brown, an Irishman who lived in nearby Fortess Road. I sent him a list of works to be done and he sent me his estimates, both of which documents I still have. I find it hard now to believe the prices. He provided a full estimate for all the jobs, which included major structural work like knocking down a rear extension containing an outside toilet and scullery, and then rebuilding it; putting in full central heating; removing our fireplaces; ripping out the bathroom entirely and fitting a complete new one; repairing the roof; and repointing back and front. The total sum was £834 and 10 shillings. I can't imagine what this work would cost today – £100,000, maybe? Of course, I didn't think it was cheap at the time, only that it was going to cost us almost 20 percent over and above what we'd already paid for the house itself. It seemed an awful lot.

So why did we never move out of our Kentish Town house? Eventually, when we both started to have our books published, we earned enough to move back to Hampstead, but we decided not to. The children were established at the local primaries and then the comprehensives. In the end, we acquired the whole house by buying a flat for the sitting tenant to move into, still on a controlled rent. We grew to love the house, and the garden.

Meanwhile, the bijou Georgian houses we'd once ogled in Hampstead grew less desirable, with their small rooms and narrow staircases. In an old Victorian house like ours, you have more space on each floor. Plus it's quieter over here, and the parking's easier. Our garden, which we never saw till the spring, faces south. In the meantime, all of the houses in our area have shot up in price and desirability. I like to think I've done my bit to help the gentrification of Dartmouth Park.

Anyway, the point of all this is to encourage you to keep and collect all the documents, scraps, records, bits and pieces from your own personal and domestic life. After all, who else is going to do it?

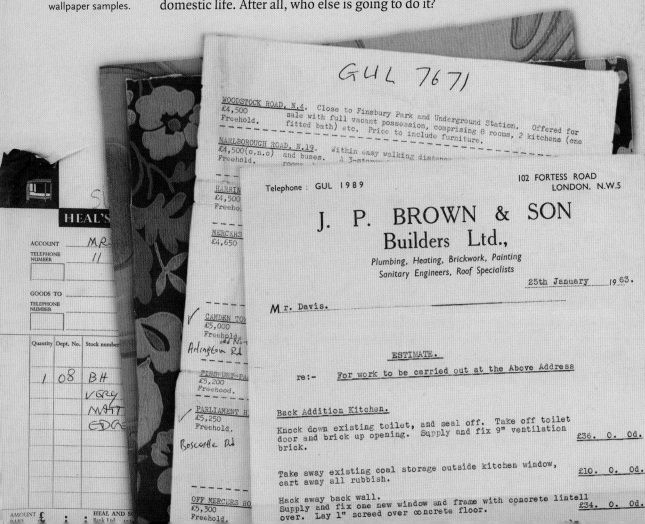

GUL 7671

WOODSTOCK ROAD, N.4. Close to Finsbury Park and Underground Station. Offered for
£4,500 sale with full vacant possession, comprising 8 rooms, 2 kitchens (one
Freehold. fitted bath) etc. Price to include furniture.

MARLBOROUGH ROAD, N.19. Within easy walking distance
£4,500(o.n.o) and buses. A 3-sto
Freehold. rooms

HARRIN
£4,500
Freeho

MERCERS
£4,650

CAMDEN TO
£5,000
Freehold
and No
Arlington Rd

FINSBURY PA
£5,200
Freehold.

PARLIAMENT H
£5,250
Freehold.
Boscastle Rd

OFF MERCERS RO
£5,300
Freehold.

Telephone : GUL 1989

102 FORTESS ROAD
LONDON. N.W.5

J. P. BROWN & SON
Builders Ltd.,
Plumbing, Heating, Brickwork, Painting
Sanitary Engineers, Roof Specialists

25th January 19 63.

Mr. Davis.

ESTIMATE.

re:-   For work to be carried out at the Above Address

Back Addition Kitchen.

Knock down existing toilet, and seal off. Take off toilet
door and brick up opening. Supply and fix 9" ventilation   £36. 0. 0d.
brick.

Take away existing coal storage outside kitchen window,   £10. 0. 0d.
cart away all rubbish.

Hack away back wall.
Supply and fix one new window and frame with concrete lintell   £34. 0. 0d.
over. Lay 1" screed over concrete floor.

HEAL'S

ACCOUNT   MR
TELEPHONE   11
NUMBER

GOODS TO
TELEPHONE
NUMBER

Quantity	Dept. No.	Stock number
1	08	BH
		VERY
		MATT
		EDGE

AMOUNT £   HEAL AND S
DATE   Bank Ltd

Last Words

I've tried to describe my 16 broad areas of collecting, but there are others I could have mentioned. For instance, I've left out my old photographs, which I've got loads of. I really should have worked them in. I've also tried at various points through the book to explain the rationale behind collecting, to get inside the mind of the collector. Which is to say, to get inside my own mind. No easy feat – but I'll attempt it once more here, anyway . . .

I have to admit that there are times when I am confused about my own motives, wonder why I do it. I can feel sickened, ashamed, weary, guilty, fed up, irritated by myself and my collections. With fellow collectors, of course, you don't have to try to rationalize collecting. Once you are in its grip, it's like a love that lasts forever. Collectors may get bored with certain collections, wondering why they bothered and how they could have got so obsessed with what began as just a passing fancy. But they tend to go on collecting forever, even if particular passions ebb and flow.

When asked why I collect certain things, I often say that there's nothing I couldn't find a reason for collecting. This is the collector talking, for we never look down upon anyone else's collections. We sympathize, empathize, try to look interested and impressed, even if we can't quite see the fascination of airline sick bags, but we still recognize the mentality and motivation.

Life is collecting. We all indulge in it as we trundle along between birth and death. We collect memories and objects at every stage of our lives. We start off with nothing, then find we have a partner, children, a house, furniture, documents, and so on. Stuff continues to pile up. And then we die.

The speed of technological change in the last few decades has made many objects almost instantly collectable, as they quickly go out of fashion. I'm constantly surprised to see people collecting old telephones – of the type I'm still using – and old Amstrad word processors, on one of which I am writing this book. Typewriters are now entirely obsolete, and have therefore become extremely collectable. Likewise old radios and TV sets, and even early mobile 'phones, videos and computers. In contrast, two hundred years ago the pace of change was slow and leisurely. Most things lasted for a lifetime, if not longer, without the need to be updated or replaced by a new model.

In modern developed countries, where people are increasingly affluent and have more leisure time and disposable income, I imagine that collecting will always continue to flourish and grow.

I often wonder what will happen to all my stuff after I'm gone. As for my Beatles collection, I know roughly what will happen to that. The best items are in the British Library and will remain there. As for the rest, I haven't a clue. I don't think I'll ever sell anything, unless I'm really, really hard up. I wouldn't want to, as the objects are so personal, part of me. I'd also be afraid to find that items I paid a lot for were now in fact worth bugger all.

I'm looking forward to enjoying them all in the years to come, even more so than I do now. If, of course, I reach my dotage. When work dries up, and nobody wants me any more, I'll get out my stuff, some of which I haven't looked at properly for years, and spend happy hours working my way through it all, mumbling to myself 'oooh, ahhh, wow, hmm, goodness, now where did I get that from?' Now and again, I might even exclaim, 'Why on Earth...!?'

As none of my three children is a collector, they won't want to take over any of my collections. My wife has never been interested either. So, when I'm gone, I suppose they'll send things like my football books and programmes to an auction house. After all, I've told them enough times that some of it is valuable. But mostly, they won't know what's good and bad, interesting or boring. My Suffragette postcards look cheap, even though they're not, while my early Beatrix Potter books are rather tatty. Naturally, I would like my collections to end up with other collectors, to the last syllabub of recorded time, for them to enjoy and treasure, even the rubbishy, piddling stuff. I know it would all find a new home, if given half a chance.

But my family might not realize this and might just tell some rag-and-bone man (or their modern equivalent, the 'house clearance' operators) to take this old junk away, burn it or dump it, just get rid of it, we don't care.

So I've already decided what my last words will be. When I'm on my death bed, I'll turn to my dear wife and croak: 'Now don't chuck anything out...'

Index

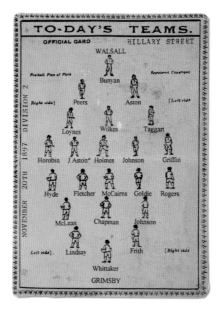

The single most expensive item in my collection of football programmes (see page 121): a single sheet of card showing the teams for a Walsall v. Grimsby game in 1897, with the line-ups on one side, and two local adverts on the other.

Acknowledgements

The objects, documents and assorted treasures that appear in this book are from my own collections of objects, documents and very assorted treasures. Wherever possible, I have tried to credit and date them. I'd like to thank and apologize to those authors, artists, copywriters, designers and publishers – many of them long gone – whose work I have used but have not been able to acknowledge.

I am also most grateful to the talented and dedicated team who brought this project to fruition; in particular Richard Milbank for setting the ball rolling and guiding everyone's endeavours, Nick Clark for the splendid design, Mark Winwood for his excellent photos and Peter Lewis, Martin Anderson and Austin Taylor for knocking it all into shape with such panache.

The following images are reproduced by kind permission of the relevant agencies: 9 Topham/Chapman 51 Topham/ Picturepoint 64 Donoso Julio/Corbis Sygma 69 'Hair of the Immortal George Washington', 1829 (mixed media)/ Atwater Kent Museum of Philadelphia/Courtesy of Historical Society of Pennsylvania Collection/The Bridgeman Art Library 80 Hulton Archive/Getty Images 104 Lake County Museum/Corbis 108 Bennett Dean; Eye Ubiquitous/ Corbis 138 Hulton-Deutsch Collection/Corbis 139 Hulton-Deutsch Collection/Corbis 145 Britain On View/Richard Watson 149 Rob Cousins/Alamy 151 Topham/PA 164 Colin McPherson/Corbis 187 McPherson Colin/Corbis Sygma 193 Land Lost Content/HIP/Topfoto 197 Sydney O'Meara/Evening Standard/Hulton Archive/Getty Images.

Every effort has been made to credit the source of materials used in this book and to discover any existing copyright holders. The author and publishers apologize if any have been missed and invite anyone claiming ownership not identified above to contact Quercus Publishing Plc.

Project manager/editor	Peter Lewis
Designers	Martin Anderson, Austin Taylor
Publishing Director	Richard Milbank
Art Director	Nick Clark
Photographer	Mark Winwood
Indexer	Helen Peters
Proofreader	Briony Ryles

First published in Great Britain in 2009 by

Quercus
21 Bloomsbury Square
London
WC1A 2NS

Copyright © 2009 by Hunter Davies

The moral right of Hunter Davies to be identified as the author of this work has been asserted in accordance with the Copyright, Designs and Patents Act, 1988.

A CIP catalogue record for this book is available from the British Library.

ISBN 978-1-84724-604-2

10 9 8 7 6 5 4 3 2 1

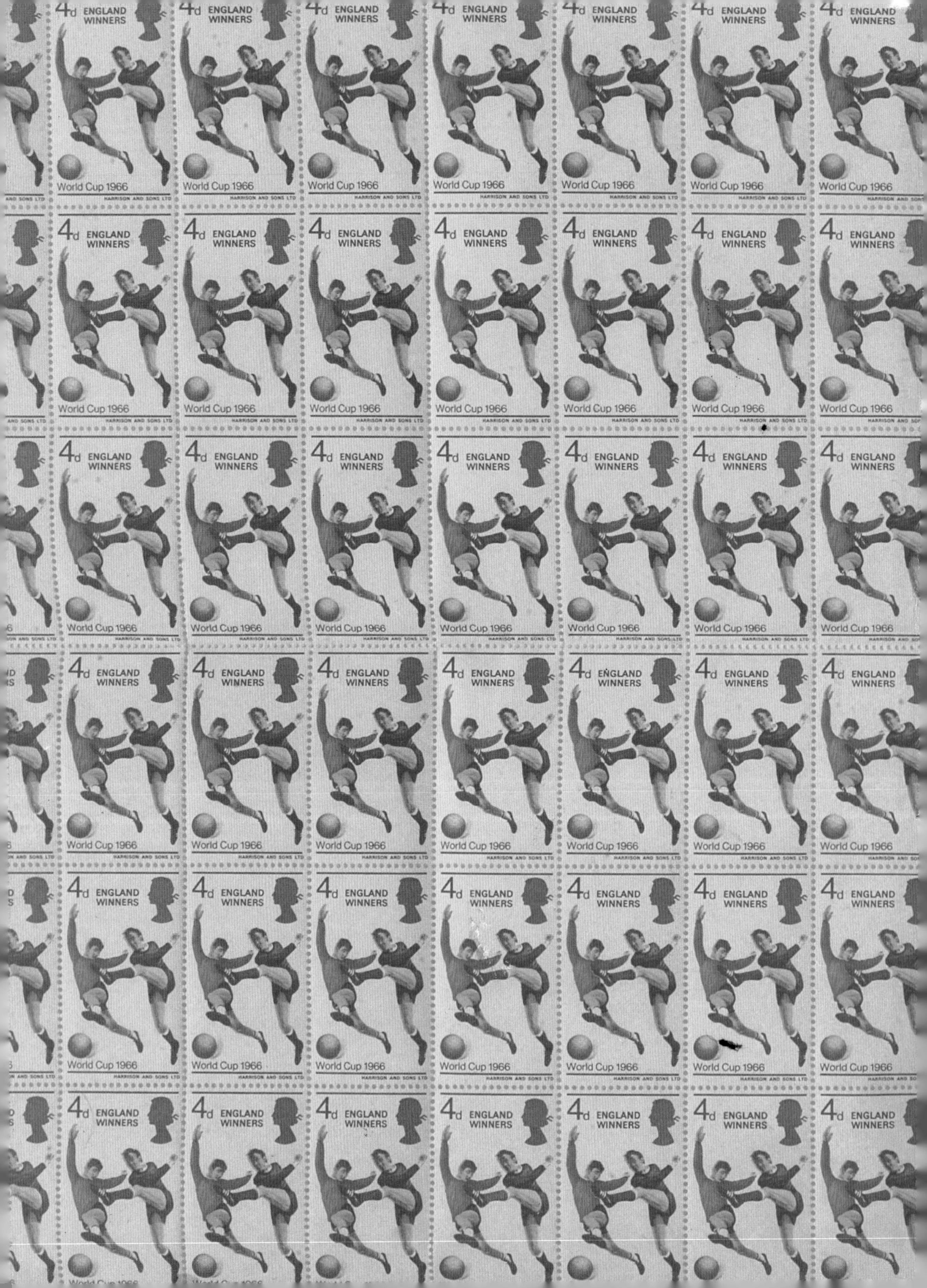
4d
ENGLAND
WINNERS
World Cup 1966
HARRISON AND SONS LTD